Brian Heap's

'A' Level Series

CONSTITUTIONAL LAW

Textbook

Thirteenth Edition

Edited by P A Read LLB, DPA, Barrister

HLT Publications

HLT PUBLICATIONS
200 Greyhound Road, London W14 9RY

First published 1979
Thirteenth Edition 1993

ISBN 0 7510 0339 5

ACKNOWLEDGEMENT
The publishers and author would like to thank The Incorporated Council of Law Reporting for England and Wales for kind permission to reproduce extracts from the Weekley Law Reports.

British Library Cataloguing-in-Publication.

A CIP Catalogue record for this book is available from the British Library.

Printed and bound in Great Britain.

CONTENTS

FOREWORD BY BRIAN HEAP

'A' Level work comprising two, three or even four subjects is a challenging course of study. It follows a period of general education leading to the GCSE in which you have experienced a 'taster' course of up to ten subjects presented to you in a highly structured teaching system. Thereafter, it becomes necessary to make a choice of specialisms for a more concentrated period of two years in which more time will be spent in private study – literally, teaching yourself.

Inevitably, private study is a new experience for most students and the time normally allocated is rarely used to the best advantage. The assimilation of facts, while working on your own, can be difficult since it also necessitates identifying the important issues from a range of books and a wealth of information. The framework of your course is naturally vital, not simply in terms of passing your 'A' Level exams but in achieving the right grades you need to enter the university or college degree course of your choice.

My 'A' Level series therefore aims to provide you with this essential framework. This book will give you the support you need to work through your syllabus and to reinforce the knowledge you will need to be sure of success at the end of your school or college career.

Brian Heap

PREFACE

Every book is shaped to a great extent by the requirements of the audience to whom it is addressed. This book is aimed specifically at those studying 'A' and 'S' Level Constitutional Law as examined by the Associated Examining Board. However, it is hoped that it will prove equally useful for students studying for other examinations, the syllabus for most 'A' Level Constitutional Law courses being very similar. But, the student *must* first verify the extent to which the various courses diverge or coincide.

Since the last edition of this book it has been substantially revised and updated to take into account all major new legislation and case law. Arranged in such a way as to follow the sequence of the syllabus, this book has been written to take into account the special needs of students sitting 'A' Level examinations.

The developments in this edition represent the law as of 1 March 1993.

TABLE OF CASES

1 THE SOURCES AND CHARACTERISTICS OF THE UNITED KINGDOM'S CONSTITUTIONAL LAW

1.1 Sources – introduction

The sources of the United Kingdom's Constitutional Law are the same as the sources of any other area of law, eg contract law. The sources are: statutes, case law and custom. Each of these is discussed briefly below.

1.2 Statutes

This manual will refer to a great number of statutes (Acts of Parliament) which have constitutional implications and it is not thought worthwhile to list them here or to make brief comments about them now, the reader will see just how important statutes are as a source of constitutional law by working through the following chapters. However, it is worthwhile to look at one particular statute, The Bill of Rights 1689, which historically is the most important source of constitutional law. In this statute, Parliament laid the foundations of the present United Kingdom constitutional arrangements by asserting its dominance over the King, in particular over the King's prerogative powers and by requiring parliamentary consent for taxation and legislation. The articles of the Bill of Rights are:

Article 1: That the pretended power of suspending of laws or the execution of laws by regal authority without consent of Parliament is illegal.

Article 2:	That the pretended power of dispensing with laws or the execution of laws by regal authority as it has been assumed and exercised of late is illegal.
Article 3:	(Ecclesiastical courts illegal)
Article 4:	That levying money for or to the use of the Crown by pretence of prerogative without grant of Parliament for longer time or in other manner than the same is or shall be granted is illegal.
Article 5:	That it is the right of the subjects to petition the King
Article 6:	That the raising or keeping a standing army within the kingdom in time of peace unless it be with the consent of Parliament is against law.
Article 7:	(Subjects-arms)
Article 8:	That election of members of Parliament ought to be free.
Article 9:	That the freedom of speech and debates or proceedings in Parliament ought not to be impeached or questioned in any court or place out of Parliament.
Article 10:	That excessive bail ought not to be required nor excessive fines imposed nor cruel and unusual punishments inflicted.
Article 11:	That jurors ought to be duly impanelled and returned
Article 12:	(Grants of forfeiture illegal)
Article 13:	And that for redress of all grievances and for the amending, strengthening and preserving of the laws Parliament ought to be held frequently.

1.3 Case law

The same comments apply for this source as for statutes; caselaw is a very important source of constitutional law and the reader will come across a great number of cases which have constitutional implications in the following chapters.

Case law may be a primary source of constitutional law or a secondary source. It is a primary source where a court lays down a principle in an area of law where statute plays no part.

For example, in a number of cases the courts have laid down that a Bill becomes an Act of Parliament once passed by the Commons and the Lords and assented to by the Queen.

It is a secondary source where the Court interprets a statute of constitutional law importance.

For example, in *Fox v Stirk* (1970) CA the court considered what degree of permanence of residence was required for an elector to be placed on the Electoral Register for a constituency under the Representation of the People Act as amended by the Family Law Reform Act 1969.

1.4 Custom

One particular area of constitutional law which is rooted in customary law is Parliamentary privilege. But constitutional rules are also derived from a source not found in other areas of the law, constitutional conventions, which are binding rules of constitutional practice, but not laws.

Many would consider that constitutional conventions should not be regarded merely as customs for they are followed and regarded as binding because they represent 'constitutional morality' or a code of ethics for politicians and there are certainly customs which would not rank as conventions because no moral outrage would ensue if they were broken.

For example, the tradition that the Chancellor of the Exchequer uses a particular case in which to carry his speech on Budget Day.

1.5 Characteristics – introduction

The principal features of the United Kingdom constitution are set out below, most are only briefly listed here as they will all be developed and considered in detail in later chapters.

1.6 Unwritten

Nearly every country in the world has a written constitution, a document or group of documents which sets out the fundamental principles of law which apply to the system of government and the rights and freedoms of the country's citizens. In most countries some of these principles and liberties are given the status, by the constitution itself, of 'higher' or 'fundamental' law. This usually means that they are either made unrepeatable (unalterable) by the legislature or repeatable (alterable) by it, but only after following a special procedure, eg that an amendment must be passed with a two-thirds majority in the legislature. Another feature of most foreign constitutions is the power of the courts to 'review' legislation and to check/test its validity against the fundamental principles of the constitution. In such systems if legislation is found to be contrary to the constitution the courts can declare the legislation invalid. But the United Kingdom's constitutional law is not to be found in any one document or set of documents called the 'Constitution' and because of this it is described as 'unwritten'. The United Kingdom's constitutional law is derived from statute and case law but none of its principles are considered to be fundamental in the sense of being unalterable or only alterable after following some special parliamentary procedure. The United Kingdom does not have any entrenched or 'higher' law and in place of this feature, which is normal in so many foreign constitutions, the United Kingdom's constitutional arrangements are dominated by the concept of parliamentary supremacy (see below). It follows, therefore, that the courts do not have the power to declare Acts of Parliament unlawful or unconstitutional simply because there is no higher law than an Act of Parliament and there is no 'constitution' against which statutes can be held to test their validity.

To summarise:

The unwritten nature of the United Kingdom constitution involves these principles:

a) There is no higher/fundamental law;

b) There are no special procedures for amending certain laws, an ordinary Act of Parliament is all that is necessary;

c) There is no judicial review of the constitutional validity of legislation.

1.7 Historical continuity of development

The main reason why the United Kingdom does not have a written constitution is because its system of government has gradually evolved and since the 'Glorious Revolution' of 1688 there has not been a breach in this historical continuity of development. Most foreign countries adopt a written constitution after some major breach in the legal/historical development of the country, eg after independence or revolution, but in the United Kingdom constitutional principles have slowly evolved over hundreds of years. There have been huge changes in the constitutional arrangements in that time, but these have been developed through evolutional progress and not through sharp breaks in constitutional continuity.

1.8 Parliamentary supremacy (or sovereignty)

This is the most important characteristic of the United Kingdom's constitutional arrangement. Government is conducted through Parliament which has vast legal powers to make or unmake any law whatsoever. Parliament is the dominant authority and all other authorities, eg the courts, are subordinate to it.

1.9 Flexible

Parliament can change any law simply by passing an Act using normal parliamentary procedures. The United Kingdom's constitutional arrangement is, therefore, flexible; constitutional laws can be repealed or altered at Parliament's will, as can any other laws, there are no constitutional provisions specially entrenched against repeals or alteration.

1.10 Conventions

Some of the most important principles of the United Kingdom's constitution are derived not from laws but from conventions (binding rules of political practice).

1.11 Responsible government

Ministers, including the Prime Minister, are the most powerful members of the Executive and conventions have developed to make them collectively and individually responsible (accountable and answerable) to Parliament.

1.12 Executive dominance of Parliament

Whilst, as indicated in 1.8 above legislation must be made by Parliament and the courts are subordinate to Parliament and in 1.11 ministers are responsible to Parliament, it is necessary to understand that the Government dominates Parliament by issuing instructions to the majority of Members of Parliament in the House of Commons which support it on how to vote on legislative proposals and matters of policy.

1.13 Limited monarchy

The vast legal powers of the monarch are by convention exercised only in accordance with the advice of ministers and because of this, these powers have been completely limited to establish a system of 'limited' or 'constitutional' monarchy in the United Kingdom.

1.14 Democracy

The most important part of the United Kingdom Parliament (the House of Commons) is democratically elected through an electoral system based on a universal adult franchise (all adults can vote).

1.15 Unitary

The United Kingdom is constituted by a union of England, Wales, Scotland and Northern Ireland. These countries are not part of a federal system.

1.16 Bicameral

Parliament is made up of two Houses: the Commons and the Lords.

1.17 No strict separation of powers

There is no formal demarcation and separation between the executive, legislative and judicial functions of government.

1.18 The rule of law

The government's powers are based on law and must conform to the law.

2 CONSTITUTIONAL CONVENTIONS

2.1 Introduction

Conventions are a very important source of constitutional rules. In later parts of this textbook, it will be seen that some of the most vital features of the United Kingdom's constitution are based on conventions. Conventions have allowed the evolutionary development of the constitution through changes in political practices. This chapter will consider certain principles which are common to all conventions, but for a detailed discussion of individual conventions in operation the reader should refer to later chapters.

2.2 What is a convention?

A convention is a rule of political practice which is binding in the sense that it is generally accepted and observed and regarded as obligatory by those to whom it applies. A convention is *not* a rule of law, but a rule of political practice. Conventions operate effectively because they are regarded as binding by the politicians, eg the Prime Minister, the Cabinet, ministers, etc and other persons, eg the Queen, to whom they apply.

2.3 Some examples of conventions

a) *Limited monarchy*

The monarch's most important common law prerogative powers, eg to appoint ministers as she pleases, to summon and dismiss Parliament as she pleases, etc, by convention can only be exercised on and in accordance with the advice of ministers.

b) *Ministerial responsibility*

Ministers by convention are responsible (accountable and answerable) to Parliament both collectively – ministers can fall from power as a group if they lose the support of the Commons and a vote of no confidence is carried against the government; and individually – each minister is responsible to Parliament for his acts and the actions of his department and in a severe case the Commons could force a minister to resign by passing a vote of censure against him.

c) *The Prime Minister and Cabinet*

The existence of these, the most powerful authorities in the system of government, is derived from conventions, as are their respective powers and the relations between them and between them and Parliament.

d) *Relations between the House of Commons and the House of Lords*

The House of Commons is the dominant House of Parliament and by convention (now reinforced by statute) the House of Lords has to give way to the clear will of the Commons in a case of conflict between the wishes of the two Houses.

e) *Various important parliamentary rules*

Many parliamentary rules are derived from conventions, eg that Parliament must be summoned annually; that the Speaker of the Commons must be impartial; that the Law Lords do not actively take part in political debates in the House of Lords; and the lay peers do not sit with the Law Lords when the latter are deciding an appeal.

f) *Relations between the United Kingdom and the Dominions*

The most important principle governing the relationship between the United Kingdom Parliament and Dominion Parliaments, that the United Kingdom Parliament would not legislate for a Dominion without the Dominion's request and consent, developed firstly as a convention (it is now supplemented by statutory provisions).

g) *Judges*

Once appointed judges should resign any political affiliations and take no further part in politics.

2.4 Conventions distinguished from laws

The basic distinction between conventions and laws is that conventions are not enforced by the courts, whereas if there is a breach of law there will generally be a legal remedy available. Dicey, writing in the late 1800s, pointed out that no court will take notice of a violation of a convention. A clear example of this distinction occurred in *Madzimbamuto* v *Lardner-Burke* (1969) Privy Council. Southern Rhodesia was a colony of the United Kingdom. Southern Rhodesia's legislative assembly had a considerable degree of independence and considerable powers of self-government, but it was subject to the overriding supremacy of the United Kingdom Parliament. A convention had developed that the United Kingdom Parliament would not legislate without the competence of Southern Rhodesia's Legislative Assembly. In 1965 the Southern Rhodesia government declared that it was no longer a colony (Unilateral Declaration of Independence). In response to this unlawful declaration, the United Kingdom Parliament enacted the Southern Rhodesia Act 1965 which declared that Southern Rhodesia was still part of Her Majesty's Dominions and reasserted legislative authority over Southern Rhodesia. The 1965 Act was not passed with the consent of the Southern Rhodesia government.

An appeal was made to the Privy Council concerning the legality of the detention of Madzimbamuto under laws passed by the Southern Rhodesia government acting under the constitution it had adopted on Unilateral Declaration of Independence. A question arose as to the validity of the Southern Rhodesia Act 1965 and whether it was in any way affected by the fact that it had been passed in breach of a convention.

It was held that the Southern Rhodesia government was not lawfully in office and that the law under which Madzimbamuto was detained was itself unlawful. The Privy Council rejected the contention that the breach of convention that had occurred could affect the validity of the Southern Rhodesia Act 1965.

> '... the convention ... was a very important convention but it had no legal effect in limiting the legal power of Parliament.
>
> It is often said that it would be unconstitutional for the United Kingdom Parliament to do certain things, meaning that the moral, political and other reasons against doing them are so strong that most people would regard it as highly improper if Parliament did these things. But that does not mean that it is beyond the power of Parliament to do such things. If Parliament chose to do any of them the courts could not hold the Act invalid. It may be that it would have been thought, before 1965, that it would be unconstitutional to disregard this convention ... Their lordships in declaring

the law are not concerned with these matters. They are only concerned with the legal powers of Parliament.'

per Lord Reid.

The court in declaring the law was not concerned with whether or not a convention had been broken. This clearly shows that the breach of a convention does not have the same effect as a breach of a law. In other words conventions have a lesser authority than laws and can be removed by statute.

Another authority which illustrates this distinction arose in the events leading up to the passing of the Canada Act 1982. This Act contained provisions to give Canada full power to amend its constitution which prior to this the United Kingdom Parliament had retained. The passing of the Act had been requested by the Canadian Federal Government which wanted to end the last trace of Canada's subordinate Dominion status. The United Kingdom Parliament could pass such an Act, by convention, only with the request and consent of the Canadian government, but Canada is a federal state made up of ten provinces and at one time only two of the provincial governments supported the federal proposals.

In *Re an Amendment of the Constitution of Canada* (1982) the Supreme Court of Canada had to decide whether the approval of a majority of the provinces was required for the Federal Government to have a valid power to make a request.

It was held that by convention (political practice) the consent and approval of a majority of the provinces was required but that in law there were no such restrictions on the Federal Government's powers. Therefore, the Federal Government could ignore the convention and no legal remedy would lie against it.

'The convention could not be enforced by the grant of legal remedies.'

NOTE: In the end, nine of the ten provinces (all except Quebec) did approve the proposals and a request was duly made to the United Kingdom Parliament which passed the Canada Act 1982.

It must be pointed out though that the courts do recognise that conventions exist and, while they cannot enforce them, they do sometimes use them as a factor to help them reach a decision. For example, in *Carltona Ltd* v *Commissioners of Works* (1943) the Court of Appeal, in deciding that the officials in a government department could act in the name of their minister, referred to the convention that the minister was responsible to Parliament for such decisions.

A breach of law generally gives rise to a legal remedy becoming available but this is not invariably the case. There are statutes which impose a duty on a person but where by another provision that duty is rendered unenforceable by the general public (eg Post Office Act 1969) and statutes which prevent a particular issue being justiciable (eg under the Parliament Act 1911 the speaker has to certify what is a Money Bill with regard to particular criteria but no one may challenge his designation). In these cases no legal remedy is available for a breach of the law.

2.5 Why do conventions exist?

Conventions have allowed the flexible and gradual development of democratic government in the United Kingdom. Conventions are the rules that make the constitution work. The United Kingdom has a tradition of historically continuous constitutional development, at least from 1688, and the most effective way of gradually altering the relations between, and the respective powers of, the various branches of government was (and is) to bring in changes by developing and altering political practices, conventions.

An important example of the role of conventions in keeping the Constitution up to date has been in the sphere of the powers of the monarch. In 1689 the monarch, though now clearly in position subject to the will of Parliament under the terms of the Bill of Rights, still wielded his prerogative powers to appoint and dismiss such Ministers as he personally chose and generally had far greater power than today. Gradually conventions grew up that Minsters should be chosen from one political party and that they should be the choice of the Prime Minister rather than the monarch. In the twentieth century the powers of the monarch to choose his Prime Minister have given way to the convention that he chooses the leader of the party with a majority in the House of Commons. The convention that the monarch exercises her prerogative powers on the advice of her government has evolved since 1689 and is one of the paramount principles of the British constitution.

Conventions fine-tune the constitution, as political practices change and new rules become regarded as binding so the constitution changes and is kept up to date with new political ideals. Thus the development through conventions of responsible government kept the constitution in line with the growing ideals of democracy (ministers responsible to Parliament, which is elected).

At any one time while some conventions are very clearly established, others are coming into existence and yet others are falling into disuse, in such ways the constitution flexibly develops. Sometimes, conventions are modified in statutes, eg the Statute of Westminster 1931.

2.6 Why are conventions observed?

If a breach of a convention does not lead to a legal sanction, then why are conventions observed? Dicey believed that breach of a convention will 'sooner or later' lead to a breach of the law. Dicey gave the example of the convention that Parliament should be summoned to meet every year. If broken, certain annual statutes that give the government the power to raise taxes would not be passed and, therefore, any attempt to raise essential taxes without such authority would involve the government in a breach of the law. Thus, a breach of a convention would have led to a breach of the law. But it is impossible to use such an example to found a general statement of principle, as Dicey did, because in reality most conventions if broken would not lead to a breach of the law. For example, if the Queen refused her Royal Assent to a Bill it simply would not become an Act but no law would have been broken.

Conventions are observed for political reasons; either:

a) because of the political consequences and difficulties that would result if they were not observed, eg if a minister broke the convention of ministerial responsibility he would be open to bad publicity, reprimand, disrepute and perhaps loss of office; or

b) because those to whom conventions apply believe that the constitutional purposes which conventions serve are justifiable, necessary and right. In other words, because politicians believe that the constitutional balance maintained by conventions is a correct and desirable one.

It is essential to realise that conventions can and do lose their binding force when they are no longer accepted as obligatory political practices, at which time a new and different convention might arise to replace the old one. In such ways, the United Kingdom constitution has evolved from one with an absolute monarchy to one with a democratic, representative and responsible government.

2.7 Should we codify conventions?

Some have argued that the constitutional conventions which we presently have, since they are not, for the most part, written down lead to undesirable uncertainty and that for the sake of clarity and to ensure that conventions are obeyed they should be codified (listed and enacted as law). This would be a very difficult task since conventions may be found in all areas of the constitution, and it may often be a difficult task to decide at what point a practice is regarded as so important it takes on the sanctity of a convention.

For example, at what point between 1902 when Lord Salisbury was the last Prime Minister from the House of Lords and 1963 when Lord Home disclaimed his peerage to become Prime Minister after fighting a House of Commons by-election did the convention that the Prime Minister must have a seat in the House of Commons crystallise?

Furthermore conventions of their very nature are flexible and are intended to be general rules to which exceptions may be made if the need arises. It would therefore be very difficult to formulate many in precise terms. If this were achieved then a code of conventions would lead to a more rigid system. Since the conventions would be laws they would be applied to every situation even if this did not achieve the most desirable effect. Conventions would not be allowed to wither and die if changed social conditions meant they were no longer required and how would new rules to cater for changing circumstances be accepted?

For all these reasons it would be difficult to enact a code of conventions and, many would argue, also undesirable since for the most part conventions are followed and are sufficiently clearly understood to be operated.

2.8 Conclusion

The importance of conventions must be emphasised. A totally inaccurate picture of the United Kingdom constitution would be gathered from a study that did not pay regard to conventions. Some conventions are more important than laws, eg the convention that completely limits the monarch's powers to assent to Bills passed by Parliament is far more important than the monarch's common law power to refuse to give such assent.

Indeed Jennings' famous description of conventions that 'they are the flesh which covers the dry bones of the Constitution' is no exaggeration.

3 PARLIAMENTARY SUPREMACY

3.1 Introduction

As Dicey wrote, the 'very keystone' of United Kingdom constitutional law is that Parliament has 'under the English Constitution the right to make or unmake *any* law whatever'. The most important common law constitutional principle is that Parliament is the supreme law-making authority and there are *no* legal limitations on its powers to enact law. It is vital to grasp this fundamental principle; the United Kingdom does not have a written constitution from which legislative authority stems and the highest authority to make laws belongs to Parliament itself. The nature of parliamentary supremacy is best seen when the position of the courts in relation to Acts of Parliament is considered. The courts' constitutional role is to interpret and apply statutes, the courts do not have the power to review the validity of a statute or to strike one down because the court considers it to be, for some reason, invalid. This is because there is no higher law in the United Kingdom above Parliament nor a supreme written constitution against which statutes can be held to test their validity.

In summary:

Parliament is the most powerful law-making authority; it can pass any law it wants to; the courts can only interpret and apply such laws, not question their validity.

3.2 The root of parliamentary supremacy

Parliament's constitutional dominance stems from the 'Glorious Revolution' of 1688 when King James II fled the country, after a protracted struggle between the King and Parliament for legal and political supremacy, and effectively left the Lords and Commons to find a new monarch. 'Parliament' offered the Crown to Prince William of Orange on terms which primarily asserted Parliament's legislative authority over the Crown, set out by it in the Declaration of Right 1688. These terms were accepted by Prince William who thus became the next King. Parliament had seized an opportunity to make itself the most powerful authority. After Parliament had been able to offer the Crown to a potential King on its own terms, how could its supremacy be questioned? The terms of the new constitutional arrangement (the redistribution of power between Crown and Parliament) were enacted in The Bill of Rights 1689 and in its Articles Parliament expressed the subordination of the Crown's prerogative powers to the authority of Parliament. (For the Articles, see paragraph 1.2.) The principles of this constitutional settlement are the heart of the United Kingdom's constitution. After the Glorious Revolution, the courts accepted and complied with those principles and this judicial acceptance set the seal on the constitutional arrangement declared by the Bill of Rights. Political change, therefore, led to Parliament's supremacy over all other authorities. There had been a breach of legal continuity between the pre- and post-1688 constitutional arrangements and the dominant feature of the new settlement was the emergence of the principle of parliamentary supremacy.

3.3 Parliamentary supremacy in operation

To illustrate the principle that Parliament can 'make or unmake any law whatever':

a) While there is a presumption of statutory interpretation that, Parliament when it passes an Act does not intend that Act to contravene the principles of international law, if a statute is clearly inconsistent with such principles then the courts simply apply the provisions of the Act. Parliament's supremacy extends so far that, according to the United Kingdom courts, it has the power to make law which is inconsistent with international law.

   In *Mortensen* v *Peters* (1906) Scottish High Court of Justiciary, M, the Danish master of a trawler registered in Norway, was convicted of an offence under the Herring Fishery Act 1889. The offence took place outside British territorial waters, but the 1889 Act extended to cover it. M argued on appeal that as a foreigner acting outside British territorial waters, he was not subject to the provisions of the Act. The court dismissed the appeal. On the question whether Parliament could enact provisions that were inconsistent with international law Lord Justice General Dunedin held that:

   > 'In this court, we have nothing to do with the question of whether the legislature has or has not done what foreign powers may consider a usurpation in a question with them. Neither are we a tribunal sitting to decide whether an act of the legislature is ultra vires (beyond its powers) as in contravention of principles of international law. For us an Act of Parliament is supreme.'

   In *Cheney* v *Conn* (1968) High Court, Cheney appealed against tax assessments on the ground that, as some of the funds raised by the tax would go to pay for the construction of nuclear weapons, the statute which authorised the charging of the tax (the Finance Act 1964) was in breach of provisions of international treaty law, the Geneva Convention.

   It was held that:

   > 'If the statute is unambiguous, its provisions must be followed even if they are contrary to international law.
   >
   > What the statute itself enacts cannot be unlawful, because what the statute says and provides is itself the law and the highest form of law that is known to this country. It is the law which prevails over every other form of law and it is not for the court to say that a parliamentary enactment, the highest law in this country, is illegal ... therefore the taxpayer's case fails.'

   per Ungoed-Thomas J.

Parliament can legislate on any topic, thus it has:

b) Prolonged its own maximum duration (The Septennial Act 1715, The Parliament Acts 1911, 1949);

c) Placed limitations on the powers of one of its elements (The Parliament Acts 1911, 1949);

d) Regulated and altered the succession to the throne (Bill of Rights 1689, Act of Settlement 1700, His Majesty's Declaration of Abdication Act 1936);

e) And has even passed retrospective legislation (ie having application to the past) (The War Damage Act 1965).

3.4 Parliamentary supremacy and dominions and former colonies

One way of grasping the real nature of parliamentary supremacy is to consider the extent of Parliament's powers to legislate for self-governing Dominions and even for former colonies.

By s4 of the Statute of Westminster 1931, Parliament recognised the Dominions as self-governing countries and enacted that it would not legislate for a Dominion without the express request and consent of the Dominion government. But, as Parliament is supreme, no Parliament can limit the legislative powers of a future Parliament (each Parliament is supreme); therefore, Parliament could enact laws in breach of the terms of s4 and if it did so, the United Kingdom courts would have to comply with the later statutory provisions. For:

> 'It is often said that it would be unconstitutional for the United Kingdom Parliament to do certain things. But, that does not mean that it is beyond the power of Parliament to do such things. If Parliament chose to do any of them, the courts could not hold the Act of Parliament invalid.'
>
> per Lord Reid in *Madzimbamuto* v *Lardner-Burke* (1969).

The ratio of *Madzimbamuto* v *Lardner-Burke* (1969) was clear – that while it would seem to be a politically insensitive thing for Parliament to enact laws in breach of the provisions of s4 of the Statute of Westminster, Parliament has the power to do so if it wishes. However in *Manuel* v *Attorney-General* (1982) the Court of Appeal took a rather different stance when, without deciding the issue, the Court stated obiter that it was prepared to assume s4 could tie future Parliaments. It based its decisions in the case on the fact that the court could not look behind the express declaration in the Canada Act 1982 that the Dominion had requested and consented to the legislation, in order to check that each of Canada's states had indeed been consulted and agreed.

The same principle applies even to former colonies of the British Empire which have been granted full independence by the United Kingdom Parliament. Although statutes granting independence always contain provisions which declare that all legislative power for the newly independent country is transferred to it, and despite the dicta of Lord Denning in *Blackburn* v *Attorney-General* (1971) that:

> 'Freedom once given cannot be taken away. Legal theory must give way to practical politics,'

there can be no doubt that, as a matter of constitutional principle, Parliament could enact laws that broke the terms of such freedom. But, of course, it would be politically rash to pass such laws and the courts in the independent country would doubtless completely disregard the United Kingdom statute. Only the United Kingdom courts would be bound to comply with it. That is the distinction between legal theory and political reality.

Therefore, parliamentary supremacy at its extreme and theoretical limits, amounts to the legal authority, according to United Kingdom common law, to enact any law on any topic for any territory but Parliament's political power is far narrower and obviously in practice political reality is far more important than the apparently boundless legal theory outlined above.

3.5 Express and implied repeal

Parliament's supremacy is a continuing supremacy, therefore one Parliament cannot limit the powers of a future Parliament. Each Parliament is supreme and can repeal any provisions enacted by a previous Parliament, even if that previous Parliament has tried to protect the provisions against later repeal in some way. Such protection is known as entrenchment. There are two different ways in which an Act can repeal a previous Act:

a) *Express repeal*

   This which occurs when an Act expressly states that the provisions of an earlier Act are repealed. This power of express repeal is an essential part of parliamentary supremacy, for if Parliament is supreme, it must be able to repeal earlier enactments.

b) *Implied repeal*

   This occurs when the provisions of an Act are inconsistent with the provisions of an earlier Act. By the operation of the rule of implied repeal, the earlier Act is repealed to the extent of the inconsistency between the Acts. In other words, when Parliament passes an Act any previous inconsistent legislation is repealed by implication. Parliament does not have expressly to state that the earlier provisions are repealed, the courts imply this when two Acts conflict with each other: *Vauxhall Estates Ltd* v *Liverpool Corporation* (1932) High Court and *Ellen Street Estates Ltd* v *Minister of Health* (1934) Court of Appeal.

Both these cases concerned the Acquisition of Land (Assessment of Compensation) Act 1919 which laid down provisions for assessing the compensation to be paid on the compulsory acquisition of land by public authorities. It was argued that s7(1) of the 1919 Act in some way limited the power of Parliament to amend the provisions of the 1919 Act at a later date, by passing inconsistent provisions in the Housing Act 1925.

In *Vauxhall Estates* Avory J said:

> 'We are asked to say that by a provision of this Act of 1919 the hands of Parliament were tied in such a way that it could not by any subsequent Act enact anything which was inconsistent with the provisions of the Act of 1919 ... such a suggestion is inconsistent with the constitution of this country ... no Act of Parliament can effectively provide that no future Act shall interfere with its provisions.'

In *Ellen Street Estates* Scrutton LJ said, of the argument that the 1919 Act had limited the powers of future Parliaments:

> 'That is absolutely contrary to the constitutional position that Parliament can alter an Act previously passed and it can do so by repealing in terms the previous Act (or) by enacting a provision which is clearly inconsistent with the previous Act.'

Once this concept of implied repeal is understood, it seems entirely logical that Parliament can always expressly repeal an earlier statute.

NOTE: The paragraph above must be read in the light of the apparent limitation of this rule by the European Communities Act 1972.

3.6 What is a valid Act of Parliament?

The courts attach a very special status to Acts of Parliament, but exactly what is an 'Act of Parliament' and how far do the courts assert any right to determine this question?

According to the common law a Bill has to be passed by Lords and Commons and be assented to by the Queen for it to have the status of an 'Act of Parliament'. This common law definition has itself been modified by statute (The Parliament Acts 1911, 1949) but the common law does not recognise a resolution of the Commons alone as an Act of Parliament, *Stockdale* v *Hansard* (1839). The remaining question is how do the courts determine that a purported Act is in fact one?

In *Pickin* v *British Railways Board* (1974) House of Lords, the Bristol and Exeter Railway Act 1836 provided that if a railway line, covered by the Act, was ever abandoned the land should go to the landowners adjoining the track. A later Act, the British Railways Act 1968, abolished this provision. P owned some land which adjoined an abandoned railway line and claimed that he was entitled to part of the abandoned track land. P argued that the 1968 Act was inapplicable because:

a) it had been fraudulently obtained by the British Railways Board (the 1968 Act was a 'private' Act) in that Parliament had been fraudulently misled by the Board; and

b) the British Railways Board had not complied with parliamentary Standing Orders before the statute's enactment.

It was held that these claims of P be struck out:

> 'The idea that a court is entitled to disregard a provision in an Act of Parliament on any ground must seem strange and startling to anyone with any knowledge of the history and law of our constitution. In earlier times, many learned lawyers seem to have believed that an Act of Parliament could be disregarded, but since the supremacy of Parliament was finally demonstrated by the Revolution of 1688, any such idea has become obsolete.
>
> The function of the court is to construe and apply the enactments of Parliament. The court has no concern with the manner in which Parliament or its officers carrying out its Standing Orders perform

these functions. Any attempt to prove that they were misled by fraud or otherwise would necessarily involve an inquiry into the manner in which they had performed their functions in dealing with the Bill which became the (1968) Act.

For a century or more both Parliament and the courts have been careful not to act so as to cause conflict between them.'

per Lord Reid.

The principles that can be derived from *Pickin* are:

a) The courts do not have the jurisdiction to examine parliamentary proceedings (this applies to both public and private Acts). Parliament's internal proceedings are covered by parliamentary privilege and the courts are excluded from examining them. This principle is clearly seen in Article 9 of the Bill of Rights 1689.

   It follows from (a) that:

b) If the courts cannot examine parliamentary proceedings, they cannot declare that an Act of Parliament is invalid because Parliament failed to follow some procedural step in its enactment.

c) Finally, the courts are subordinate to Parliament and will not declare Acts invalid because this would offend against the supreme constitutional position of Parliament.

If the courts cannot examine parliamentary proceedings, how do they determine whether a purported Act is in fact one?

It was said in *Edinburgh and Dalkeith Railway* v *Wauchope* (1842) that:

> 'All that a court can do is to look at the Parliamentary Roll, if from that it should appear that a bill has passed both Houses and received the royal assent, no court can inquire into what was done previous to its introduction or what passed in Parliament during its progress through Parliament.'

per Lord Campbell.

Therefore, if a statute was entered on the Roll, which occurred when the original of an Act was written in manuscript on the ancient record of parliamentary proceedings (the Roll), then the courts would consider the Act completely valid and beyond any investigation as to what happened in Parliament, etc. When Acts were entered on the Roll, the answer to the question above was easily answered; if it was on the Roll it was a valid Act.

But the Roll is *not* maintained today. The nearest modern equivalents are the two vellum prints of an Act signed by the Clerk of Parliaments. In practice, it seems that if a statute bears the customary words of enactment:

> 'Be it so enacted (etc) ...'

it is highly unlikely that a court would go any further to establish proof of due and valid enactment.

The judicial reasoning in *Edinburgh and Dalkeith Railway* and that in *Pickin* is the same, a judicial refusal to examine parliamentary proceedings or to declare Acts invalid; the only modification between the cases is that today the courts have to rely on another technical device to serve the function that the Roll used to.

NOTE: On 30 July 1982 the Court of Appeal delivered judgment in *Manuel* v *Attorney-General*; the case is noted here, although relevant to other parts of this chapter too.

The plaintiffs sought declarations that the Canada Act 1982 was ultra vires (beyond the powers of Parliament), and therefore void, on the ground that it did not comply with the requirements of s4 of the Statute of Westminster 1931. Under s4:

> 'No Act of Parliament shall extend to a Dominion unless it is expressly declared in that Act that that Dominion has requested and consented to, the enactment thereof.'

The plaintiffs' propositions were:

a) That Parliament could tie the hands of its successors and, therefore, that s4 had to be complied with in the Canada Act 1982.

b) That the conditions of s4 had not been complied with, because:

   i) the actual request and consent of the Dominion of Canada had to be given to the 1982 Act; and

   ii) that meant the consent of the Federal Parliament and all the provincial legislatures (and the Indian nations); but

   iii) the provincial legislature of Quebec (and the Indian nations) had not joined in giving consent or in making the request.

The Court of Appeal had to decide a preliminary issue: whether the claim of the plaintiffs disclosed no arguable case and should, therefore, be struck out.

The Court of Appeal held (per Slade LJ):

On proposition (a): On the face of it, the ordinary, elementary rules of constitutional law left the court with no choice but to construe and apply Acts (*Pickin* v *British Railways Board*). The argument that s4 could tie the hands of future Parliaments conflicted with *Ellen Street Estates*, but had found some support from academic lawyers. For the purposes of this case, the Courts were content to assume that s4 could tie future Parliaments but the court was not deciding the issue.

On proposition (b): All that s4 required was an express declaration in the Canada Act that the Dominion had requested and consented. If the 1982 Act contained such a declaration, that was conclusive. (The court could not investigate whether there actually had been such a request etc and from whom). The Canada Act did contain such a declaration and, therefore, if and so far as the conditions of s4 had to be complied with, they had been.

The plaintiffs' claim disclosed no arguable case and, therefore, should be struck out. Even if the case had gone to trial (ie if the claim had not been struck out and the plaintiffs' case had gone ahead to a proper court hearing) the trial judge sitting in an English court and applying English law would on any footing be bound to follow and apply the House of Lords' decision in *Pickin* v *British Railways Board*.

3.7 Entrenchment

Could Parliament pass a statute which in some way entrenched (protected) its provisions from future repeal, either absolutely or partially? On the basis of the principles discussed above, the answer is clear – Parliament could not do so. But, could Parliament modify the common law rule of continuing supremacy? For example, if Parliament enacted a Bill of Rights (ie a charter of civil liberties) could it protect the provisions from repeal by stating that a special majority (eg two-thirds) would have to be achieved in Parliament to pass an amending Act? If Parliament did try to introduce a special majority system, this would be an attempt to delimit the 'manner and form' of future statutes.

There are Commonwealth authorities which show that if there are 'manner and form' limitations on the powers of a legislature imposed by some *higher* authority then the courts will enforce the limitations. For example, in *Attorney-General for New South Wales* v *Trethowan* (1932) Privy Council. By the Colonial Laws Validity Act 1865 which applied to New South Wales (as a colony) the legislature of New South Wales had full power to make laws changing the constitution, powers and procedure of the New South Wales legislature provided that such laws were passed in accordance with any existing requirements laid down by an Act of Parliament or Colonial Law. The New South Wales legislature had passed a Constitution Act in 1902 (amended in 1929) a 'colonial law', which restricted the powers of the New South Wales legislature to abolish its second chamber by requiring that before a bill to do so could be presented for royal assent, it had to be approved by the electorate in a referendum (s7A). This same restriction also applied to restrict the power of the New South Wales legislature to repeal s7A.

In 1930, the New South Wales legislature sought, in two bills, to repeal s7A and abolish the second chamber without complying with the restrictive provisions.

The Privy Council held that s7A was binding on the New South Wales legislature which could only repeal it by complying with its provisions. An injunction was upheld to restrain the presentation of the bills for royal assent.

The powers of the New South Wales legislature were restricted by the higher authority of the United Kingdom Parliament. The Colonial Laws Validity Act, passed by the United Kingdom Parliament, placed restrictions on the (inferior) New South Wales legislature. To pass certain laws, the New South Wales legislature had to comply with existing 'colonial laws'. There are no similarities between the inferior position of the New South Wales legislature in this case and the United Kingdom Parliament's supremacy. But, the case does illustrate how the courts will review the validity of legislation if given the power to do so by some form of higher law.

How could Parliament enact an effective form of higher law to limit the 'manner and form' of future legislation? The most important factor in the present rule of parliamentary supremacy is the subordinate attitude of the courts. The only way in which entrenchment could be effective is if the courts changed their attitudes to the investigation of parliamentary proceedings and the review of legislation. It is suggested that given a clear enough indication of popular approval (eg a referendum) and clear prompting from Parliament, the courts could change their attitudes. The present attitudes stem from the revolution settlement of 1688-9. It is arguable that a parliamentary desire to change the constitutional balance and restrict Parliament's powers could amount to a sufficient jolt to lead the courts to reformulate their attitudes.

Parliament has already apparently modified the traditional rule of supremacy to a limited extent by the enactment of the European Communities Act 1972. This is considered in the next chapter.

4 PARLIAMENTARY SUPREMACY AND THE EUROPEAN ECONOMIC COMMUNITY

4.1 The European Economic Community: foundation and objectives

The European Economic Community was created when the six founding states (Belgium, France, Germany, Italy, Luxembourg, the Netherlands) signed the Treaty of Rome in 1957. Since then, six additional states have signed treaties of accession to become members (Denmark, Ireland, the United Kingdom, Greece, Spain and Portugal). Primarily, the European Economic Community is a customs union which has, as a central feature, a common external tariff on imported goods and which has as its guiding objectives the achievement of: a common inter-community trade policy; the free movement of persons, services, capital and goods between the member states; a common agricultural policy; and the harmonisation of various laws, eg competition and company laws.

4.2 Institutions

a) *The Commission*

This is an independent guardian of the interests of the Community as a community. It has 17 members appointed by the governments of the member states all of which have to agree to each appointment. The Commission's independence is guaranteed by the provisions of the Treaty of Rome. Its main functions are: to ensure that the provisions of Community law are enforced; and to initiate and make proposals for Community legislative action, based on the provisions of the Treaty of Rome and other Community treaties and the objectives of the Community, to the Council of Ministers.

b) *The Council of Ministers*

This is made up of one representative from each member state chosen by the state's government. The Council's main function is to try to resolve conflicts of national interests between the member states and, in doing so, to accept or reject proposals made by the Commission. Often the representative is each country's Foreign Minister but if agricultural matters were under discussion it could be the Agricultural Minister, and so on.

c) *The European Parliament*

The European Parliament is made up of directly elected MEPs (Members of the European Parliament) from each member state, who form and sit in party political groups and not by nationality. The European Parliament is essentially a debating forum and has the right to be consulted on most legislative proposals. By virtue of the Single European Act, the European Parliament will in future play a greater part in the legislative process.

d) *The Court of Justice*

This has 13 judges appointed unanimously by the governments of the member states. The court sits with either three or seven judges, depending on the type of case it is dealing with, has a continental procedural system and has as its main task the interpretation of the Treaty of Rome and Community law referred to it under Article 177 Treaty of Rome.

These four institutions are recognised by the European Economic Community Treaties but a European Council now operates in addition. This body is made up of all the Heads of Government of the Member States and meets several times each year, at which meetings many of the most important Community decisions are taken.

4.3 Community law

a) *Articles of the Treaty of Rome*

These are the primary and fundamental source of Community law. They establish some of the most important principles and priorities of the European Economic Community and are the heart of Community law. The Treaty of Rome gives powers to the Council and the Commission to decide on and make laws for the Community.

The various other types of Community law are:

b) *Regulations*

The main form of Community legislation, generally made by the Council. By Article 189, they are binding on and directly applicable to all member states and therefore take immediate effect (see paragraph 4.4 below)

c) *Directives*

These are made by the Council or Commission. They are addressed to all member states and specify an end result which the states must achieve, eg the harmonisation of company law, while leaving the states themselves to decide exactly what measures to take to do so. Normally a time limit is set within which harmonisation is to be achieved.

d) *Decisions*

Decisions made by either the Council or Commission are addressed to and binding on particular member states and are designed to enable the implementation of Community principles.

e) *Note: Decisions of the European Court of Justice*

The European Court of Justice does not operate a system of binding precedent and its decisions are, as a source of Community law, just of persuasive authority.

4.4 Direct applicability

Under this Community doctrine particularly important provisions of Community law, eg regulations, do not require any measures to be taken by the member states to implement their terms, a directly applicable provision comes into force in each member state simply by virtue of its being made. Also, directly applicable provisions automatically render inapplicable any existing conflicting national law and prevent the legislatures of the member states from adopting any new conflicting measures. NOTE: this doctrine is one of Community law and is an essential part of the theory of Community supremacy.

4.5 Direct effect

Under this Community doctrine, any provisions of Community law – if they satisfy certain conditions – can have directly effective, ie they can confer rights on the nationals of member states which can be invoked by them in the national courts. If a provision is directly effective, a person can enforce it in the courts of his country and this operates despite any provisions of national law. NB: this is a doctrine of Community law.

4.6 The Community view of supremacy

According to the principles of Community law, it is supreme over all the individual legislatures of the member states and, therefore, it takes absolute priority in any case of conflict between Community law and national law. Just how absolute this supremacy is can be seen from the following decisions of the European Court of Justice (note, whether or not this supremacy is accepted by the member states is another question).

In *Costa* v *ENEL* (1964) European Court of Justice which arose from an Italian reference, the European Court of Justice stated that:

> 'The law stemming from the Treaty (of Rome) could not be overriden by domestic (national) legal provisions without being deprived of its character as Community law and without the legal basis of the Community itself being called into question. The transfer by the states from their domestic legal system to the Community legal system of the rights and obligations arising under the Treaty carries with it a permanent limitation on their sovereign rights, against which a subsequent unilateral (national) act incompatible with the Community cannot prevail.'

In *Internationale Handelsgesellschaft* (1972) European Court of Justice, which arose from a German reference, the court had to decide whether a fundamental provision of a member state's written constitution could have any effect on a conflicting provision of Community law. The European Court of Justice stated that:

> 'The validity of a Community measure or its effect within a member state cannot be affected by allegations that it runs counter to either fundamental rights formulated by the constitution of that state or the principles of a national constitutional structure.'

In *Simmenthal* v *Italian Minister of Finance* (1977) European Court of Justice, which arose from an Italian reference, the European Court of Justice stated that:

> 'Any national court must apply Community law in its entirety and must set aside any provision of national law which may conflict with it, *whether prior or subsequent* to the Community rule.

A national court is under a duty to give effect to (the provisions of Community law) if necessary refusing to apply any conflicting provisions of national legislation even if adopted subsequently and it is not necessary for the court to audit the setting aside of such provisions by legislative means.'

These three cases show the Community doctrine of Community supremacy. This is based on the view that the Treaty of Rome established a new legal order. Note, in particular the priority of Community law over national law whether national law is enacted before or after Community law. The Community view is obviously entirely incompatible with the United Kingdom's common law rule of parliamentary supremacy.

4.7 The European Communities Act 1972

Has the United Kingdom's membership of the European Economic Community affected the traditional rule of parliamentary supremacy?

a) It is a principle of United Kingdom constitutional law that the United Kingdom courts cannot take notice of the provisions of any treaty signed by the United Kingdom government unless an Act of

Parliament is passed to give statutory effect to the provisions of the Treaty and introduce them into the English legal system. The courts will only give effect to the provisions of the Treaty to the extent that the legislature directs. (*Attorney-General for Canada* v *Attorney-General for Ontario* (1937) Privy Council.)

This principle applied to the Treaty of Rome:

> 'Even though the Treaty of Rome has been signed, it has no effect, so far as these courts are concerned, until it is made an Act of Parliament. Once it is implemented by an Act, these courts must go by the Act.'
>
> per Lord Denning MR in *McWhirter* v *Attorney-General* (1972) Court of Appeal.

Therefore, a statute had to be enacted to bring the Treaty of Rome into national effect. This was done by introducing the European Communities Act 1972.

b) *The European Communities Act 1972*

The major provisions are:

i) Section 2(1)

> 'All such rights, powers, liabilities, obligations and restrictions from time to time created or arising by or under the Treaties and all such remedies and procedures from time to time provided for by or under the Treaties, as in accordance with the Treaties are without further enactment to be given legal effect or used in the United Kingdom shall be recognised and available in law and be enforced, allowed and followed accordingly.'

Comment

This subsection gives full legal effect and introduces into United Kingdom law (ie 'shall be recognised and available ... and be enforced, allowed and followed') all existing *and* future (ie 'from time to time created or arising') directly applicable or directly effective provisions of Community law (ie 'as in accordance with the Treaties are without further enactment to be given legal effect or used in the United Kingdom'). Therefore, if a provision of Community law is either directly applicable or directly effective then whenever it was or is made, it is part of United Kingdom law by virtue of s2(1).

ii) *Section 2(4)*

> '... any enactment passed or to be passed shall be construed and have effect subject to the foregoing provisions of this section.'

Comment

Preliminary points:

1. 'any enactment passed or to be passed'. The last three words make it clear that s2(4) is meant to apply not only to Acts that were already in existence in 1972, but also to Acts that are passed in the future, ie after 1972.
2. 'subject to the foregoing provisions of this section'. The provisions referred to include s2(1) which introduced directly applicable and directly effective provisions of Community law into United Kingdom law.

   Therefore, the subsection can be read:

   > '... any enactment passed or to be passed shall be construed and have effect subject to those provisions of Community law which are directly applicable or directly effective.'
3. There is no attempt made in s2(4) or anywhere else in the 1972 Act to try to entrench its provisions against express repeal by a future Parliament. But, s2(4) may be an attempt to modify implied repeal.

Comment

Possible interpretations of s2(4)

Either:

1. Section 2(4) is an attempt to entrench the directly applicable and directly effective provisions introduced by s2(1) against implied repeal by a later statute. That the words 'subject to' mean that post-1972 statutes cannot repeal those provisions merely by being inconsistent with them;

Or

2. Section 2(4) merely introduces a presumption of statutory interpretation that applies in cases of possible conflict between directly applicable and directly effective provisions and statutes passed *after* those provisions. The courts should try to interpret such statutes so that they do not conflict with the Community provisions. If such a statute has two possible meanings, one consistent, the other conflicting, with the Community provision, then the courts should adopt the consistent meaning. To reach this result, the courts could use the Community provision as an aid to the interpretation of the statute and interpret the statute in the light of the provision, trying to ensure that there is no conflict between them. The presumption of interpretation would be rebutted if a statute passed after the Community provision could *not* be reconciled with it. In such a case, the statute, as the later expression of Parliament's will, would prevail over the earlier Community provision. This would simply be implied repeal in operation.

NOTE: There is no difficulty if a statute, which conflicts with a directly applicable or directly effective provision, was passed before the introduction of the Community provision. In such cases, the normal rule – the later repeals the earlier – applies. But when the statute post dates (comes after) the Community provision, it becomes vital to determine which of the interpretations (1) and (2) given above is correct.

iii) *Section 3(1)*

'... any question as to the meaning or effect of any of the Treaties, or of any Community instrument, shall be treated as a question of law for determination in accordance with the principles laid down by any relevant decision of the European Court.'

Comment

The main purpose of s3(1) is to ensure that United Kingdom courts apply European Court of Justice methods of interpretation to Community provisions so as to ensure that the United Kingdom courts do not, by applying their normal rules of interpretation, reach a decision on the meaning of such a provision which is inconsistent with the approach of the European Court of Justice.

> '... the English courts must follow the same principles (of interpretation) as the European court. Otherwise, there would be differences between the countries of the (European Economic Community). That would never do. They should all apply the same principles. It is enjoined on English courts by s3.'

per Lord Denning MR in *Bulmer* v *Bollinger* (1974) Court of Appeal.

4.8 The reaction of the courts: *Macarthys Ltd* v *Smith*

In *Macarthys Ltd* v *Smith* (1979) and (1981) Court of Appeal, Mrs S was employed by M to manage a stockroom. S was paid £50 a week whereas the man who had filled the post immediately before her had been paid £60. S claimed that she was entitled to receive the same pay (equal pay) as her male predecessor had received.

The relevant provisions were:

a) Section 1(2)(a)(i) Equal Pay Act 1970 which was amended by the Sex Discrimination Act 1975. Therefore, the operative statutory provision dated from 29 December 1975 when the SDA came into force. The provision stated that:

> 'Where (a) woman is employed on like work with a man in the same employment if ... any term of the woman's contract is less favourable to the woman than a term of a similar kind in the contract under which that man is employed, that term of the woman's contract shall be modified as not to be less favourable.'

b) Article 119 of the Treaty of Rome which is directly applicable and which was introduced into United Kingdom law by s2(1) of the 1972 Act. Article 119 states that:

> 'Men and women should receive equal pay for equal work.'

c) A directly applicable Council Directive made in February 1975 designed to ensure implementation of Article 119 and introduced into United Kingdom on being made in February 1975 under the provisions of s2(1) of the 1972 Act.

The problem that arose for the court's consideration was whether S could compare her pay to that of a man who had worked in her position prior to her employment. Was it necessary for the man and woman to be employed at the same time for the woman to be able to claim equal pay to the man? This problem became acute because it was arguable that the provisions of Article 119 (1972) and the Directive (February 1975) did not require contemporaneous (at the same time) employment, whereas the provisions of the Sex Discrimination Act 1975, amending the Equal Pay Act, did. As the statutory provisions postdated the Community provisions, the court had to face the problem of what to do in cases of such conflict.

It was held (Court of Appeal (1979) decision) per Lord Denning MR:

> 'Article 119 is part of our English law. It is directly applicable in England. What is the position? Suppose that England passes legislation which contravenes the principle contained in the Treaty or which is inconsistent with it or fails properly to implement it.
>
> Under s2(1) and (4) of the European Communities Act 1972, the principles laid down in the Treaty are "without further enactment" to be given legal effect in the United Kingdom; and have priority over "any enactment passed or to be passed" by our Parliament. So we are entitled and bound to look at Article 119 of the European Economic Community Treaty because it is directly applicable here and also any directive which is directly applicable here. We should, I think, look to see what those provisions require about equal pay for men and women.
>
> Then we should look at our own legislation on the point, giving it, of course, full faith and credit, assuming that it does fully comply with the obligations under the Treaty. In construing our statute, we are entitled to look to the Treaty as an aid to its construction; but not only as an aid but as an overriding force. If on close investigation it should appear that our legislation is deficient or is inconsistent with Community law by some oversight of our draftsmen, then it is our bounden duty to give priority to Community law. Such is the result of s2(1) and (4) of the European Communities Act 1972.
>
> I pause here, however, to make one observation on a constitutional point. Thus far, I have assumed that our Parliament, whenever it passes legislation, intends to fulfil its obligations under the Treaty. If the time should come when our Parliament deliberately passes an Act with the intention of repudiating the Treaty or any provision in it or intentionally of acting inconsistently with it and says so in express terms then it would be the duty of our courts to follow the statute of our Parliament. Unless there is such an intentional and express repudiation of the Treaty, it is our duty to give priority to the Treaty. In the present case, I

assume that the United Kingdom intended to fulfil its obligations under Article 119. Has it done so?

... A 119 is reasonably clear on the point; it applies not only where the woman is employed at the same time with a man ... but also when she is employed in succession to a man.

Now I turn to our Act.'

(Lord Denning then considered the statutory provisions and continued)

'... Now stand back and look at the statutes as a single code intended to eliminate discrimination against women. They should be a harmonious whole. To achieve this harmony, the Equal Pay Act should not be read as if it included the words "at the same time".

By so construing the Treaty and the statutes together, we reach this very desirable result ... there is no conflict between (them).'

Comment

a) Lord Denning in this judgment seems to fuse the two possible approaches to the interpretation of s2(4) by deciding that Community provisions should be used as an aid to the interpretation of the statutory provisions; but that if there is an irreconcilable conflict between them then because of s2(1) and (4) European Communities Act 1972, the Community provisions prevail whenever they were introduced into United Kingdom law.

b) Lord Denning interpreted the statutory equal pay provisions in the light of the Community ones and concluded that there was no conflict between them.

c) On a 'constitutional point' Lord Denning clearly accepted that Parliament could expressly repeal the provisions of the European Communities Act 1972.

However, the majority, Lawton and Cumming-Bruce LJJ, adopted a different approach to Lord Denning's. They decided that they could not understand whether Article 119 applied to non-contemporaneous employment and, therefore, referred its interpretation to the European Court of Justice, a step which national courts are entitled to take under Article 177 of the Treaty of Rome. This postponed the determination of the decision of what the court should do in a case of conflict, until the European Court of Justice had ruled on the meaning of Article 119. The majority did make some observations on this problem:

Lawton LJ observed that Article 119 could not be ignored. The court was obliged to apply it. However:

'I can see nothing in this case which infringes the sovereignty of Parliament.'

Parliament had introduced Community law, but it could withdraw it at a later date. But:

'There is nothing in the Equal Pay Act 1970 as amended by the Sex Discrimination Act 1975 to indicate that Parliament intended to amend the European Communities Act 1972 or to limit its application.'

Cumming-Bruce LJ:

'If the terms of the Treaty are adjudged in Luxembourg (by the European Court of Justice) to be inconsistent with the provisions of the Equal Pay Act 1970, European law will prevail over that municipal legislation.'

NOTE: These were just preliminary observations; the majority of the court were in doubt as to the meaning of Article 119 and so referred it to the European Court of Justice.

The European Court of Justice decided that Article 119 did apply to cases such as Mrs Smith's, ie where there was non-contemporaneous employment of men and women.

The Court of Appeal applied this decision in 1980.

Lord Denning gave the leading judgment; he held:

> 'It is important now to declare that the provisions of Article 119 take priority over anything in our English statute which is inconsistent with Article 119. That priority is given by our own law. It is given by the European Communities Act 1972 itself. Community law is now part of our law and whenever there is any inconsistency, Community law has priority.'

Lord Denning went on to apply the decision of the European Court of Justice on Article 119. Mrs Smith was entitled to receive the same pay as her male predecessor.

Lawton and Cumming-Bruce LJJs agreed. Cumming-Bruce LJ did add a few words on the use of Community law as an aid to statutory interpretation; he said that if:

> 'There was an ambiguity in the English statute ... it was appropriate to look at Article 119 in order to assist in resolving the ambiguity.'

The Court of Appeal therefore applied the Community provisions over and above the later statutory provisions. This decision clearly provides authority for the proposition that the normal rule of implied repeal has been suspended in relation to the provisions of Community law. If implied repeal had been applied in this case, the later statutory provisions would have impliedly repealed the earlier Community provisions as they conflicted. But, the Court of Appeal gave priority to the Community provisions. This therefore indicates that the effect of s2(4) European Communities Act 1972 is to entrench Community provisions against implied repeal.

It is interesting to note that Lord Denning (in 1979) and Cumming-Bruce LJ (in 1980) considered that Community provisions could be used as an aid to statutory interpretation in some cases. But if there is an irreconcilable conflict Community provisions will prevail.

The House of Lords has, since *Macarthys* v *Smith*, considered s2(4).

4.9 *Garland* v *British Rail*

The facts concerned BR's post-retirement travel facilities schemes which differentiated in their treatment of former male and female employees. The relevant provisions were Article 119 and s6 of the SDA 1975, but both the Employment Appeal Tribunal and the Court of Appeal dealt with the case as a matter which solely concerned the application of s6, ie without reference to Article 119, and reached different results on the meaning of s6.

The House of Lords held that:

a) Even if Article 119 had not been part of United Kingdom law, there is:

   'A principle of construction of statutes that the words of a statute passed after (a) Treaty has been signed and dealing with the subject matter of the international obligation of the United Kingdom are to be construed, if they are reasonably capable of bearing such a meaning, as intended to carry out the obligation and not to be inconsistent with it.'

   per Lord Diplock.

b) Article 119 was a directly applicable Community provision and part of United Kingdom law (by s2(1) European Communities Act 1972) and therefore it should have been considered by the courts in this case.

c) There were two possible interpretations which could be applied to s6 SDA; one was consistent with Article 119, the other not. The consistent interpretation should be adopted. This was a case in which the consistent interpretation could be adopted

   'without any undue straining of the ordinary meaning of the (statutory) language used.'

   per Lord Diplock.

d) The Lords did not therefore need to consider what should happen in a case of conflict. Lord Diplock felt that it was not 'an appropriate occasion' to consider whether only:

> 'An express positive statement in an Act passed after (the coming into force of the European Communities Act 1972) that a particular provision is intended to be made in breach of an obligation assumed by the United Kingdom under a Community treaty, would justify an English court in construing that provision in a manner inconsistent with a Community treaty obligation.'

The House of Lords in *Garland* took a simple route. It adopted an interpretation of a statute that was consistent with an earlier Community provision. But the court did not consider the question which arose in *Macarthys* v *Smith*, ie what to do in a case of irreconcilable conflict. It is suggested though that the Lords would have considered *Macarthys* v *Smith* to have been correctly decided.

In *Duke* v *GEC Reliance Ltd* (1988) the House of Lords refused to consider the terms of an European Economic Community Directive to assist in the interpretation of an Act of Parliament and Lord Diplock's action in using a Directive to reach a decision in *Garland* was criticised by Lord Templeman. The Lords emphasised the difference between the effect of a regulation and that of a Directive. The former is directly applicable, the latter is not. This case has been criticised by some academics.

A number of important new cases have had the effect of clarifying the situation and confirming the supremacy of European law over United Kingdom law.

In *R* v *Secretary of State for Transport, ex parte Factortame (No 2)* (1991) unqualified acceptance of the Community principles of direct effect and supremacy was accorded by the House of Lords. On the same matter in *Factortame (No 3)* (1991) the European Court of Justice ruled that the British Merchant Shipping Act 1988 unfairly discriminated against foreign nationals (viz Spanish fishermen). It has been announced that the 1988 Act is to be amended to comply with Article 52 of the Treaty of Rome.

In *Stoke on Trent CC* v *B & Q plc* (1991) the present attitude of the judiciary was summed up by Hoffman J as follows:

> 'The EEC Treaty is the supreme law of this country taking precedence over Acts of Parliament. Our entry into the EEC meant that (subject to our undoubted but probably theoretical right to withdraw from the Community altogether) Parliament surrendered its sovereign right to legislate contrary to the provisions of the Treaty on matters of social and economic policy.'

The constitutional functions of United Kingdom courts when resolving differences between the two systems of law now seems quite clear in the light of the above case.

4.10 What if the United Kingdom does break its Treaty obligations?

If an Act of Parliament did repeal a directly applicable provision of Community law, then the United Kingdom would be in breach of its obligations under the Treaty of Rome. Under Article 121 the European Court of Justice can find that a member state has failed to fulfil its Treaty obligations and, according to Community law, the member state shall then 'be required to take the necessary measures to comply with the judgment'. Whether the United Kingdom obeyed such a judgment would really be a political, not a legal, decision. It would depend on whether the United Kingdom wanted to remain a proper member of the European Economic Community.

In fact, the United Kingdom was adjudged by the European Court of Justice to be in breach of the Treaty of Rome over the introduction of tachographs and the United Kingdom government complied with the judgment and introduced regulations to give effect to the European requirements.

4.11 The European Communities (Amendment) Act 1986

The 12 member states in 1986 signed the Single European Act, a treaty designed to bring about a 'single' Europe and closer European 'union'. The treaty was given effect in the United Kingdom by the European Communities (Amendment) Act 1986. Lord Denning stated in a Lords debate that the treaty would further diminish Parliament's sovereignty in favour of Community sovereignty. This is so, for the treaty gives Community institutions greater scope in an attempt to harmonise the laws of member states and allows decisions on European Economic Community law to be made by 'qualified majority' in the Council. The qualified majority is 54 out of the total 76 votes and since the United Kingdom will have only 10 votes it cannot block legislation. Prior to the treaty most decisions were made unanimously but even now decisions on certain matters involving vital national interests such as taxation must be made unanimously.

4.12 The Maastricht Treaty

This was expected to be signed as a formal Treaty in March 1992, but at the time of writing Denmark and the United Kingdom have yet to ratify the Treaty provisions.

The main items are:

a) *EMU – Economic and Monetary Union*

To create a single currency in Europe to be introduced between 1997–99. A European bank to be established to issue ECUs (the European currency) and determine currency policies independent of national governments.

NB: Britain will be able to opt out of EMU. Whether to do so or not will be decided by Parliament before 1997.

b) *European Parliament*

New consultation procedures will be established between the Council of Ministers and the European Parliament. For the first time, the European Parliament will have a right of veto over certain types of legislation, including consumer protection, education, environmental policy, transport and health.

c) *Enlargement*

Any democratic European country is free to apply for membership. Sweden and Austria are expected to be the next countries to apply.

d) *Policy*

All members (again with Britain allowed to opt out) will aim for harmonised social policy (in areas such as employment and welfare law).

5 THE RUL OF LAW

5.1 Introduction

There are many different ways of explaining what the 'rule of law' is and pursuing them all would be a futile exercise. In this chapter, two particular ways of formulating the concept will be examined.

5.2 First formulation

That the rule of law signifies that all persons, including those exercising governmental powers, are subject to the law; 'be you ever so high, the law is above you'.

Dicey in 1885, in his *Introduction to the Study of the Law of the Constitution* examined the rule of law which he felt was a 'guiding principle' of the United Kingdom constitution and divided it into three principles:

a) 'The absolute supremacy of regular law as opposed to the influence of arbitrary power and excludes the existence of arbitrariness, of prerogative or even of wide discretionary authority on the part of the government ... a man may be punished for a breach of the law, but for nothing else.'

b) 'Equality before the law, or the equal subjection of all classes to the ordinary law of the land administered by the ordinary law courts.'

c) 'The constitution is the result of the ordinary law of the land.'

Comment

On principle (a): Dicey felt that one aspect of the rule of law was that power, eg the power to arrest or detain someone, should be subject to clear legal rules ('the regular law') and limitations. The other side of this principle was that there could be no discretionary powers ('arbitrary power') which were so wide in their terms that they were not subject to clear legal rules and limitations.

As will be seen later in this manual (a brief outline only is given below, points will become clearer as later chapters are studied), many powers vested in members of the executive are subject to clear legal limitations. Therefore, eg the powers of the police are formulated in various statutes and common law cases and there are limits on those powers, thus a man may not be detained against his will without being arrested. There are though many very wide discretionary powers vested in members of the executive. Many statutes give ministers and other administrative authorities the power to do something if they 'think fit'. It could be argued that such widely drafted powers give 'arbitrary power' to the authorities concerned, for how can such wide powers be subjected to legal limitations? Fortunately, the courts have formulated and apply legal limitations even to such wide powers. Thus, a discretionary power vested in an administrative authority must not be exercised 'unreasonably' and if it is, the courts can declare it to be unlawful. Certain of the Crown's prerogative powers (common law discretionary powers) are still not subject to legal limitations in the sense that, if they are exercised unreasonably, the courts cannot grant a remedy to an aggrieved citizen, but since the GCHQ decision other prerogative powers are reviewed by the courts. Even unreviewable prerogative powers are subject to the rule of law in the sense that they can be abrogated by an Act of Parliament. ('The absolute supremacy of the regular law'.)

On principle (b): Dicey felt that all persons should be subject to the ordinary law and, in particular, that there should not be special courts administering different rules for particular people (as in the French administrative courts). 'Equality before the law' is a grand principle and is reflected in most countries' written constitutions. Some United Kingdom statutes aim to ensure equality for groups who might otherwise be discriminated against eg women (Sex Discrimination Act 1975) and racial groups (Race Relations Act 1976). But, while everyone is eventually subject to the supremacy of 'the law', in the sense that Parliament can make laws which affect anyone and everyone, in practice inevitably some are 'more equal' than others. Some people are given special powers, privileges and immunities, eg the police, the Crown, which others lack. Also, with the growth of the welfare state, many administrative tribunals have been established to administer special codes in particular areas.

The difficulty would seem to lie in defining exactly what 'equality before the law' means: we are all subject to Parliament's supreme law-making powers, but in exercising those powers, Parliament may give some of us greater authority than others and inevitably make people unequal.

On principle (c): Dicey felt that (leading on from (a) and (b)) another aspect of the rule of law was that the United Kingdom's constitutional principles were derived from the ordinary law (statutes, common law) and not from a special written document (as in nearly every other country). In reality, it seems that the lack of a written constitution in the United Kingdom, to rule over and above Parliament as some form of higher law, may be a considerable weakness of the United Kingdom constitutional system.

If the rule of law means rule by Parliament's laws, then the United Kingdom complies with it, but if the rule of law requires there to be certain fundamental principles, eg guaranteed civil liberties, then the United Kingdom system is totally subject to the ability of Parliament to remove these liberties, etc as it pleases. The courts can look to no higher wisdom than Parliament's, hence the decision in *BR Board* v *Pickin*.

Summary

It is arguable that the most important aspect of the rule of law is that all persons, including those exercising governmental powers, are subject to the law. In the United Kingdom the courts generally apply principles which accord with this aim, but of course, under the United Kingdom system, Parliament (in reality the Prime Minister and Cabinet who through their control of the dominant party in the Commons can usually decide exactly what Parliament will enact) can alter the law without any legal restraints but subject only to political commonsense.

5.3 Second formulation

That the rule of law should also establish certain minimum standards for the fair government of the people.

Some formulations of the rule of law set out not only the principle, explained in 5.2 above, that all are subject to the law, but also the minimum requirements that the law should satisfy. Various international treaties, such as the European Convention on Human Rights, set out minimum requirements of liberty and freedom. In the 1959 Declaration of Delhi, formulated on the basis of the opinions of lawyers from all across the world, the rule of law was formulated to require, among other things; representative and responsible government; the existence of remedies against state authorities for their wrongful actions; certain freedoms and civil liberties, eg freedom of religious belief, freedom of association and assembly; fair trial and criminal process; an independent judiciary.

In practice, the United Kingdom's constitutional rules satisfy these basic requirements and arguably protect them in a better fashion than many countries which have written guarantees of them, but of course there are some deficiencies in the law. Most importantly, the law can be changed by Parliament as it pleases and so the present position of overall respect for the fine principles set out above can be changed radically by Parliament. This aspect of the rule of law is, therefore, legally in a very delicate position in the United Kingdom.

6 SEPARATION OF POWERS

6.1 The powers of government

The three powers (functions) of government are:

a) *Legislative power*, ie the power to make laws (primarily vested in Parliament).

b) *Executive power*, ie the power to implement laws. (The executive covers a diverse range of persons and authorities, from those who determine important policies (ministers) to those who implement the detailed rules established under those policies (the civil service, local authorities, the police, etc).)

c) *Judicial power*, ie the power to interpret laws (primarily vested in the courts).

6.2 Montesquieu

Montesquieu developed the theory of the separation of powers. In the early eighteenth century he argued that the best constitutional way to avoid tyrannical government was to vest each power of government in different persons and authorities. If the powers are combined:

> 'there can be no liberty'

but instead there would be arbitrary control and oppression and

> 'an end to everything'.

Or, as Locke wrote in 1690, there would be:

> 'too great a temptation to human frailty'.

It is arguable that the theory of separation of powers involved two aspects:

a) That each power should be vested in different and separate organs of government; and

b) By implication, that each organ of government can check and balance the powers held by the other organs of government and act as a restraint on them, to prevent them abusing and misusing their powers.

6.3 The United States constitution

The United States constitution (1787) was drafted to reflect Montesquieu's theory of separation of powers. It embodies both aspects, separation of persons holding powers and mutual checks and balances between them. To illustrate:

a) *Separation of persons*

The federal powers of government are separated as follows:

i) *Article I:*

> 'All legislative powers shall be vested in a Congress of the United States, which shall consist of a Senate and House of Representatives.'

ii) *Article II:*

'The executive power shall be vested in a President of the United States of America.' The President is elected separately from the members of Congress and is not a member of, or responsible to, Congress.

iii) *Article III:*

'The judicial power of the United States shall be vested in one Supreme Court and in such inferior courts as Congress may establish.'

b) *Mutual checks and balances*

i) *Article I s7*

The President can veto measures passed by Congress, but Congress can override that veto.

'Every bill which shall have passed the House of Representatives and the Senate shall, before it becomes a law, be presented to the President; if he approves it, he shall sign it, but if not, he shall return it, to that House in which it originated, who shall reconsider it. If after such reconsideration, two-thirds of that House shall agree to pass the bill, it shall be sent to the other House and, if approved by two-thirds of that House, it shall become a law.'

ii) *Article II s2*

The President can make treaties, but the Senate must approve them. The President appoints officers of the State, eg judges, but the Senate must approve them.

'The President shall have power to make treaties, provided two-thirds of the senators concur; and he shall nominate and with the consent of the Senate shall appoint ambassadors, other public ministers and consuls, judges of the Supreme Court and all other officers of the United States.'

iii) *Article II s4*

Impeachment by congress.

'The President and all civil officers of the United States shall be removed from office on impeachment for and conviction of treason, bribery or other high crimes and misdemeanours.'

The Supreme Court decided in *Marbury* v *Madison* (1803) that it could review the acts of the legislature and the executive to check their constitutional validity.

6.4 The United Kingdom constitution

In preparing his theory of separation of powers Montesquieu referred to the United Kingdom constitution and this is why the doctrine is so discussed in the United Kingdom context.

However, the United Kingdom constitution does not reflect and never has reflected the theory of separation of powers. The United Kingdom constitution has never been formulated into a written document, as the United States constitution has, and therefore there has not been the occasion deliberately to distinguish between the different functions of government and vest them in separate persons and authorities. The United Kingdom constitution has evolved gradually and in so evolving has mixed up the functions of government, although some checks and balances have developed. Indeed:

> 'The blending of executive and legislature is a fundamental characteristic of the British system of government. To discard it would be a more startling change than the introduction of federalism and entrenched civil liberties in a written constitution.'

a) *Are there any ways in which the United Kingdom constitution follows the separation of powers?*

Montesquieu's theory envisages that each of the organs of government should be quite separately staffed so that members of the Legislature should not also be members of the Executive or the Judiciary. To some degree there are rules to effect this in the United Kingdom although there are major respects in which this separate staffing rule is not followed set out in the next section.

The ideal of separate staffing is behind the electoral rules which prevent members of the civil service, police, and armed forces (all part of the Executive) from standing for election to the House of Commons. Similarly apart from lay magistrates no judges may stand for election to the legislature. One group of judges, the Law Lords, are part of the Legislature by virtue of their membership of the House of Lords.

b) *The non-separation of powers under the United Kingdom constitution*

For example:

i) The Queen is head of the Legislature (the Queen in Parliament), the Executive (the Queen's ministers) and the Judiciary (the Queen's courts).

ii) The most important members of the Executive, ie the Prime Minister and his/her ministers, must by convention be members of either the Commons or Lords (the legislature).

iii) Ministers and other executive authorities are often vested by Acts of Parliament with the power to make statutory instruments setting out rules of general application and thereby exercise legislative powers.

iv) The Lord Chancellor is a Cabinet Minister (Executive), is the most senior judge (Judiciary) and is Speaker of the House of Lords (Legislature).

v) The Law Lords are part of the House of Lords (Legislature).

vi) Some judicial functions are vested in members of the Executive, eg appeals in planning law cases lie to the Secretary of State for the Environment.

vii) The courts make law (exercise a legislative function) through the doctrine of precedent.

viii) Administrative tribunals, over which the Executive exercises some control, make judicial decisions.

ix) Parliament in Parliamentary privilege and contempt cases makes judicial decisions.

b) *Checks and balances*

For example:

i) Parliament, by passing a vote of no confidence, can by convention force the Prime Minister and ministers to resign.

ii) The courts, by applying the doctrine of ultra vires, can review the abuse of power by the Executive in making statutory instruments or judicial decisions and can by the same doctrine control the administrative tribunals.

iii) Parliament can remove a judge from office, on an address by both Houses, for misbehaviour. (This has only happened once since 1700, when in 1830 an Irish judge was removed.)

c) *Conventions*

And in reality conventions have developed to limit some of the possible dangers of the lack of separation of powers. For example:

i) The Queen must assent to Bills passed by the Commons and Lords.

ii) The Queen must exercise her power in accordance with the advice of ministers.

iii) The Law Lords do not take part in politically contentious debates in the House of Lords.

iv) The lay peers do not participate with the Law Lords when hearing appeals.

The checks and balances that have developed do, at least, ensure that powers are not grossly misused.

6.5 Elective dictatorship?

Finally, reference must be made to the supremacy of Parliament. During a period of majority government, Parliament's supreme powers are controlled by the Prime Minister and his/her Cabinet. It is arguable that one of the checks and balances of the United Kingdom constitution, the ability of Parliament to oust a government on a vote of no confidence, is in reality illusory:

> '... the sovereignty of Parliament has increasingly become, in practice, the sovereignty of the Commons and the sovereignty of the government which, in addition to its influence in Parliament, controls the party whips, the party machine and the Civil Service. This means that what has always been an elective dictatorship in theory, but one in which the component parts operated, in practice, to control one another, has become a machine in which one of those parts has come to exercise a predominant influence over the rest.'
>
> Lord Hailsham, 1976 Dimbleby Lecture.

7 THE ELECTORAL SYSTEM

7.1 Introduction

As explained in Chapter 1 the United Kingdom has a bicameral Legislature comprising the House of Commons and the House of Lords. The Commons is the representative chamber and the dominant House and is the main subject matter for the next four chapters.

Elections to the House of Commons must, by the Parliament Act 1911, take place at least every five years when one Member of Parliament is chosen for each of the 651 constituencies (the number of constituencies increased by one from 650 as from the 1992 election). A constituency is a geographical area, and constituencies vary in size according to the density of population in the area. In major cites they will cover a small area whilst in rural areas may stretch over many miles. The rules relating to who may stand as a candidate for election and the qualifications of the voter are covered in the next chapter. In this chapter a feature of the United Kingdom system which has been causing increasing criticism in recent years is considered. This is the first past the post, 'relative' or 'simple majority system' and what it means is that when the votes for each candidate are counted the winning candidate is the one who has polled the largest number of votes, regardless of whether he has a mere one vote more than his nearest rival or many thousands. There is no requirement under this system for a successful candidate to reach a particular quota of votes, eg 51 per cent.

7.2 United Kingdom parties

Although this chapter and the following deal with the United Kingdom Parliament ie England, Wales, Scotland and Northern Ireland, in fact the parties and some of the electoral rules in Northern Ireland are different. These parties and rules are not considered in this textbook.

The main United Kingdom parties are as follows:

a) *The Conservative Party*, presently led by John Major, which has formed the government for the last thirteen years. The present Government was elected in 1992.

   The Conservative Party has a long history going back to the formation of the political parties in the eighteenth century, it was formerly known as the Tory party and is still sometimes referred to by this name. It is thought of as a right wing party and believes in the freedom of the individual and his right of choice and responsibility to care for himself and his family. It espouses policies such as a strong defence capability, privatisation of the nationalised industries, law and order, freedom of choice in education and health matters, increasing competition for commercial concerns and rejects ideas that government should subsidise uneconomic industry etc. A Conservative government took the United Kingdom into the European Economic Community but the present government resists precipitate entry into a European Monetary and Economic Union.

   The party is well organised nationally and would expect to field candidates in almost all the English, Welsh and Scottish constituencies. These candidates, approved by the Conservative Central Office, are selected by the constituency committees. Although fielding candidates on a national basis the party's main strength lies in England, and particularly southern England and rural areas. Its representation in Scotland was severely cut in the 1987 election.

b) *The Labour Party*, presently led by John Smith. The Labour party was last in government from 1975 to 1979. The Labour Party's history can be traced to the end of the last century when in 1893 the Independent Labour Party was formed and in 1900 the Labour Representation Committee, an affiliation of various unions and socialist societies. In 1918 the party improved its organisation and in 1924 a first Labour government was elected. From that time Labour had clearly replaced the Liberal Party as the second major party in British politics.

   The party is considered a left wing party and believes in equality of opportunity and care for the less able in society. Its policies have recently been overhauled by a review commissioned after its defeat in the 1987 election. Broadly speaking it now believes in a strong welfare state, non-selective education, a strong National Health Service, and full membership of the European Monetary and Economic systems. Again this is an oversimplification designed to give the student who knows nothing of United Kingdom parties an introduction.

   The party is well organised nationally and like the Conservatives will field candidates in almost all, if not all, constituencies in a General Election. Again the candidate for a constituency is selected by the party's constituency association from a list of candidates approved by central office. If the party association fails to select a candidate Labour central office will, as a last resort, impose its own selection as happened at the recent Vauxhall by-election.

   The party's main strength in electoral terms lies in industrial and inner city areas of England, parts of Wales and throughout Scotland. This is because the party was formed to champion the cause of the working classes who were suffering appalling conditions in the industrial revolution and traditionally the party is seen as a working class one, whose supporters can therefore be found in industrialised areas. In the June 1989 European Parliament election it won 45 European seats to the Conservative party's 32.

c) *The Liberal Democrats*, presently led by Paddy Ashdown.

   This party has a complicated history. It was formed in 1988 (as the 'Social and Liberal Democrats' (SLD)) by a merger of the Liberal Party with a majority of the SDP (Social Democratic Party) after the Alliance between those two parties failed to perform as well as expected in the 1987 General Election. The Liberal Party has an impressive history which can be traced to the eighteenth century. Until the period after 1920 the Liberals (formerly the Whig Party) were the alternative to the Conservatives, but with the rise of the Labour Party the Liberals gradually lost support so that by the 1970s they would be expected only to win from 6 to 14 seats in the Commons at a General Election.

   The Liberal Democrats are considered to occupy the middle ground of politics but are presently suffering a very poor electoral showing because of the turbulent fashion in which the party was formed, its lack of clarity on policies and, probably, because its leader was, before his election to the post, relatively unknown. In the European Assembly Elections in June 1989 it came fourth in electoral support behind the Labour, Conservative and Green parties.

d) *The Green Party*. This is the British manifestation of a party to be found all over Europe, but which is particularly strong in West Germany. It is included here because at the European Assembly election in June 1989 it polled 15 per cent of the national vote. Because of the first past the post system no Green Party Members of the European Parliament were elected. Its policies are designed to protect the environment and are very radical – unilateral nuclear disarmament, leaving the North Atlantic Treaty Organisation (NATO), anti-pollution programmes, etc. It had never previously had any election success in the United Kingdom and polled only 89,000 votes in the 1992 Election, securing no seats.

e) *The SDP.* Formed in 1980 by four rebel labour Members of Parliament, who could no longer support the trend to the left taken by the Labour Party. Led, for most of its short lifespan by David Owen; it finally fragmented to such a degree that the party was formally liquidated in 1990–91 and David Owen retired as a Member of Parliament. Most existing members had long since joined the SLD (see c) above). It is included here because it still has minimal support at local government level.

7.3 The present United Kingdom electoral system

a) *Disadvantages*

The United Kingdom first past the post system of counting votes is simple, but also crude. Its disadvantages are:

i) *Wasted votes*

The present system often leads to Members of Parliament being elected with a minority of the total votes cast in their constituency. For example:

In February 1974, 408 (approximately two-thirds) of the 635 Members of Parliament elected received fewer than 50 per cent of the votes cast in their constituencies.

Some 41 Members of Parliament were elected with fewer than 40 per cent of the votes cast.

Similar results occur at each election. The disadvantage revealed here is that votes cast for unsuccessful candidates are completely wasted; the voters who cast them receive absolutely no representation in Parliament, even though (on the figures above) these wasted votes might amount to a majority of the votes cast in the constituency.

This wasting of votes in the constituencies and the election of Members of Parliament on a minority of votes cast in large numbers of constituencies, works through to the overall result of any general election. Since 1935 no government has had an overall majority of the votes cast on a national basis and, notably, in the February 1974 election the Labour Party won 5 more seats than the Conservatives and formed the Government, when it had actually polled fewer votes nationally than the Conservatives. Despite the fact that no Government has won an overall majority of the national vote since 1935 each Government since then (with the sole exception of the 1974 to 1979 Labour Government) has had a clear majority of the seats in the House of Commons. The end result of this is that United Kingdom governments traditionally have a strong Commons base, ie a majority of Members of Parliament, but they do not represent the overall political opinion of the electorate. It must be a disadvantage for any democratic electoral system consistently to lead to government by a party which represents the minority of the electorate.

ii) *Over representation of the two major parties*

The present system leads to the gross over representation of the two main political parties, Conservative and Labour, in Parliament and the gross under representation of smaller political parties. This can be illustrated by looking at the comparative figures for votes cast/seats gained by the parties in the general elections from 1970 to 1992.

VOTES	'000	SEATS	% VOTES	% SEATS
1970				
CONSERVATIVES	13,144	330	46.4	52.4
LABOUR	12,179	287	42.9	45.6
LIBERAL	2,117	6	7.5	0.9
1974 (FEB)				
CONSERVATIVES	11,963	296	38.2	46.6
LABOUR	11,655	301	37.2	47.4
LIBERAL	6,063	14	19.3	2.2
1974 (OCT)				
CONSERVATIVES	10,459	276	35.8	43.4
LABOUR	11,459	319	39.3	50.25
LIBERAL	5,348	13	18.3	2.05
1979				
CONSERVATIVES	13,698	339	43.9	53.5
LABOUR	11,506	268	36.9	42.3
LIBERAL	4,314	11	13.8	1.7
1983				
CONSERVATIVES	13,013	397	42.4	61.1
LABOUR	8,457	209	27.6	32.2
LIB-SDP Alliance	7,781	23	25.4	3.5
1987				
CONSERVATIVES	13,738	375	42.2	57.6
LABOUR	10,033	229	30.8	35.2
LIB-SDP Alliance	7,339	22	22.6	3.4
1992*				
CONSERVATIVES	14,048,283	336	41.9	51.6
LABOUR	11,559,735	270	34.4	41.4
LIB-DEMOCRATS	5,999,384	20	17.8	3.1

* Excluding N Ireland seats

The figures tell their own story; eg in February 1974 the Liberals polled over half the number of votes that either the Labour or Conservative parties did and yet the Liberals only won 14 seats, compared to the 301 Labour and 296 Conservative seats. If the Liberals had received seats in proportion to the number of votes cast for them, they would have won approximately 120 seats! On occasion, this system even turns 'winners' into 'losers', eg in February 1974 when the Conservatives polled more votes than Labour and yet won fewer seats. But the third party, in 1992 the Liberal Democrats, in 1983 and 1987 the Liberal SDP Alliance, prior to that the Liberals, always suffers. The United Kingdom system does not represent the true preference of the voters. In 1983, for example, the Conservative party had the biggest Parliamentary majority of any since the war. Moreover, the Alliance gained over one-quarter of the votes cast but received only one twenty-eighth of the seats available. The Labour party gained less than one million votes more than the Alliance but won nine times as many seats! In the 1987 General Election, the Alliance gained over one-fifth of the national vote but was awarded only 22 seats. Similarly in 1992 the Liberal Democrats gained nearly half the vote that Labour polled, but gained only 20 seats compared to Labour's 270.

b) *Advantages*

i) *Strong government*

If the object of an electoral system is to ensure fair representation of the voters' preferences, then the United Kingdom system fails miserably to do so, but if the object is to elect a strong government, then the system is remarkably successful. Since 1935, there has only been one government with a minority of Commons seats. The United Kingdom system avoids the problems, often found in European countries, which use different systems, of coalition/minority governments which can find it difficult to govern effectively because of their delicate electoral position.

ii) *Constituency/Member of Parliament link*

The United Kingdom system is based on one-member constituencies and arguably this produces a strong link between Members of Parliament and their constituencies. This is not present in some other voting systems which work on large multi-member constituencies.

7.4 Alternative voting systems

a) *Alternative vote system*

This is merely a modification of the United Kingdom system. Under the alternative vote system there are single member constituencies. The electors place the candidates in order of preference on the ballot paper, ie 1, 2, 3 etc. If no candidate polls an absolute majority, ie over 50 per cent of the first preferences than the candidate who polled the least first preferences is eliminated and his second preferences are distributed. This process of elimination of the bottom candidate and redistribution of preferences is repeated until one candidate ends up with an absolute majority and is elected.

i) *Advantages*

This system allows voters' preferences to be taken into account and it does ensure that the elected candidate has to receive a majority of votes, albeit often redistributed ones, to be elected.

ii) *Disadvantage*

The system is not a proportional one. It is not designed to lead to national representation proportionate to the votes cast for each party. Churchill described the redistribution of preferences entailed in the system as the distribution of the 'most worthless votes given for the most worthless candidates'.

b) *Proportional representation*

i) *Single transferable vote (STV)*

A single transferable vote is a system which (along with the party list system considered below) is designed to ensure results proportionate to votes cast. Under single transferable vote, there are multi-member constituencies, ie each constituency returns several Members of Parliament and each constituency has large numbers of voters in it. The voters mark their preferences numerically on the ballot paper, 1, 2, 3, 4, etc. Each constituency has a quota of votes which is arrived at by:

	Example
dividing the number of votes *cast*	100,000
by the number of seats in the constituency) plus 1)	(4 + 1 =) 5 = 20,000
plus 1 = the quota	+ 1 = 20,001 (the quota)

If a candidate attains the quota when the first preferences are counted, then he is elected to one of the constituency's seats. On the election of a candidate or candidates, by attaining the quota on first preferences cast, the second preferences cast on the successful candidate's *surplus* votes (ie the second preferences on his first preference votes over the quota) are distributed to the candidates for whom they have been cast. In order to ensure fairness in the distribution of the surplus votes, all the votes cast for the candidate are recounted on the basis of the second preference expressed and then a proportion of the votes reallocated to the other candidates is added to each of their totals. This proportion is arrived at by dividing the surplus votes by the total votes for the candidate and then multiplying the result by the votes reallocated to each of the other candidates. This system is repeated until all the seats are filled.

Example:

If there are four seats to be filled, 100,000 votes cast and the quota is 20,001; and

Candidate A receives 35,500 first preferences

Candidate B receives 33,000 first preferences

Candidate C receives 17,000 first preferences

Candidate D receives 14,500 first preferences

(100,000)

then

Candidates A and B are elected.

Their surplus first preference votes are:

Candidate A has 35,500 – 20,001 = 15,499 surplus votes

Candidate B has 33,000 – 20,001 = 12,999 surplus votes

and these surplus votes are taken to one side

and the second preferences on them are distributed.

For example, if of Candidate A and B's second preferences (worked out as above) 10,000 are cast for Candidate C, then C has reached the quota (17,000 + 10,000 = 27,000) and so on until all the seats are filled.

If at any count no candidate achieves the quota then the bottom candidate is eliminated and his second preferences are distributed.

The single transferable vote system has been used in Northern Ireland for elections to the Assembly in 1973 and to the European Assembly and is in use in Eire and in Australia. There are also many variants on this basic system and in many European countries eg, Sweden, Switzerland, Italy, Denmark, single transferable vote is mixed with the Party List System.

ii) *Party list*

Under this system, each party publishes a national list of candidates in order of rank and each elector casts his vote for whichever party list he prefers. The votes cast for each list are counted and worked out as a percentage, eg if one party has polled 40 per cent of the votes cast then the top 40 per cent of that party's list are elected. There is usually a threshold requirement to eliminate the smaller parties. This system is used with single transferable vote with some seats filled under each system, in many European countries. Israel uses the list system. In 1982 the European Parliament recommended that a regional party list system should be used for elections to it.

7.5 Proportional representation reviewed

a) *Advantages*

The major advantage of proportional representation is that it achieves legislative representation which accords with the relative electoral strengths of the political parties and by doing this, proportional representation reduces the number of wasted votes. This is a considerable advantage for a democratic electoral system.

b) *Disadvantages*

i) proportional representation by using either multi-member constituencies (single transferable vote) or a national constituency (party list) leads to there being a severely weakened or no link at all between Members of Parliament and constituencies. (But do voters vote for candidates or parties?)

ii) It is also argued that proportional representation is unduly complex, eg Belgium, where in the party list system election for the Brussels seats in 1981, the ballot paper had 816 candidates printed on a sheet the size of a broadsheet newspaper page. (But, is complexity a valid reason for failing to use a fair system?)

iii) Finally, it is arguable that proportional representation, according to European experience, eg Italy, often produces coalition or minority governments which usually rely for their political survival on arrangements with one or more of the smaller parties. This in turn leads to giving these smaller parties political importance out of proportion to their popular support. (But, if on votes cast the electorate do not favour any one party over and above the others, then aren't minority or coalition governments more democratic?)

7.6 Prospects for reform of the United Kingdom system

a) In 1910, a Royal Commission recommended that the alternative voting system should be adopted in the United Kingdom, but a bill introduced in 1918 to partially give effect to this failed in the Commons.

b) The Liberals and more recently the SDP and SLD have applied almost constant pressure for reform since, which has been consistently resisted by the two major parties.

c) During the debates on elections to the Scottish and Welsh Assemblies under the devolution proposals, in 1978 proposals were made to use single transferable vote, but without success.

d) The normal system was used for the first direct elections to the European Parliament from England, Scotland and Wales, despite the aim of the Treaty of Rome to have a uniform system across the Community. However, Northern Ireland has used a proportional system. England, Scotland and Wales are the only places in the European Economic Community not to use proportional representation for European elections.

e) The most recent hope for reformers was the formation of the SDP/Liberal Alliance (now the Liberal Democrats) which is committed to the introduction of proportional representation and which, apparently, would demand this as a term of forming a pact with another party to enable a government to be formed after an election which did not produce a clear winning party. The Alliance published a report on 23 July 1982 which adopted single transferable vote as the system favoured by it. However, given the recent electoral collapses of the Liberal Democrats they are unlikely to be in a position to achieve such reform.

8 THE COMPOSITION OF THE HOUSE OF COMMONS

8.1 Who can vote?

The franchise is based on 'adult suffrage' and is defined by the Representation of the People Act 1983 as amended by the Representation of the People Act 1985. To be entitled to vote, a person must be entered on the electoral register for the constituency and:

a) have attained the age of 18 years at the date of the poll;

b) be a 'Commonwealth citizen' or a citizen of the Republic of Ireland;

c) not be subject to any of the following incapacities: ie not be an alien (someone who is not within category (b)), a peer, in prison or disqualified due to a conviction for an electoral offence;

d) either:

    i) be 'ordinarily resident' in the constituency on the qualifying date, 10 October, ie 'to have one's settled or usual abode' there. (In *Fox* v *Stirk* (1970), it was held by the Court of Appeal that university students were ordinarily resident in their university town); or

    ii) be qualified as a British overseas elector in accordance with the Representation of the People Act 1985. This provides that a person temporarily overseas may continue to be registered on the Electoral Register for a constituency provided that at some time in the preceding five years he was ordinarily resident in that constituency.

e) at the time of the poll, have the capacity to understand what he is doing. At common law, it appears that the presiding officer at the poll can refuse to allow someone who is mentally ill or drunk or infirm and, therefore, unable to understand what he is doing, to vote.

8.2 Who can become a Member of Parliament?

Under various statutes, the following are disqualified from membership of the House of Commons:

Persons who are (i) aliens; (ii) under 21 years old; (iii) suffering from mental illness; (iv) peers; (v) bankrupts; (vi) disqualified due to a conviction for an election offence; (vii) clergymen – the provisions are piecemeal and do not disqualify non-conformist ministers, such as the Reverend Ian Paisley; (viii) holders of certain public offices, eg judges, civil servants, members of the armed forces, the police etc (under the House of Commons Disqualification Act 1975); (ix) detained in prison, serving a sentence of at least 1 year's imprisonment, in either the British Isles or the Republic of Ireland. This disqualification was entered by the Representation of the People Act 1981 to prevent convicted terrorists such as Bobby Sands being elected.

If a person subject to a disqualification is nominated and elected as a Member of Parliament, the House of Commons can exercise its privilege to regulate its own composition and declare the seat vacant; or

An election petition can be presented, eg by an elector, to the Election Court which is made up of two High Court judges who can declare the election void and require a by-election to be held, or award the seat to the runner-up. The court's decision has to be reported to the Speaker and approved by the Commons.

8.3 How are constituency boundaries determined?

For a vote to carry equal value wherever it is cast, it is essential that constituencies contain approximately equal numbers of voters. This means firstly that constituencies must be established to try to implement this requirement and secondly, that they should be kept under review so that changes can be made to reflect population shifts. Under the House of Commons (Redistribution of Seats) Acts 1949, 1958, 1979, four Boundary Commissions, one each for England, Scotland, Wales and Northern Ireland are established. Each Commission is made up of:

a) A chairman, who for each commission is the Speaker of the Commons;

b) A deputy chairman, who is a High Court judge, appointed by the Lord Chancellor;

c) Two other members, not Members of Parliament and not active in politics, one of whom is appointed by the Home Secretary, the other by the Secretary of State for the Environment.

The Commissions are assisted by public officials, such as the Registrar-General of Births and Deaths and the Director-General of the Ordnance Survey.

The object of the legislation is to ensure that the sensitive task of boundary redistribution is conducted by people who are not actively involved in politics. The Boundary Commissions review parliamentary constituencies and report their recommendations, for constituency redistribution and boundary changes, to the Home Secretary. Boundary Commissions' general review reports must be at intervals of not less than 10 years, but not more than 15 years. They can report on individual constituencies at any time. The Home Secretary must lay the report before Parliament, together with a draft Order in Council to give effect to the recommendations. The Home Secretary can modify Boundary Commission recommendations, but cannot ignore them. If the Order is approved by resolutions of the Commons and Lords, then the Order will be made and take effect.

In 1969, the Home Secretary did not want the Boundary Commission recommendations fully implemented, but wanted them implemented only in so far as they applied to Greater London. He did not present the required Orders to Parliament. On an application brought by a citizen, McWhirter, for a court order to require the Home Secretary to lay the Orders as required by law, he undertook to do so. The Orders were laid, but the Labour members were instructed by the party whips not to vote for them. The Orders were rejected. The 1970 general election took place on unaltered boundaries. The Conservatives won and Orders were introduced to give effect to the Boundary Commission recommendations. It is intended, before the next general election to revise the existing constituency boundaries. It may not ultimately affect the number of parliamentary constituencies (presently 651) but it is planned to secure greater representation for the heavily populated South East of England, probably at the expense of the less populous Northern and North Eastern areas. Exact details for the redrawing of the boundaries have not so far been released by the Government.

8.4 Rules

The Boundary Commissions have to follow certain statutory rules in reviewing parliamentary constituencies:

a) Great Britain must have not substantially more nor less than 613 constituencies of which Scotland must have at least 71 and Wales must have at least 35;

b) Northern Ireland, under the 1979 Act, must have in future not less than 16, but not more than 18;

c) Boundary Commissions should try to ensure that constituencies are approximately equal in size to each other, with similar numbers of voters in them; BUT

d) Boundary Commissions can deviate from (c) in order to follow local government boundaries, or for geographical reasons such as the size, shape and accessibility of the area being considered.

In the 1979 election:

England had 516 constituencies } }
Scotland had 71 constituencies } total Great Britain 623 } total United Kingdom 635
Wales had 36 constituencies } }
N Ireland had 12 constituencies }

In the 1983 election:

England had 523 constituencies }
Scotland had 72 constituencies } total United Kingdom 650
Wales had 38 constituencies }
N Ireland had 17 constituencies }

After the major 1983 boundary review a mere 66 constituencies were unaltered. The review reduced the number of seats in the inner cities and created new constituencies in some surburban areas. The reason for this was a movement of the population away from the inner city to more rural areas but the effect was in favour of the Conservatives, for inner city seats are traditionally Labour strongholds whereas more rural areas are the heartland of the Conservative Party. The Labour Party leader, Mr Michael Foot, challenged the Boundary Review (*R* v *Boundary Commission, ex parte Foot* (1983) CA) on the grounds that insufficient notice had been taken of the electoral quota for each constituency and the practice of following local government boundaries had been too slavishly followed. However, the court refused to entertain these points as the Commission should be able, provided it followed the guidelines in the legislation, to attach the importance it thought fit to each of them.

8.5 Criticisms

a) The effect of the rules relating to constituencies is that Scotland and Wales are over-represented because they have fewer electors per member.

b) The Boundary Commissions have not succeeded in achieving constituencies of equal size; therefore, the principle 'one man, one vote, one value' does not apply. Even after the 1983 Boundary Review there was a difference of 48,850 votes between the largest Parliamentary constituency, Isle of Wight, and the smallest, Hammersmith.

8.6 What rules apply to the conduct of election campaigns?

a) The Representation of the People Act 1983 provides for various election offences; either corrupt practices, eg bribing or unduly influencing voters, or illegal practices, eg exceeding the amounts allowed for election expenses. If an election offence is alleged, the Election Court can be petitioned and it can declare the election void and require a by-election to be held. This paragraph will be concerned with a provision of particular importance.

b) *Election expenses*:

The Representation of the People Act 1991 amends the 1983 Act; in particular it relates to returning officers' charges and expenses. It came into effect on 22 July 1991. Returning officers will be entitled to receive reasonable expenses, to an extent as specified by the Treasury.

The main Act is still the 1983 Representation of the People Act.

The Act limits the amount of expenditure which a candidate can incur. Every candidate must have an agent, which may be the candidate himself. Under s75 of the 1983 Act (previously s63 of the 1949 Act), expenditure to promote the election of a candidate at an election must be authorised by the candidate or the candidate's agent. Under s76 each candidate can only authorise, himself or through his agent, expenditure up to a total of £2,700 plus 3.1 pence for each elector in a county constituency or 2.3 pence for each elector in a borough constituency. The total is the maximum expenditure which can be incurred.

NOTE: Election expenditure is controlled on a constituency basis, but not on a national basis. There are no limits on the amounts that can be spent in a national campaign to promote a political party.

In *R* v *Tronoh Mines Ltd* (1952) a company incurred expenditure on a national newspaper campaign to promote political parties other than the Labour party. Alleged breach of Representation of the People Act provisions on the basis that this national campaign must have helped a Conservative candidate in a particular constituency and as such, it was unauthorised expenditure.

It was held that the provisions were:

> 'Not intended to prohibit expenditure incurred on advertisements designed to support, or having the effect of supporting, the interests of a particular party generally in all constituencies and not supporting a particular candidate in a particular constituency.
>
> Even although that general political propaganda does incidentally assist a particular candidate among others.'

per McNair J.

(See too: *Grieve* v *Douglas-Home* (1965).)

NOTE: In the 1979 general election the parties incurred the following national expenditure.

Conservative	£2.25 million
Labour	£1.25 million
Liberal	£129,000

It is clear from *DPP* v *Luft* (1977) House of Lords, that expenditure incurred against a particular candidate (in *Luft*, against a National Front candidate) can be treated as expenditure which promotes the other candidates and, therefore, needs authorisation to be legal.

> 'Where there are more than two candidates for a constituency, to persuade electors not to vote for one ... must have the effect of improving the collective prospect of success of the other candidates.
>
> On a prosecution under s63 ... it is sufficient to establish an intention on the part of the person incurring the expense to prevent the election of a particular candidate or candidates.'

per Lord Diplock.

8.7 Suggested reforms

In September 1991 the Hansard Society issued a series of recommendations for changes in the law regulating elections. These include:

a) *Fixed-term Parliament*

This would remove the power of the Prime Minister to choose the date of an election, although in theory an earlier dissolution of Parliament would still be possible if the Government failed to command a majority.

b) *Boundaries*

There should be one Boundary Commission to replace the current four. The constituency boundaries should be re-drawn according to electoral criteria to achieve a fairer redistribution of seats.

c) *Party expenditure*

Political parties should be compelled to publish audited accounts, showing not only expenditure but source of income.

d) *Electoral Commission*

An independent statutory body should be created to administer elections, and generally act as a permanent advisory body on electoral matters.

9 THE HOUSE OF COMMONS

9.1 Introductory notes

To enable the reader to understand this chapter, the following preliminary points are made:

a) Parliament is made up of the House of Commons, the House of Lords and, in a formal role, the sovereign.

b) A 'Parliament' lasts from general election to general election and is divided into 'sessions', which usually run from the November of one year to the end of October in the next year. Each session is divided into 'sittings'. The summoning of a Parliament, the proroging of a session and the dissolution of a Parliament, are matters of royal prerogative. The adjournment of a sitting is a matter for determination by each House. In practice, Parliament meets every year and is active for the vast majority of every year, although under the terms of section 1 of the Meeting of Parliament Act 1694, the minimum legal requirement is for Parliament to meet at least once in three years.

c) At the beginning of every session the Queen's Speech is read, which is a summary of the government's proposed legislation for the forthcoming session. Public Bills that have not gone through all their parliamentary stages by the proroging of a session are 'lost' and cannot just be continued with in the next session from the point reached in the previous session.

d) Each party in the House of Commons has officers known as 'Whips' whose function it is to act as a channel of communication between, in the Government case, ministers and backbenchers and in the case of opposition parties their front bench spokesmen and other Members of Parliament in their party, and most notably to impose a discipline to ensure that for the most part the Members of Parliament in each party vote according to the party line on any policy or proposed legislation.

e) A backbench Member of Parliament is one who has no ministerial responsibility and he may come therefore from either the government party or the opposition parties. The Government relies on the support of the backbench Members of Parliament in its party to remain in power.

9.2 The Speaker

At the beginning of each new Parliament, the Commons elects from its members a Speaker. The Speaker traditionally acts as a spokesman for the Commons to the sovereign and to the Lords. The procedure for electing a Speaker is as follows: the most senior member of the Commons, at the end of the first day of a new Parliament, proposes the election of a Member of Parliament whose name has previously been agreed between the party leaders. The Commons will then vote for the election of the nominated Member of Parliament to be the Speaker. For the first time at the election of the present Speaker, Betty Boothroyd, the convention that the nominated candidate will be automatically elected (the choice having been agreed previously by the Party leaders on an alternate basis) was not followed. The previous Speaker having been a Conservative, the successor should traditionally have been chosen from among Labour Members of Parliament and Betty Boothroyd's name was put forward. Unusually however, Tory Members of Parliament suggested a rival claimant and a 'true' election had to be held, instead of election being a mere formality as it always had been in the past. It remains to be seen whether this will form the pattern for the election of future Speakers, or whether Parliament will revert to the convention of formal pre-agreed selection. Royal approval of the election is required by convention and this is given by the Lord Chancellor in the name of the sovereign. The Speaker's functions are:

a) to act as a channel of communication from the Commons to the sovereign and to the Lords;

b) to preside over the Commons, to maintain order, to determine questions of practice and privilege;

c) to protect the rights of minority parties and impartially to ensure that all parties have an opportunity to speak on matters before Parliament.

The Speaker does not participate in debates and, except in the event of a tie, does not vote. If there is a tie then the way in which he casts his vote is determined by conventions requiring him to cast it in such a way as to retain the existing position. He or she must, by convention, refrain from party political activities and, therefore, cannot fight for his seat at a general election as a member of a political party. Traditionally, to enable the Speaker to be returned despite his/her inability to campaign, the Speaker's seat is not fought for by other political parties. In some recent elections, this tradition has not been complied with. There have been some criticisms of the post of Speaker. It has been argued that the Speaker's constituents are effectively disenfranchised because of the convention that Speakers are impartial. Certainly it is true that Speakers do not take a party political line but the Speaker may fulfil the other role of a Member of Parliament to take up his/her constituents' grievances by private communication with Government departments and Ministers.

9.3 A typical week in the Commons

To illustrate how the Commons functions, set out below is the course of a typical week in the Commons (Monday 5 July – Friday 9 July 1982). At this stage many of the terms will seem strange, but they are explained in various places in this chapter. This illustration is set out now so that it can be referred to during reading of this chapter.

Monday 5 July

Met 2.30 pm
Prayers
Oral answers to questions – Secretary of State for Wales
Minister for the Arts
Debate – BR Dispute
Supply debate – Unemployment
Second reading of a bill
Adjournment debate
Adjourned 11.59 pm

Tuesday 6 July

Met 2.30 pm
Prayers
Oral answers – Secretary of State for Employment
Prime Minister
First reading of a bill
Debate – Defence
Motion to annul a statutory instrument
Adjournment debate
Adjourned 12.12 am

Wednesday 7 July

Met 2.30 pm
Prayers
Oral answers – Secretary of State for Foreign Affairs
First reading of a bill
Lords amendments to a bill considered
Motion to approve statutory instruments
Adjournment debate
Adjourned 2.46 am

Thursday 8 July

Met 2.30 pm
Prayers
Oral answers – Minister for Agriculture
Prime Minister
Debate – Falkland Islands review
Supply debate – The army
Adjournment debate
Adjourned 11.04 pm

Friday 9 July

Met 9.30 am
Prayers
Lords amendments to bills considered
A bill reported and read a third time
Second reading of a bill
Adjournment debate
Adjourned 3.03 pm

9.4 Functions

Apart from being a grand debating chamber where Members of Parliament can make attempts to redress grievances and can speak freely under the protection of their special privileges, the Commons (as part of Parliament) has three main functions:

a) to make laws;

b) to analyse and scrutinise government policy decisions and the administration of the central government;

c) to check, control and scrutinise government expenditure.

9.5 Legislation – types of bills

Approximately one-half of a parliamentary session is taken up by debates on Bills introduced by the government, most of which are passed (a government with a majority of seats in the Commons is almost certain to achieve this). The different types of Bill are:

a) *Public Bills*, ie a Bill which will have a general effect which is either:

   i) Government sponsored, ie introduced on behalf of the government or

   ii) Private members', ie introduced by a backbench Member of Parliament (an ordinary Member of Parliament of any of the parties who does not hold a ministerial post).

b) *Private Bills*, ie a Bill which will have a local effect or character only, eg a Bill sought by a local authority to give it special powers.

   In May 1991 the Government announced its intention to introduce new legislation to reform the present system whereby changes in rail, waterway and harbour projects may be authorised by Private Bills.

   At present, Private Bills are required to be approved in principle, after the public inquiry stage. If Parliament does reject the Bill, promoters and objectors alike will have been put to needless expense.

   The new system will require projected schemes to be put before Parliament by ministerial order, before the inquiry stage. Assuming parliamentary approval to be forthcoming, the subsequent public inquiry would be more limited in scope than at present.

9.6 Procedure – government-sponsored public bills

The Bill will be introduced in either the Commons or Lords, although if the Bill authorises taxation or expenditure, it must be introduced in the Commons by a Minister. The procedure for a Bill introduced in the Commons is:

a) The Bill is introduced and receives its first reading, which means that the Bill's title is read and then the Bill is printed and published.

b) *Second reading*: at this stage, the Commons will debate the principles of the Bill but no amendments can be made to individual clauses in the Bill. It can be rejected, but only as a whole.

c) *Committee stage*: at this stage, the Bill will be considered by a Standing Committee of the Commons. These Committees are made up of between 16 and 50 Members of Parliament and reflect party strengths in the Commons. Generally, all public bills are sent to a Standing Committee, but if the Bill is either an uncontroversial one or one that involves a major constitutional issue (eg the European Communities Bill 1972, the Canada Bill 1982, the Northern Ireland Assembly Bill 1982) then the committee stage will be taken on the floor of the House, ie a Committee of the whole House, where the House of Commons as a body will consider it.

   At the committee stage, amendments proposed either by the government or the Opposition, to individual clauses of the Bill, will be debated. Votes are taken to decide whether a proposed amendment should be made or not. The chairman of the Committee has the power to select which amendments are debated and in what order. In principle, the Committee should go through the Bill clause by clause, but often there is no time to do this. Every amendment which involves the authorisation of central government expenditure or taxation must be introduced by a Minister.

   In 1980, the government introduced an experiment under which representations from the public and from interest groups were received at the committee stage hearings of certain bills. The bills selected for this experiment were:

   The Criminal Attempts Bill
   The Deep Sea (Mining) Bill
   The Education Bill

Although Members of Parliament were almost completely satisfied with this new procedure and useful amendments were made to some of the Bills' clauses directly because of evidence received from witnesses at the new style hearings, the government announced in December 1981 that the experiment was not going to be continued, although it might be revived at a later date.

d) *Report stage*: at this stage, the Bill is reported back to the Commons from the Committee and amendments can be moved in the House to individual clauses.

e) *Third reading*: at this stage, minor amendments can be made to the Bill and in theory, it could be rejected as a whole.

f) *Sent to the Lords*: after passing all the above stages in the Commons, the Bill will be sent to the House of Lords where a similar procedure will be followed, although the Committee stage will always be in the Whole House. Often the government puts forward amendments in the Lords.

g) After passing through its stages in the Lords, if the Lords make any amendments to the Bill, these have to be considered by the Commons, which can either accept or reject them.

h) Finally, the Bill, having passed all its Commons and Lords stages, will receive the Royal Assent. This is today a purely formal stage as by convention the Queen must assent to a Bill passed by Commons and Lords.

9.7 Procedural devices to curtail debate

There are two main devices which are used to cut down debate and prevent measures being held up against the government's wishes. They are:

a) *Guillotine*

This is used only in legislative procedure. Under this procedure, the Leader of the House of Commons introduces a resolution to limit the maximum number of days that will be spent at each stage of a particular Bill. If the resolution is carried by the Commons, then a certain number of days will be allotted to each stage of the Bill concerned. Under this scheme, when the end of the allotted time is reached at each stage, the 'guillotine' falls, ie the Commons has to pass onto the next stage, regardless of how far the debate has reached. This is a very effective way of preventing time wasting and, for example was used during debates on the Northern Ireland Assembly Bill in 1982 to push the measures through against the determined and delaying opposition of a small number of Members of Parliament NOTE: The Lords do not have guillotine resolutions.

b) *Closure motions*

This is used in both legislative procedure and in other business too; under this procedure an MP, usually a government whip, usually at a pre-arranged time, during a debate will move (propose) that the 'question be now put'. If this resolution is carried by the Commons, then the question or issue which the Commons were debating immediately before the resolution will be put to an immediate vote. The debate on that topic will be terminated.

9.8 Private Members' Bills

Private Members' Bills go through the same procedure as described above, but a few points must be made to explain how such Bills arise. These Bills are introduced by backbench Members of Parliament and are not often passed, although some significant Bills do originate as Private Members' Bills eg National Audit Act 1983, Abortion Act 1967. In each parliamentary session ten Fridays are set aside on which Private Members' Bills have priority. Six of these are particularly for earlier stages, the other four are for later stages. Also, on another ten Fridays in each session, such Bills can be dealt with after Private Members' motions. A ballot takes place between backbench Members of Parliament to allocate time on the days when Members of Parliament Bills can be considered to some of the backbenchers. A Member of Parliament who has been lucky in the ballot and who has won a place to introduce a bill, will often be lobbied by pressure groups, seeking to persuade him to introduce a bill that they have drafted.

Another way in which Private Members' Bills can be introduced is through the ten minute rule (under Standing Order 13). Under this procedure, a Member of Parliament can ask the Commons for leave to introduce a bill. Such motions are limited to one a day and are very briefly dealt with. The proposer of the Bill will explain its purposes, a short speech opposing it will be allowed and then a vote will be taken.

NOTE: If a Private Members' Bill is introduced via the ten minute rule, or if it gets through some of its stages on the allotted Fridays, the Bill will often only have a chance of going through all its stages and becoming law if the Government is prepared to give up some of its time for it. Therefore, government support is often necessary for a Private Members' Bill to become law. Such support may be forthcoming if the Bill has proved popular in the Commons, eg National Audit Act 1983

If a PM Bill involves the authorisation of governmental expenditure then a Minister has to move a financial resolution to introduce and seek parliamentary approval of such provisions.

Guillotine motions are not used on Private Members' Bills and

Closure motions need the support of at least 100 Members of Parliament to be carried.

Private Members' Bills often deal with controversial issues, eg abortion, divorce law reform, matters of social reform, of minority interest, of law reform. Some of these issues are ones which the government itself would not like to introduce bills on openly.

The following table is an indication of the way in which the government dominates the legislative process:

Government Bills	1979–80	1980–1	1981–2	1982–3
Introduced	71	58	47	48
Passed	71	57	46	41
Not passed	0	1	1	7
Private Members' Bills				
Introduced	125	80	93	81
Passed	10	14	10	10
Not passed	115	66	83	71

9.9 Scrutiny of the government's policies and administration

Government business takes priority in and dominates the Commons, but the Commons has several opportunities to scrutinise the government. In 1979, new reformed select committees were introduced which are proving to be important in this area, but nevertheless there are criticisms.

a) *Firstly*: What parliamentary opportunities are there for the Opposition to analyse and scrutinise the government, by giving the Opposition the opportunity to decide what matters are debated in Parliament? Mainly, the following:

    i) During debates on the Queen's speech;

    ii) Opposition days (formerly known as 'Supply days');

    iii) Second readings of Bills;

    iv) Consolidated Fund Bills; Appropriation Bill;

    v) At Question Time.

    Also, if the Opposition proposes a motion of censure, or of no confidence, then the government is required to give up one day for a debate on the motion.

b) *Secondly*: What opportunities do backbench Members of Parliament have?

Mainly, the following:

i) During debates on the 20 Fridays in each session set aside for Private Members' business;

ii) Daily adjournment – half an hour is set aside at the end of each day for a short debate on a topic proposed by a backbencher;

iii) Consolidated Fund Bills; and

iv) At Question Time.

Also, at any time, ordinary business may be interrupted (under s9) to discuss a matter of urgency. The procedure is: a motion is proposed by a Member of Parliament; if the Commons approves this, then debate will follow on the urgent matter.

NOTE: On Opposition days.

In 1982–3 the 29 supply days used by the Opposition to debate Government policies were replaced by three estimate days (see section 9.12) and 20 Opposition days. On 17 of these Opposition days the major Opposition party chooses the subjects for debate and the remaining three are allocated to other minority parties. These days are therefore an opportunity for the Commons to scrutinise the Government's record in areas which the Opposition choose.

9.10 Question time

Question time is one of the key opportunities for backbench and opposition Members of Parliament to try to check the Executive. Most of the procedural rules which govern question time were worked out in the late 1800s. At the turn of the century, time restrictions were introduced which limited question time to one hour. The general object of question time is to question Ministers about matters within their responsibilities.

a) Questions, of which advance notice must generally be given to the Clerk of the House, can be of three different types:

i) If an oral answer is required, then the question is starred when notice is given, ie a star is put on the notice. A Member of Parliament is limited to two oral questions a day.

ii) If the question is unstarred then a written answer will be given to it. Each year approximately 30,000 unstarred questions are asked. A written answer may take some time to produce and, therefore:

iii) If a 'W' is placed by an unstarred question with a specific date, eg 'W 1 July', then the written answer will be given on the specified date.

There seem to be no obvious reasons to determine which of the above forms is used for a question.

Each day, apart from Fridays, when question time is reached, a rota, fixed by the government after inter-party consultation, determines which Minister or Ministers are answering questions on that particular day. Each day a different Minister will begin at question time, according to the rota and questions will be grouped to ensure that all those questions for that particular Minister are put together. The average number of questions answered orally each day is 20, but there are usually some 60 questions set down for oral answers each day. Questions not orally answered on the day are answered in writing the next day. There just is not the parliamentary time available to answer all the starred questions orally.

Questions to a Minister must relate to matters within his responsibilities. There are other restrictions, eg a question must be a question (not a statement) and a question must not cast imputations on private character. The Speaker is the sole judge of whether a question is allowable or not. A Minister can refuse to answer a question, eg on grounds of public policy or national security.

NOTE: Once a question is answered orally, the questioner can put a supplementary question to the Minister, ie a follow up question. Often, the supplementary is far more important than the original question. If skilfully used, an element of surprise can be achieved and a Minister will be shown in a bad light if he does not answer well. There is no advance notice of supplementaries except that in 1984 the Speaker made a ruling that a supplementary must relate to the question asked of the Minister.

b) *Why are questions asked?*

i) Questions enforce the convention of ministerial responsibility. Parliament confers powers on Ministers who are answerable and accountable to it. Question time is a major way of ensuring that Ministers are literally answerable to Parliament, to ordinary Members of Parliament, for the way in which they exercise their powers.

ii) Because questions are grouped together for one or two Ministers each day, Parliament is given a chance to see how particular Ministers perform under pressure, especially in the way supplementaries are answered. Ministers' reputations can be made or broken during question time.

iii) Questions are one way of bringing to the direct attention of a Minister a decision that has been taken by his department in his name.

iv) Questions are a very important way of getting information from the civil service; departmental officials are responsible for answering written questions and will provide a brief for their Minister to enable him to answer oral questions.

c) *Prime Minister's questions*

The Prime Minister answers questions for quarter-of-an-hour on Tuesdays and Thursdays. As the Prime Minister has few statutory powers, Members of Parliament usually begin by asking the Prime Minister a question about his/her engagements for the day. Once this is answered, the Member of Parliament can then ask, in the form of a supplementary, the question he really wanted to put in the first place!

Criticisms of question time

Although question time provides backbench Members of Parliament with an opportunity to question Ministers and check the Executive it is easy to overstate its usefulness. There are a number of factors limiting its effectiveness:

a) The time allowed is too short for oral questions to be fully dealt with.

b) Members of Parliament may be poorly informed and therefore fail to ask the correct question to elicit the required information.

c) Ministers become expert at 'stonewalling' ie giving no proper answer.

d) Both Members of Parliament and Ministers tend to use question time as an opportunity for political point scoring. This is particularly true of Prime Minister's question time.

9.11 Select Committees

Perhaps the most exciting development in parliamentary procedure is the reform of the Select Committee system. The new Select Committee system provides an extremely good opportunity for the Commons to analyse and scrutinise the government's policies and administration. In 1979 the new Select Committee system was introduced, the major reform being that under the new system each Select Committee monitors a particular government department. (Most of the old Select Committees and the Expenditure Committee were abolished by the 1979 reforms.)

a) Prior to the General Election of 1992, the organisation of Select Committees was as set out below:

NAME OF COMMITTEE	*PRINCIPAL GOVERNMENT DEPARTMENT(S) CONCERNED*	*MAXIMUM NUMBER OF MEMBERS*	*QUORUM*
1. AGRICULTURE	MIN OF AGRICULTURE, FISHERIES & FOOD	11	3
2. DEFENCE	MIN OF DEFENCE	11	3
3. EDUCATION, SCIENCE AND ARTS	DEPT OF EDUCATION & SCIENCE. OFFICE OF ARTS AND LIBRARIES	11	3
4. EMPLOYMENT	DEPT OF EMPLOYMENT	11	3
5. ENERGY	DEPT OF ENERGY	11	3
6. ENVIRONMENT	DEPT OF THE ENVIRONMENT	11	3
7. FOREIGN AFFAIRS	FOREIGN & COMMONWEALTH OFFICE	11	3
8. HOME AFFAIRS	HOME OFFICE	11	3
9. SCOTTISH AFFAIRS	SCOTTISH OFFICE	13	5
10. SOCIAL SERVICES	DEPT OF HEALTH & SOCIAL SECURITY	11	3
11. TRADE & INDUSTRY	DEPT OF TRADE & INDUSTRY	11	3
12. TRANSPORT	DEPT OF TRANSPORT	11	3
13. TREASURY & CIVIL SERVICE	TREASURY; BOARD OF INLAND REVENUE; BOARD OF CUSTOMS & EXCISE	11	3
14. WELSH AFFAIRS	WELSH OFFICE	11	3

The task of a Select Committee is to scrutinise and examine the expenditure, administration and policies of its particular designated government department. The membership of Select Committees is entirely backbench and reflects party strengths in the Commons. Select Committees have the power to 'send for', ie demand, departmental papers, records and documents and to require persons, eg Ministers, civil servants, to give evidence. These powers are backed by contempt provisions; it may be a contempt of Parliament to refuse a Select Committee request. The Select Committees are assisted by a limited number of specialist advisors and research workers.

b) *How effective have the Select Committees been?*

As an example, one can take the Treasury Select Committee which, despite having a Conservative chairman and a membership that reflects the Conservative government's majority in the Commons, has produced highly analytical and critical reports of the government's economic policy decisions, eg among its early reports the Select Committee, one week before the March 1981 budget, criticised the government's economic policies as being 'not soundly based'. The Select Committee has produced reports, among many others, which criticise the government's budget strategy and its controls over expenditure. The Select Committee frequently subjects the Chancellor of the Exchequer to close public questioning and examination. The Treasury Select Committee is a perfect example of how the new Select Committees should work, of how a Select Committee made up of backbenchers from different political parties can work together to scrutinise the Executive.

The advantages of the Select Committees have been:

i) Backbench Members of Parliament who are members of Select Committees are selected for a Parliament and over that prolonged period may become well versed in the affairs of the department they are scrutinising and therefore provide expert, informed criticism.

ii) Select Committees themselves decide into what matters they wish to investigate and have access to question not only Ministers and civil servants but also academic experts and other witnesses.

iii) as a result of the activities of Select Committees it seems that more information on the workings of the various government departments is routinely published.

iv) the quality of Ministerial decision making should be higher because of the psychological effect of the Minister knowing he may later have to justify his decision to a Select Committee.

Despite these advantages one must not lose sight of the fact that on every Select Committee there is a majority of backbench Members of Parliament from the Government party and Select Committees may sometimes split on party lines which means that they are not effective in checking the Government. Furthermore, Select Committees have not always been treated with proper respect by Government which has on occasion frustrated Select Committee attempts to get to the truth of a matter by refusing to allow Select Committees to question civil servants, or by Ministers or former Ministers refusing to answer questioning.

For example, after the 1986 Westland Helicopter Affair (see chapter 14) the former Secretary of State for Trade and Industry, Leon Brittan, refused to give details requested by the Defence Select Committee and that Committee was not allowed to question civil servants involved in the leaking of a letter from the Solicitor General to Michael Heseltine. It was only allowed to interview the head of the Civil Service who had conducted an inquiry.

In 1989 after the resignation of the Health Minister, Mrs Edwina Currie, over the issue of salmonella in poultry it was only by threats of coercion that the Agriculture Select Committee persuaded her to submit herself to questioning over the affair.

Even when highly critical reports are produced these may not be accepted by Government and there is often insufficient time available for critical reports to be fully debated.

A final example of the limitations on the effectiveness of Select Committees is the fact that for the first six months after the 1987 General Election there were no Select Committees set up and because so few Conservative Members of Parliament were elected in Scotland there remained in June 1989 no Scottish Select Committee to monitor government activities in Scotland.

In May 1991 the Second Report of the House of Commons Select Committee on Procedure was issued (Cmnd 1532 HMSO). Among other changes introduced was the establishment of a Select Committee on Northern Ireland and increased jurisdiction for the Home Affairs Select Committee. This has now been given power to scrutinise the workings of the offices of the various Law Officers of the Crown: the Lord Chancellor's department, the Attorney-General's office, the Treasury Solicitor's office and the Crown Prosecution Service. Its terms of reference are limited, however; it will not, for example, have the power to consider individual cases before the court.

9.12 Scrutiny of government expenditure

By convention, this is a task for the Commons. Approximately two-thirds of the government's expenditure requires annual statutory authority which, in theory, gives the Commons the opportunity to scrutinise the government's expenditure proposals before approving them.

NOTE: Consolidated fund expenditure, which provides, eg moneys for the Queen's civil list, judges' salaries, the Speaker's salary, does *not* need annual authority and, therefore, is not subject to annual debate.

Procedure

Every summer the various government departments prepare estimates of the moneys required to provide the necessary services, etc for the following financial year beginning on 1st April in the next year. These estimates have to be agreed with the Treasury.

Each year in about February the government publishes a Public Expenditure White Paper detailing its proposed expenditure plans. This is later followed by volumes of estimates which are divided up to show how much money each government department will require to implement the White Paper proposals. The end result is that Parliament will pass an Appropriation Act authorising the proposed expenditure. But, before this Act is passed, the Commons has to debate the estimates and the expenditure plans because the redress of grievances precedes supply, ie the authorisation of the proposed expenditure.

Three days are set aside as 'estimate days'. During these days, particular departmental estimates will be examined, debated and voted on by the Commons. Exactly which estimates will be debated on these days will be decided according to the recommendations of a Liaison Committee made up of the Chairmen of the Select Committees. The Liaison Committee will make its recommendations after considering recommendations from the Select Committees as to which particular estimates each Select Committee would like considered by the Commons. Since supply matters are matters of confidence the results of such debates are a foregone conclusion as government Members of Parliament will be instructed by the party whips to vote in favour of the proposals. Nevertheless the fact that estimates are to be scrutinised is valuable since before estimate days were introduced in 1982-3 the 29 supply days were simply devoted to debating subjects chosen by the Opposition which need have nothing to do with government expenditure.

The decision to allow the Select Committees to, in effect, decide which estimates should be considered by the Commons, is significant. Certainly, this reform is a step towards better parliamentary scrutiny of government expenditure and is to be welcomed, but the time is too short and many Members of Parliament are not sufficiently financially trained to make these debates fully effective.

9.13 The Public Accounts Committee

The Public Accounts Committee is a well established and respected Select Committee. It dates from 1861. It is made up of 15 Members of Parliament and its membership reflects party strengths in the Commons, but its Chairman is, by convention, an Opposition Member of Parliament. By tradition, the Public Accounts Committee performs its tasks in an independent way. The Public Accounts Committee looks at governmental expenditure that has already been spent. It checks and scrutinises how the government has actually spent the monies voted to it by Parliament. The Public Accounts Committee's task is to discover financial irregularities in governmental spending and wasteful, extravagant and imprudent expenditure. The Public Accounts Committee is guided by the reports of an independent public officer, the Comptroller and Auditor General, who with a very large departmental staff and with a view to find irregularities, etc, audits the government's accounts and examines how efficiently the departments have spent their moneys. The Public Accounts Committee's reports are debated by Parliament and it often uncovers gross financial mismanagement in government departments. Sometimes, this involves the careless and wasteful spending of millions of pounds.

The main difficulty with the Public Accounts Committee as a control over government expenditure is that it only covers money already spent and, therefore, mistakes already made. On the other hand, it can be pointed out that the knowledge that the Public Accounts Committee will closely scrutinise a department's expenditure must have some effect on the civil servants that staff them and the discovery of mismanagement by the Public Accounts Committee does lead to departmental reforms.

The Public Accounts Committee is a good watchdog – but barks too late; is there any other means of controlling government expenditure?

A step in this direction was taken with the passing of the National Audit Act 1983. The independence of the Comptroller and Auditor General was strengthened and he has complete discretion in the exercise of his duties. In liaison with Parliament it is hoped that the National Audit Office set up under the Act will provide closer scrutiny of government policy, administration and proposed expenditure.

9.14 The role of the backbench Member of Parliament

A backbench Member of Parliament is a Member of Parliament with no ministerial responsibility who therefore sits on the backbenches in the House. The government relies on the support of its own backbenchers to remain in office and they as a group therefore have a greater influence than the backbenchers in Opposition parties.

For example, Conservative backbench pressure was responsible for the resignations of Leon Brittan in the 1976 Westland Helicopter Affair and Mrs Edwina Currie in 1989 after the controversy over salmonella in eggs.

The backbenchers' influence is mainly felt:

a) In the part they take in standing committees on government sponsored Public Bills but the government always has a majority in the committees and there are various devices outlined above for the curtailment of debate.

b) Backbenchers may introduce their own Private Members' Bills but very few of these reach the statute book (see above).

c) In question time, but the time is too short for effective scrutiny of government. Members of Parliament may be too poorly informed to frame an effective question and Question Time is often misused for party political point scoring.

d) In Select Committees, perhaps the most effective form of control over government, but these still have their limitations (see above).

e) In debates on the Queen's speech, on Opposition days and at second reading debates. However once again the vote at the end of the debate will normally be a foregone conclusion because of the whip system.

10 PARLIAMENTARY PRIVILEGES

10.1 Introduction

Definition:

> 'The sum of the peculiar rights enjoyed by each House collectively and by members of each House individually, without which they could not discharge their functions and which exceed those possessed by other bodies and individuals.'
>
> Erskine May.

Parliamentary privileges exist to enable the Houses of Parliament to carry out their tasks as effectively as possible, without interference from those outside, or abuse of position by those inside Parliament. Privilege stems from the law and custom of Parliament. Neither House can by its own resolution establish new privileges. If a privilege affects someone outside Parliament, then its limits can be determined by the courts and on such occasions, privilege forms part of the common law. This chapter will concentrate on:

10.2 Privileges of the House of Commons

At the opening of a new Parliament, the Speaker claims from the Crown the 'ancient and undoubted rights and privileges' of the Commons and names separately:

a) Freedom of speech;

b) Freedom from arrest;

c) Freedom of access to Her Majesty (through the Speaker); and

d) That the most favourable construction be placed upon all their proceedings.

There are other privileges of the Commons which are not specifically named by the Speaker, eg freedom to regulate its own composition and proceedings; the right to punish for breaches of privilege and for contempt of the House; exclusive jurisdiction over all financial matters.

10.3 Freedom of speech

Nothing said in Parliament by a member acting as such can be treated as an offence or civil wrong by the courts of law. (The case of *Sir J Elliott, Denzil Hollis and Others* (1666).)

The principle set out in this case was adopted in Article 9 Bill of Rights 1689:

> 'The freedom of speech and debates or proceedings in Parliament ought not to be impeached or questioned in any court or place out of Parliament.'

Therefore, a Member of Parliament speaking in the course of parliamentary proceedings cannot be prosecuted, eg for sedition, for breach of the Official Secrets Acts, or sued, eg for defamation, for the things that he says. This is the most important privilege and it exists to enable Members of Parliament to speak their minds freely without fear of being prosecuted or sued for their words. While this privilege can be abused, and sometimes is, its importance can readily be seen. The privilege only covers Members of Parliament acting as such, in parliamentary proceedings.

Proceedings in Parliament cover: debates, questions, committee hearings and 'everything said or done in either House in the transaction of parliamentary business'. The essential aspect is the carrying out of parliamentary business, not just speaking in the Houses of Parliament.

Even speeches outside the Palace of Westminster can be protected by absolute privilege if parliamentary business, eg the hearings of a Select Committee, are involved. However it should be noted that meetings of Members of Parliament in their constituencies, etc are not Parliamentary business and so speeches at such meetings are not covered by absolute privilege. If a Member of Parliament is sued for defamation for something said which is not covered by the term 'proceedings in Parliament' then the plaintiff cannot use anything said by the Member of Parliament in Parliament to support his case, eg as evidence of bad faith (eg *Church of Scientology* v *Geoffrey Johnson-Smith* (1972)).

The meaning of 'proceedings in Parliament' was considered by the Committee of Privileges and the Commons in the *Strauss Case* (1957). Strauss, a Member of Parliament, wrote to a Minister complaining of the activities of the London Electricity Board but since the Minister considered that the day-to-day administration of a nationalised industry was concerned he simply referred the matter to the Chairman of the Board who threatened libel proceedings against Strauss. Strauss considered that his letter was covered by absolute privilege as it was 'proceedings in Parliament' and a threat to sue for defamation was a breach of his parliamentary privilege. The Speaker referred the matter to the Committee of Privileges which agreed with this point of view but the Commons disagreed. Although this decision is not binding on later Parliaments it worried Members of Parliament sufficiently that the Speaker later made a ruling to the effect that a letter from a Member of Parliament to a Minister could be 'proceedings in Parliament' and thus be covered by absolute privilege if the letter had been invited by a Minister, eg by a Minister at question time asking Members of Parliament to let him have written information.

In the *Strauss Case* no further action was taken against Strauss by the London Electricity Board but, had it been, Strauss could not have pleaded absolute privilege. However, qualified privilege is a defence available to anyone (not just a Member of Parliament) provided that he can establish that he had a legitimate interest in the information communicated, that he communicated it to another who had a legitimate interest to receive it and that he was acting bona fides (in good faith). It may have been the likely success of this defence in the *Strauss Case* which deterred the London Electricity Board from taking the matter any further.

If parliamentary proceedings are published they attract privilege in the law of defamation. If parliamentary papers are published with the authority of either House, they are absolutely privileged against civil or criminal proceedings and media reports of such papers have qualified privilege (ie they are privileged unless published with notice of their falsity); The Parliamentary Papers Act 1840.

The privilege of freedom of speech is essential to protect the independence of Members of Parliament in another way too. Many Members of Parliament are sponsored by organisations outside Parliament, eg Trade Unions. If the privilege of freedom of speech did not exist such organisations might attempt to dictate to the Member of Parliament what he should say and how he should vote during parliamentary proceedings. The initial agreement between a Member of Parliament and a sponsoring organisation does not offend against the privilege unless its terms are such that the Member of Parliament is not free to follow the dictates of his own conscience in speaking and voting in the House. Even termination of such an agreement will not breach the privilege. In the case of *W J Brown* (1949) his position as consultant to a trade union was terminated because the union were dissatisfied with his performance. This was no breach of privilege. However by contrast in 1974 the Yorkshire branch of the National Union of Mineworkers warned its sponsored Members of Parliament that if they failed to speak and vote in support of the Union's policies in Parliament then their sponsorships would be terminated. The Committee of Privileges concluded that this was a breach of privilege in that it was a quite clear attempt to threaten Members of Parliament into following a line dictated to them from outside Parliament and party.

In the case of *K Barron* (1991), Mr Barron was a Labour Member of Parliament sponsored partly by the National Union of Mineworkers. In January 1991, at the last formal count, he was critical of the policies of Arthur Scargill in speeches in Parliament. The National Union of Mineworkers voted to withdraw his sponsorship.

The Committee of Privileges in the House of Commons ruled that, merely because a Member of Parliament was sponsored, it did not make him a delegate of the sponsoring body. The threat to withdraw sponsorship was a breach of the privilege enjoyed by all Members of Parliament to speak out freely on any issue.

A register is now kept to record the business and other interests of Members of Parliament outside Parliament.

NOTE: Absolute privilege protects Members of Parliament from being prosecuted or sued by outsiders for the business they transact in Parliament and this immunity even protects a Member of Parliament who deliberately lies or breaches an Act of Parliament. However if the House considers that a Member of Parliament has abused the privilege of freedom of speech in this way then it may itself punish him for contempt of Parliament (see below).

10.4 Freedom from arrest

Freedom from *civil* arrest (which protected Members of Parliament from being arrested for debts) for the duration of a parliamentary session and 40 days before and after it. This privilege does not extend to arrest in criminal cases and is of little practical importance now as civil arrest can only occur in a few cases.

10.5 Freedom to regulate its own composition

Without interference from the courts, ie the courts cannot declare unlawful a decision made by the House in exercising this privilege. The Commons can:

a) order the issue of writs for by-elections to be held to fill casual vacancies;

b) determine whether a person is disqualified from sitting as a Member of Parliament;

c) expel members which the House considers to be unfit to sit and declare their seats vacant, as *John Wilkes* was on several occasions between 1769–74. (Although as Wilkes showed, the expelled member can be re-elected, upon which the House can expel him again!) Also *Allighan* in 1947, who was expelled for contempt of Parliament, for accusing Members of Parliament of acting against the interests of the House when under the influence of drink or payment.

10.6 Freedom to regulate its own proceedings

Without interference from the courts. This privilege includes the right to maintain order in the House, to enforce this Members of Parliament can be suspended from the House and the right to exclude strangers from the House. The courts will not determine the legality of actions taken by the House in relation to its internal proceedings (see *Pickin* v *British Railways Board*). Even if Parliament makes an error in the interpretation of a statute which applies to such proceedings, the courts will not allow an action against the decision. This is illustrated by one of the stages in the long parliamentary battle involving Charles Bradlaugh.

In *Bradlaugh* v *Gossett* (1884) B was elected to Parliament but as he was an atheist, the House refused to allow him to take the oath. B was excluded from the House, on its resolution by the Serjeant-at-Arms. B claimed an injunction to restrain the Sarjeant-at-Arms, G, from enforcing the order and that the order was void.

It was held, by the Queen's Bench Division, that even if the Commons' resolution was inconsistent with the provisions of the Oaths Act 1866, which required newly elected Members of Parliament to take the oath:

> '... the House of Commons is not subject to the control of Her Majesty's courts in its administration of that part of the statute law which has relation to its own internal proceedings and that the use of such actual force as may be necessary to carry into effect such a resolution as the one before us is justifiable ...
>
> The House of Commons is not a court of justice, but the effect of its privilege to regulate its own internal concerns practically invests it with a judicial character when it has to apply to particular cases the provisions of Acts of Parliament. We must presume that it discharges this function properly and with due regard to the laws ... If its determination is not in accordance with the law, this resembles the case of an error by a judge whose decision is not subject to appeal.'

per Stephen J.

(NOTE: B was elected on several occasions and on several occasions was prevented from taking the oath and was ejected. B had considerable national support and conducted brilliant campaigns. Eventually, he was elected at a general election. He went to swear the oath and kiss the Bible, as required by law. Another newly elected Member of Parliament moved a motion to prevent B from doing so. But the Speaker ruled the Member of Parliament out of order as he had not yet taken the oath himself! B swore the oath and took his seat. At last B could participate in the business of the House to which he had been elected so many times.)

10.7 Contempt of Parliament

A 'breach of privilege' is a breach of one of the defined privileges of Parliament.

A 'contempt of Parliament' is:

> 'Any act or omission which obstructs or impedes either House in the performance of its functions, or ... any member or officer of such House in the discharge of his duty, or which has a tendency, directly or indirectly, to produce such results.'

Erskine May.

The Commons can decide by resolution that any act which fits within these principles is a contempt ('even though there is no precedent for the offence') and can impose a punishment. The important element of a contempt is its obstructive nature. For example: disorderly conduct in the House, refusing to give evidence to a committee, discrediting the House, etc.

10.8 The right to punish for breach of privilege or contempt

The Commons can:

a) expel a Member of Parliament, which means that his seat is vacant and a by-election must be held;

b) imprison a Member of Parliament or an outsider, on a warrant of the Speaker, executed by the Serjeant-at-Arms. Imprisonment can last the duration of a session and the person can be recommitted at the next session. This punitive power is not used now;

c) reprimand or admonition, by the Speaker. These are the most common and least serious forms of punishment. (They amount to a 'ticking off' and having to say 'sorry'.) They may be followed by other sanctions, eg denying a journalist access to the House, which can be fairly serious in effect; but

d) it is generally believed that the Commons cannot impose a fine.

10.9 Privilege, contempt and the courts

In *Stockdale* v *Hansard* (1839) Queen's Bench, a medical book published by S was described in a report of two government officials as 'disgusting and obscene'. This report was printed and sold by H on the order of the Commons. S sued H for libel. H was directed by the Commons to plead that the report had been distributed in compliance with an order of the House, that it was part of parliamentary proceedings and that the House had passed a resolution that described such distribution as 'an essential incident to the constitutional functions of Parliament'. H's defences were:

a) the resolution; and

b) that each House was the sole judge of its privileges.

It was held that:

a) 'the House of Commons is not Parliament, but only a co-ordinate and component part of Parliament. That sovereign power can make and unmake laws; but the concurrence of the three legislative estates is necessary; the resolution of any one of them cannot alter the law or place anyone beyond its control.'

per Lord Denman CJ.

b) that the courts could determine the existence and extent of a privilege which affected someone outside Parliament (Stockdale)

> '... when a matter of privilege comes before the courts not directly, but incidentally, they may because they must, decide it.'

per Lord Denman CJ.

c) that applying this – that parliamentary privilege did *not* extend to give immunity against defamation actions to publications outside the House.

Therefore, if it is alleged in court that a parliamentary privilege places limits on a person who is not a member of Parliament, then the court can determine whether the privilege exists, and if so, how far it extends. In such cases privilege forms a part of the common law and is subject to it. But there is a distinction between privileges that affect outsiders (eg *Stockdale* v *Hansard*) and ones that affect insiders, Members of Parliament and the internal proceedings of the House. In the case of insiders, etc, the courts cannot adjudicate on the existence and extent of the privilege.

> 'Some ... rights are to be exercised out of Parliament, others within the walls of the House of Commons. Those which are to be exercised out of Parliament are under the protection of this court, which ... will apply proper remedies if they are ... invaded, and will in so doing be bound, not by resolutions of either House, but by its own judgment as to the law of the land, of which the privileges of Parliament form a part. Others must be exercised within the House of Commons ... such rights must be dependent upon the resolutions of the House.'

per Stephen J in *Bradlaugh* v *Gossett* (1884).

In *Case of the Sheriffs of Middlesex* (1840) Queen's Bench, the Sheriffs, in pursuance of a writ from the court, levied execution on the property of Hansard, to satisfy a judgment which had been made in favour of Stockdale. (This is the sequel to *Stockdale* v *Hansard* above – S had won an award of damages against H for libel.) The House of Commons committed the Sheriffs for contempt. A writ of habeas corpus was brought and the Serjeant-at-Arms, in reply, referred to the warrant of the Speaker which was authority for the commitment for contempt, but it did not set out what the contempt consisted of.

It was held that:

> '... if the warrant merely states a contempt in general terms, the court is bound by it ... we must presume that ... what either House of Parliament, acting upon great legal authority, takes upon it to pronounce a contempt, is so.'

per Lord Denman CJ.

and therefore, the court could not discharge the Sheriffs from imprisonment.

Therefore, the courts can be excluded from determining the extent of a privilege by Parliament committing a person for contempt without explaining the details of the alleged contempt.

NOTE: After these cases the Parliamentary Papers Act (1840) was enacted (see 10.3).

10.10 Commons procedure on a complaint of breach of privilege or contempt

a) Complaint raised, eg by a Member of Parliament, or committee, or Speaker;

b) Speaker has to decide within 24 hours whether there has been a prima facie breach, etc;

c) If Speaker decides it is a prima facie breach, a motion is put to refer the matter to the Committee of privileges;

d) If motion carried, matter referred;

e) Committee reports to House and recommends action;

f) House not bound to accept report or recommendations (eg *Strauss* case).

11 THE HOUSE OF LORDS

11.1 Introduction

The House of Lords is the less influential of the two Houses of Parliament and by convention and statute it cannot resist the clear will of the Commons. Despite its faults, which arguably mainly result from the fact that its members are not elected, the Lords has important functions. Many different proposals for reforming the Lords have been made and occasionally its abolition is called for. To date, the main reform that has been achieved is the introduction of Life (as opposed to hereditary) peers. It seems clear that some form of Second Chamber is necessary, but in what form and with what powers?

This chapter will consider the Lords as presently constituted and will then look at prospects for reform.

11.2 Composition

In 1991, at the last formal count, the composition of the Lords was 1,201 members, of which 422 were life peers (including law lords and bishops) and 799 hereditary peers.

Of the 422 life peers, 61 are women. The peers attending on a regular basis, from both the life and hereditary groups, number just 324.

Composition of the Lords does not depend on election. The different types of Lord are Lords Spiritual and Lords Temporal.

a) *Lords Spiritual*

These are composed of 26 churchmen, ie the Archbishops of Canterbury, York and the most senior Church of England Bishops.

b) *Lords Temporal*

i) Approximately 800 Hereditary Peers, ie peers entitled to sit by descent. Hereditary peers can be created by the Crown on the Prime Minister's advice.

ii) Approximately 350 Life Peers, ie peers created for their lifetimes only, under the provisions of the Life Peerages Act 1958.

This Act was passed to enable peerages to be created deliberately to increase the representation of non-Conservative interests in the House. The appointments are made by the Crown on the Prime Minister's advice. Life peers are drawn largely from the ranks of politicians, and the trade unions, although eminent persons from other disciplines may also be selected. Through the creation of life peers a wide range of interests and of expertise has been introduced into the House.

iii) Eleven Lords of Appeal in ordinary, ie the Law Lords, who sit to decide cases when the House acts as the final appellate court. The Law Lords are life peers and therefore when one retires he continues to sit in the House in its legislative and other non-judicial roles. By convention, the Law Lords do not align with any political party. They sit on the cross benches, do not take part in controversial political debates, but do contribute to debates where their expertise is useful, eg debates on law reform. By convention, other Lords (lay peers) do not sit with the Law Lords when the latter are acting as a court.

The 'Speaker' of the House of Lords is the Lord Chancellor who, unlike the Speaker of the Commons, takes part in debates and votes in divisions.

NOTE: Whilst it is extremely rare to find independent Members of Parliament in the House of Commons there are independent members of the House of Lords. It is true that most Lords are members of one of the major parties with a system of party whips similar to that in the Commons. There is an in-built majority of Conservative peers. However, because the Lords do not depend upon election to their seats, they may more easily, although they will not readily, defy the party whips. Additionally there are the cross – benchers, approximately 300 independent lords (including the Lords Spiritual and Law Lords) who sit on benches which run between those of the Government and the Opposition, hence their name.

These factors lead to a somewhat less politically charged atmosphere in the Lords making it easier to give attention to issues which are not purely political.

11.3 Disclaimer

Under the Peerages Act 1963, a hereditary peer can disclaim his peerage for his lifetime (ie succession on his death is not affected), provided that he disclaims within 12 months of his succession or coming of age or within one month in the case of a Member of Parliament who succeeds to a peerage.

The Act was passed as the result of a personal campaign by Lord Stansgate, who exercised the rights of disclaimer and is now better known as Tony Benn. The purpose of the Act is to enable persons who are to succeed to hereditary peerages to conduct, or aspire to, an active political life in the Commons, knowing that when they do succeed they can disclaim their peerages. (NB: Peers are barred from membership of the Commons).

NOTE: An hereditary peer may disclaim, pursue an active career in the Commons and later be created a life peer. This happened to the Earl of Home, who disclaimed and, as Alec Douglas-Home, became Prime Minister and was later created Lord Home. Also, Viscount Hailsham disclaimed his title; as Quintin Hogg he became a Member of Parliament, and was later created Lord Hailsham on being appointed Lord Chancellor.

11.4 Leave of absence

Through Standing Orders of the House, a leave of absence system has been introduced under which peers can be granted leave from attending the House. Peers who do not reply to a letter from the Lord Chancellor asking them whether they want to receive leave are deemed to have been granted leave. A peer who is subject to the leave provisions is expected not to attend the House without giving one month's notice of his intention to do so, although there are no legal restraints on such a peer to prevent him attending. This system was introduced to prevent 'backwoodsmen', those peers who rarely take an active part in the business of the House, from voting on and influencing sensitive decisions of the House.

11.5 Attendance

The average daily attendance of peers is between 250 and 275. These 'regulars' are mainly life peers, less than 10 per cent of hereditary peers attend on a regular basis. This is worth bearing in mind because it indicates that the House is not in practice dominated by peers who only have the right to sit by inheritance.

11.6 Functions

The main modern functions of the House are:

a) To try to make the Commons and the government reconsider measures that the Lords consider unsound. The Lords can be particularly assertive when there is a minority government in office (unusual), eg the 1974–9 Labour government. Even the Conservative government, with a majority of 140 in the Commons, was forced to think again by the House of Lords after an attempt to abolish local elections in certain areas of the country suffered severe criticism during the 1984–5 session.

b) To examine and revise Bills passed by the Commons. The Lords, in carrying out this function, provide an opportunity for the government, as well as the Lords, to improve a Bill's drafting, to make technical amendments and to have second thoughts about a Bill's provisions. The Lords, without the closure and guillotine motions of the Commons, has more time to examine Bills and can consider them in greater detail. The Committee stage in the Lords takes place before the whole House and therefore a wider spectrum of experts can consider the provisions. Life peers will normally only be appointed as such having risen to an eminent position after a full career in a particular industry or environment and may thus have a clearer understanding of the likely effect of proposed legislation on a particular industry than Members of Parliament.

c) Less controversial Bills can be introduced in the Lords and go through their parliamentary stages in the Lords before going to the Commons. Such Bills receive detailed examination and scrutiny before going to the Commons. This saves the government time in the Commons. Most Private Bills are dealt with in this way.

d) To debate matters of public importance, sometimes matters that the Commons just does not have the time to consider.

e) To scrutinise the activities of the Executive by question time, etc.

11.7 Relations with the Commons

The Commons is the dominant House. Money Bills, ie Bills which are certified by the Speaker as involving only taxation or expenditure, etc, must be introduced in the Commons. This means that the most crucial Bills have to be dealt with by the Commons before going to the Lords. By convention, the Lords has to give way to the will of the Commons in a case of conflict. This convention has been reinforced and given a statutory basis by the Parliament Acts 1911 and 1949.

a) *Background to the 1911 and 1949 Parliament Acts*

In 1909, the Lords rejected the Liberal Government's budget, after a series of battles between Commons and Lords. The government got the promise of the King that he would create enough new peers to outnumber resistance in the Lords. The government called an election to see if the electorate endorsed its policies. It won. The Parliament Bill, to restrict the powers of the Lords, was introduced and passed by the Commons. The Lords objected to some of its provisions. The Prime Minister made known the King's promise and the Lords then passed the Bill. The 1911 Act was amended to impose greater restrictions on the Lords when the 1949 Act was passed under the 1911 Act procedure (without the consent of the Lords). The 1949 Act was passed to ensure that the Labour Government had the means of forcing through its nationalisation plans, if necessary.

Key provisions of the 1911 Act as amended by the 1949 Act are:

i) Under s2: if a Public Bill is passed by the Commons in two successive sessions and is rejected by the Lords in both of those sessions, then on its second rejection, the Bill can be presented for royal assent to become an Act, ie even though the Lords has not passed it. One year must have elapsed between the second reading of the Bill in the Commons in the first session and the passing of the Bill by the Commons in the second session.

Section 2 allows the Lords a limited power to delay measures passed by the Commons. Basically, if the Commons passes a Bill twice, it can go for royal assent despite its rejection by the Lords. Under the 1911 Act, the delaying power was two years, this was reduced to one year in 1949. Section 2 does not apply to Money Bills.

ii) Under s1: a Money Bill, ie a Bill certified by the Speaker as including only provisions relating to central government taxation, expenditure or borrowing, which has been passed by the Commons can, if it has not been passed by the Lords without amendment within one month, be presented for royal assent to become an Act, even though the Lords has not passed it.

iii) The provisions of the Parliament Acts do *not* apply to a Bill to extend the maximum duration of Parliament beyond five years.

NOTE: The Parliament Acts do not alter the Lords' powers in respect of Private Bills or delegated legislation.

b) *Use of the 1911 and 1949 Parliaments Acts*

The Acts could be used to ensure dominance by the Commons, but in fact the special procedure has only been used on three occasions:

i) To pass the Welsh Church Act 1914;

ii) To pass the Government of Ireland Act 1914 – which did not come into force;

iii) To pass the Parliament Act 1949.

The 1949 Act powers have been used only once, although the special procedure may act as a threat in the background, the presence of which ensures that the convention of Commons dominance is not broken by the Lords.

In June 1990 the Lords rejected the War Crimes Bill which had received a comfortable majority at second reading in the Commons.

In 1991 the Government reintroduced the Bill, and it was again defeated at a Second Reading in the House of Lords. The Government used the procedures introduced by the Parliaments Acts 1911 and 1949 to send the Bill direct to the Queen for the Royal Assent. The Bill became law in the summer of 1991.

The 1949 Act itself was passed against the wishes of the Lords, and this is the first time its provisions have been used to force through legislation.

11.8 Reform

Firstly, distinguish reform, which would keep the Lords in existence, but modify and change it, from abolition, which would mean the disbanding of the Lords.

The 1911 Act in its preamble stated that Parliament intended eventually:

'to substitute for the House of Lords ... a Second Chamber constituted on a popular instead of a hereditary basis.'

The main sources of discontent within the Lords are: its largely hereditary composition; its total lack of elected members; its traditional conservatism. All these things are interlinked.

The major reform to date has been the introduction of life peers. The closest that the Lords has come to radical reform was in 1968–9.

In 1968 the Labour government introduced a Bill under which membership of the Lords was to be divided into two classes; (a) voting peers; and (b) non-voting peers.

a) *Voting* peers were to be those existing life peers who declared that they wanted to be voting peers and hereditary peers of first creation who wished to be voting peers. A voting peer would have the right to speak and vote, although this voting right would be lost if a peer failed to attend one-third of the House's sittings. There was to be a retirement age of 72.

b) *Non-voting* peers were to be all the other peers. They were to have the right to speak during debates, but not to vote.

After a general election the government was to have the power to create enough new voting peers to give the government a majority over the Opposition parties in the Lords, *but* not over the Opposition and the crossbench peers (those who do not align with any party) together.

The delaying power of the Lords was to be reduced to six months. The Bill was abandoned by the government in 1969 because it took up too much parliamentary time and the government wanted to introduce other more important legislation.

NOTE: This Bill would still have retained the House on an appointed and not elected basis. The present policy of the Labour party is that the House of Lords should be replaced by an elected assembly.

12 DELEGATED LEGISLATION

12.1 Introduction

For various reasons, but mainly because of lack of time, Parliament does not itself make all new laws. In many instances, it delegates law-making powers to subordinates, eg Ministers, local authorities or nationalised industries. Each year the amount and volume of delegated legislation is vastly greater than the amount and volume of statutes passed by Parliament. An important preliminary point is that powers to make delegated legislation are powers delegated by a superior authority, Parliament, to an inferior authority, eg a Minister. The powers are, therefore, subject to the limitations placed on them by Parliament. An inferior authority can only make laws within the powers given to it by Parliament (intra vires).

On terminology: an Act which gives an authority the power to make delegated legislation is termed 'the enabling Act' or 'the parent Act', and delegated legislation may be described as 'subordinate legislation', 'statutory instruments', regulations', 'rules', 'orders', etc, depending on the context.

12.2 Why is delegated legislation used?

a) *Lack of time*

Parliament has so many Bills to consider and such a great amount of work to do that it has very little time to consider matters of legislative detail. When Parliament passes an Act, it generally decides on the general policy of the Act but, to save time, it leaves the details of how that policy is to be put into operation to be filled in by some subordinate authority through delegated legislation.

b) *Technical details*

Delegated legislation is used to fill in those technical details in a legislative scheme that Parliament itself would not have the expertise to understand. Such details can be left to be drafted by subordinate authorities acting on the advice of and in consultation with experts.

c) *Unforeseen contingencies*

Provision is sometimes made for delegated legislation to be available to be used by a subordinate authority to deal with matters that were not foreseen at the time the parent Act was passed.

Delegated legislation is flexible and can be used to enable experimentation with new ideas, to see whether they work in practice.

d) *Emergency powers*

e) Some Acts do not come into effect immediately they are enacted. In such cases, delegated legislation is used to bring the statutory provisions into effect at some later date. Sometimes different parts of an Act are brought into effect at different times.

Also note:

'The Henry VIII clause'

Sometimes an enabling Act will give a power to make delegated legislation which modifies the provisions of other Acts and, sometimes even, the provisions of the enabling Act itself (The Henry VIII clause).

12.3 Criticisms

Legislation:

a) Often the details that are filled in by delegated legislation are the most important parts of a statutory scheme. It is arguable that such matters should be dealt with by Parliament which is directly responsible to the electors.

b) The major criticism is that, accepting that delegated legislation is very useful and indispensable, the controls over it are inadequate and ineffective. (This is considered in detail later in the chapter.)

12.4 Statutory instruments

a) *Procedure: what is a Statutory Instrument?*

There is a common set of procedural rules which apply to the making of a Statutory Instrument. What is a Statutory Instrument?

The Statutory Instruments Act 1946 s1(1):

> 'Where by this Act or any Act passed after the commencement of this Act power to make, confirm or approve orders, rules, regulations or other subordinate legislation is conferred on His Majesty in Council or on any Minister of the Crown then, if the power is expressed:
>
> i) in the case of a power conferred on His Majesty to be exercisable by Order in Council;
>
> ii) in the case of a power conferred on a Minister of the Crown, to be exercisable by statutory instrument, any document by which that power is exercised shall be known as a "statutory instrument" and the provisions of this Act shall apply thereto accordingly.'

A Statutory Instrument is therefore either an Order in Council (the Privy Council) or a piece of delegated legislation which results from a power given by a statute to make Statutory Instruments! Note that a Statutory Instrument can take the form of an order, rule, regulation, or any other type of subordinate legislation. Generally, statutes when giving the power to make a delegated legislation require it to be exercised in the form of Statutory Instruments.

b) *Making and publication*

A Statutory Instrument must be in the form of a document. The Statutory Instrument is 'made' as soon as it is drafted in its final form. The enabling Act may require the authority to consult with various specified persons and bodies before making the Statutory Instrument, or it may give the authority a discretion as to whom to consult.

The 1946 Act sets out provisions for the publication of Statutory Instruments once they have been made.

i) *Section 2(1)*

> 'Immediately after the making of any statutory instrument, it shall be sent to the King's printer of Acts ... and ... copies thereof shall as soon as possible be printed and sold by the

King's printer of Acts'. (Sometimes though a Statutory Instrument does not have to be published and made available to the public, eg if publication would be 'contrary to the public interest' or if the Statutory Instrument is only to have temporary effect.)

If a Statutory Instrument has to be published and is not, then:

the Statutory Instrument itself is still valid – *R* v *Sheer Metalcraft Ltd* (1954) a Statutory Instrument is valid on being made; but if a prosecution is brought against a person for breaking the terms of an unpublished Statutory Instrument the person has a special defence (s3(2)).

ii) *Section 3(2)*

> 'In any proceedings against any person for an offence consisting of a contravention of any such statutory instrument, it shall be a defence to prove that the instrument had not been issued by His Majesty's Stationery Office at the date of the alleged contravention unless it is proved that at that date reasonable steps had been taken for the purpose of bringing the purport of the instrument to the notice of the public, or of persons likely to be affected by it, or of the person charged.'

In other words, the defence of non-publication can be rebutted by the prosecution showing that reasonable steps were taken within the provisions of the subsection.

12.5 Parliamentary controls – 'laying' before Parliament

a) *Introduction*

Sometimes, but not always, a Statutory Instrument when made has to be laid before Parliament. Whether or not it has to be laid depends on the terms of the enabling Act. A Statutory Instrument is laid once it has been delivered to the Votes and Proceedings Office of either the House of Commons or Lords, depending on the enabling Act's provisions. This merely means that the Statutory Instrument has been received, along with many others, in a Parliamentary office. This in itself is not a control over Statutory Instruments, but the enabling Act may also make the Statutory Instrument subject to either a negative or an affirmative resolution procedure once it has been laid. It is through these procedures that Parliament has its main opportunity to try to control Statutory Instruments. (Note, some enabling Acts will not require a resolution procedure, in which case the Statutory Instruments generally go through no parliamentary scrutiny at all.)

b) *Negative resolution procedure*

Under this procedure, a Statutory Instrument will be laid before its provisions come into operation. (A Statutory Instrument can come into effect earlier than this when it is essential for it to do so. The Lord Chancellor and the Speaker must be given an explanation of the reasons.) Then, the members of either the Commons or Lords have a period of 40 days during which any one of them can propose that the Statutory Instrument be annulled. A Statutory Instrument can only be annulled by Parliament, not amended, through this procedure. Proposals (resolutions) for annulment are moved at the end of a day's business in Parliament, before the adjournment debate and there is very often little time available for debate and few members present to listen. If the resolution to annul is carried on a vote in either House then the Statutory Instrument will be annulled by an Order in Council.

NOTE: A Statutory Instrument can come into operation before the expiration of the 40-day period, but it can still be annulled during that period. Generally, Statutory Instruments come into operation at the end of the period, if not annulled.

Criticisms

This procedure relies heavily on the alertness of individual Members of Parliament and peers and their ability to spot Statutory Instruments that should be annulled. This is not an easy task given the great numbers of Statutory Instruments that have been laid and Parliament is assisted by the Joint

Special Committee (see below). But, there is very little time available for resolutions and by necessity only a few can be made. The majority of Statutory Instruments go unchecked through this procedure.

c) *Affirmative resolution procedure*

Under this procedure, the Statutory Instrument is made and laid but cannot come into operation unless it is approved (affirmed) by both Houses of Parliament. This procedure is simple and it provides very effective parliamentary control over Statutory Instruments as Parliament has to debate and positively approve them. However, the main reason why Statutory Instruments are used is to save parliamentary time. This procedure uses up far more time than the negative procedure. Few Statutory Instruments are made subject to this procedure by enabling Acts. Because Parliament does have not the time to deal with many Statutory Instruments under this procedure, it has to remain the exception and not the rule.

12.6 The Joint Special Committee

Parliament is assisted by the Joint Special Committee. It is made up of members drawn from both Houses. The Committee considers Statutory Instruments laid before Parliament to see whether any of the following conditions exist:

a) that it imposes a tax or charge;

b) that by virtue of the enabling statute, it is excluded from challenge in the courts;

c) that it purports to have retrospective effect, where no such express authority was conferred by the parent statute;

d) that there appears to have been some unjustified delay in the publication or laying of the instrument;

e) that the instrument has come into operation prior to 'laying' and the Speaker of the House has not been promptly notified thereof;

f) that it appears to make some unusual or unexpected use of the delegated power, or that there is a doubt whether the instrument is ultra vires the enabling statute;

g) that for any special reason its form or purport requires elucidation;

h) that the drafting appears to be defective.

If the Committee finds that a Statutory Instrument falls within one of these headings, it will make a report to Parliament. It is then for a member of either House to seek to get the Statutory Instrument annulled (if the report is made within the 40-day period, which is not always the case) or to raise the matter in Parliament in some other way, eg through a Question to a Minister.

12.7 Judicial controls

The courts can review the validity of delegated legislation by applying the doctrine of 'ultra vires'.

For the purposes of this chapter, there follows a brief explanation:

The power to make delegated legislation derives from statutes. Enabling Acts will expressly confine the power in some way, eg the statute may require the authority vested with the power to consult interest groups before using it, or the statute may precisely limit the subject matter that the delegated legislation can cover. If such express limitations are exceeded by an authority, eg a Minister, then the authority has exceeded its powers under the enabling Act. It has acted 'ultra vires'. In such cases, the courts can declare the delegated legislation void.

The courts also imply certain limitations into enabling Acts, eg that delegated legislation must not be grossly unreasonable nor made in bad faith. If these limitations are broken then there has been an ultra vires exercise of power. The courts can determine the validity of delegated legislation because authorities can *only* have the powers given to them by the enabling Acts within the express and implied limitations of that Act.

Note:

The legal validity of a Statutory Instrument can be reviewed by the High Court, even though the Statutory Instrument has been approved by a resolution of either or both Houses of Parliament, because such resolutions do not constitute Acts of Parliament (which are beyond judicial review): *Stockdale* v *Hansard.*

To illustrate:

a) Delegated legislation may be ultra vires if the enabling Act requires consultation and this has not been complied with: *Agricultural, Horticultural and Forestry Industry Training Board* v *Aylesbury Mushrooms* (1972) High Court. Under an enabling Act the Minister of Labour had to consult with organisations 'appearing to him' to be ones that should be consulted, before exercising his power to make a Statutory Instrument. The Minister did not comply with this requirement.

   The court held that a Statutory Instrument made by the Minister was void in relation to the members of the mushroom growers association which had not been consulted as required.

b) Delegated legislation will be ultra vires if it does not relate to the purposes of the enabling Act, or if it is grossly unreasonable.

   In *Commissioners of Customs and Excise* v *Cure and Deeley Ltd* (1962) High Court, the Finance Act 1960 gave the Commissioners the power to make regulations to give effect to the provisions of the Act. The Commissioners made a requisition under which they could determine the amount of tax due from a person if he did not make a tax return and that the amount determined would be deemed to be the proper tax due. The Commissioners made such a determination. A challenge was made in court to the validity of the regulation.

   The court held that the regulation was ultra vires and invalid because, among other reasons, it allowed the Commissioners to determine the amount of tax payable, instead of the tax payable being determined under the provisions of the Act itself.

   That is, the regulation:

   > '... renders the subject liable to pay such tax as the Commissioners believe to be due, whereas the charging sections impose a liability to pay such tax as in law is due.'
   >
   > per Sachs J.

   The regulation sought:

   > '... to substitute the rule of tax collectors for the rule of law.'

   Sachs J also held that the court should examine 'the nature, objects and scheme' of the enabling Act to determine the extent of the power given to make delegated legislation and to use that to determine whether the regulation is ultra vires.

c) The courts will also protect certain important constitutional principles, eg even though some tax rates can be varied by Statutory Instruments (eg VAT, subject to an affirmative resolution procedure in the Commons if the tax is increased), the courts will not decide that a power to make a Statutory Instrument involves any power to impose taxation unless the terms of the enabling Act clearly give this power.

   In *Attorney-General* v *Wilts United Dairies* (1921) House of Lords, an Act of 1916 established the office of Food Controller, who was given the duty of regulating the supply of food and under the Defence of the Realm Act 1914, the powers to make orders regulating the production, supply, sale, pricing of foods. The Food Controller made an Order which provided that two pence a gallon had to be paid to the Food Controller on milk from a certain area. Wilts agreed to this provision in return for a licence to purchase milk from the area concerned. Wilts then refused to pay the sums and the Attorney-General sued for the money due.

It was held that the regulation provisions were ultra vires. The charging provisions infringed Article 4 of the Bill of Rights 1689, which declared that no money could be raised for the Crown without the consent of Parliament:

> '... the Food Controller could only acquire the right to make such a charge by statutory authority.
>
> ... if an officer of the executive seeks to justify a charge upon the subject made for the use of the Crown, he must show, in clear terms, that Parliament has authorised that particular charge.
>
> ... no powers ... of imposing any such charge are given to the Minister of Food by the statutory provisions.'

per Atkin LJ (delivering judgment in the Court of Appeal, which was upheld by the House of Lords).

And also eg:

The courts will not allow Statutory Instruments to take away a citizen's right of access to the courts:

> 'This might legally be done by Act of Parliament, but I think this extreme disability can be inflicted only by direct enactment of the legislature itself.'

Chester v *Bateson* (1920) High Court.

In *R* v *Richmond upon Thames LBC, ex parte McCarthy and Stone Ltd* (1991) a local authority had charged a fee of £25 for a consultation between its local government planning officers and the developers, before the latter had made a planning application. The council relied on the Local Government Act 1972 s111 which confers on local authorities 'power to do anything calculated to facilitate or is conducive or incidental to, the discharge of their functions'. The House of Lords held that the charge was unlawful; there was no direct authority and the test of 'necessary implication' went far beyond what was proposed here. The Bill of Rights in 1689 Article 4, requires Parliamentary authority for the levying of taxation. 'Taxation' includes indirect charges such as that proposed here and the Local Government Act s111 did *not* give the necessary authority.

d) Parliament at one time sought to exclude judicial review of the validity of delegated legislation by enacting the following type of provision in enabling Acts:

> 'Regulations made shall have effect *as if enacted in this Act.*'

In *Institute of Patent Agents* v *Lockwood* (1894) the House of Lords held that regulations made in such a case were as unchallengeable in courts as if they had actually been provisions of an Act of Parliament.

But, in *Minister of Health* v *R, ex parte Yaffe* (1931) the House of Lords held that, even if an enabling Act contained such a provision, the authority given the powers could only act within the terms of the statute. If those were broken, ie if the delegated legislation was ultra vires, then the courts could intervene. The 'as if enacted' clause could not protect delegated legislation which was made outside the powers of the enabling Act. In this case, the Lords showed considerable determination to ensure that the courts retained their power to review the validity of delegated legislation. The 'as if enacted' clause is not used today.

12.8 By-laws

By-laws are a special type of delegated legislation. The power to make by-laws is given by statutes to *non*-central government authorities, ie for the purposes of this chapter, local authorities, although statutory corporations, eg BR Board, are also given such powers.

Local authority by-laws

Section 235 Local Government Act 1972 gives local authorities a general power:

> 'to make by-laws for the good rule and government of the whole or any part of the district or borough and for the prevention and suppression of nuisances therein.'

Various statutes also confer on local authorities the power to make by-laws for particular purposes, eg public health, housing, highways, etc.

The procedure used to make by-laws has some special features. A by-law once made by an authority is only effective if it is confirmed by a central government Minister, usually the Secretary of State for the Environment (depending on the enabling Act).

When a local authority makes a by-law it must advertise in local newspapers that it is to seek Ministerial confirmation of it. This is to give the public the opportunity to make representations to the Minister.

The Minister concerned, or rather his departmental officials, will consider the by-law and, in practice, will receive representations from interested groups and persons before coming to a decision.

The Minister can reject or confirm the by-law, but there is no express power given to him to modify or amend it. A confirmed by-law will come into operation soon after its confirmation. It can be reviewed by the courts if:

a) the procedural steps required by the enabling Act have not been followed; or

b) the by-law was made beyond the powers of the local authority; or

c) the by-law is vague in its terms or uncertain in operation or application; or

d) the by-law runs contrary (is repugnant) to a statutory provision; or

e) the by-law is unreasonable.

In *Kruse* v *Johnson* (1898) Lord Russell CJ said:

> 'Unreasonable in what sense? If, for instance, they (the by-laws) were found to be partial and unequal in their operation as between different classes; if they were manifestly unjust; if they disclosed bad faith; if they involved such oppressive or gratuitous interference with the rights of those subject to them as could find no justification in the minds of reasonable men, the court might well say Parliament never intended to give authority to make such rules; they are unreasonable and ultra vires.'

If a by-law is made in breach of any of these principles, then a court can declare it to be void.

13 THE CROWN, PREROGATIVE AND ACT OF STATE

13.1 The Crown and the prerogative – introduction

One of the most important characteristics of the United Kingdom's constitution is its system of limited monarchy, ie the Crown's vast array of common law prerogative powers can only be exercised constitutionally by the monarch acting strictly in accordance with the advice of her ministers, who are responsible to Parliament. While at law the monarch could personally govern in an autocratic way, conventions have developed to limit the operation of every important common law power the Crown has.

13.2 The prerogative

Dicey described the Crown's prerogative powers as:

> 'The *residue* of *discretionary* authority which at any given time is *legally left* in the hands of the Crown.'

Prerogative powers are those powers, rights, immunities and privileges, derived from the common law, which the Crown has but ordinary citizens do not.

a) *'legally left'* – ie prerogative powers stem from common law principles.

b) *'residue'* – ie the Crown can have its prerogatives taken away, or suspended, by statutory provisions. At any time the Crown's prerogative powers are those common law powers which it has which have not been affected by statute law.

c) *'discretionary'* – ie according to common law, the Crown can exercise its remaining powers at will, as the monarch pleases.

13.3 Prerogative powers

What sort of powers does the monarch have at common law?

The following is a list of some of the more important prerogative powers of the Crown. It will be appreciated, when this list has been read, that if the monarch could exercise these powers uncontrolled by constitutional principles, the United Kingdom would have a system of strong monarchic government:

a) appoint and dismiss Prime Minister and Ministers;

b) summon, prorogue and dissolve Parliament;

c) assent and refuse to assent to Bills passed by Parliament;

d) create peers;

e) give honours;

f) appoint judges and a great range of other public officers;

g) control, organise, and dispose of the armed forces;

h) negotiate treaties;

i) declare war;

j) grant passports;

k) restrain aliens entering the United Kingdom;

l) pardon criminals;

m) stop prosecutions in the courts (by entering a 'nolle prosequi').

All these powers, and many more not listed, could be exercised at common law at the will of the monarch, eg the Queen could appoint whomever she liked to be Prime Minister and Ministers (the government) and dismiss them whenever she wanted to; she could allow Parliament to sit and then suspend it whenever she wanted to, etc.

13.4 Conventions

Since 1688 and the Glorious Revolution, conventions have developed which have severely limited all of these powers and have effectively taken them out of the hands of the monarch acting personally. The Glorious Revolution led to a change in political power which gave Parliament predominance over the Crown. Conventions reflect this by requiring that the Crown's common law powers have always to be exercised in particular ways and usually only on and in accordance with the advice of ministers (responsible to Parliament).

By convention:

a) after a general election the Queen must appoint the leader of the largest party in the Commons to be the Prime Minister. She cannot appoint whomever she personally likes or prefers. A Prime Minister only loses office when his party loses control in the Commons after an election defeat;

b) the Queen can only appoint Ministers in accordance with the Prime Minister's wishes; she cannot appoint whom she likes;

c) the Queen can only order the dissolution of Parliament on the Prime Minister's advice and at a time when the Prime Minister wants a dissolution. The Queen cannot dissolve Parliament as she pleases;

d) the Queen must assent to a Bill passed by Commons and Lords. The last time royal assent was refused was in 1708;

e) the Queen creates peers and gives honours on the Prime Minister's advice;

f) the Queen appoints judges on the Prime Minister's or the Lord Chancellor's (depending on the importance of the judge) advice;

g) the armed forces are controlled (etc ...)

h) treaties are negotiated ... }

i) passports are issued ... } on the Queen's behalf by Ministers

j) criminals are pardoned ... }

k) prosecutions are stopped ... etc }

Therefore, the Crown's prerogative powers are not in any real sense exercised by the Queen, but rather are exercised only on and in accordance with the advice of Ministers or by a Minister acting on the Crown's behalf.

Conventions have transformed a strong monarchy into a constitutional, limited one.

In return, though, for exercising her powers in accordance with these limitations, the Queen is constitutionally entitled to some reciprocal respect from the government. It is a constitutional understanding that the Queen has, as Bagehot explained, the right to be consulted by, to encourage and to warn the government (in general, the Prime Minister). The Queen can express her personal views to the Prime Minister at their regular audiences (meetings). Whether or not these are paid much heed depends on the experience and wisdom of the monarch. In an interview at the time of the Queen's sixtieth birthday the former Conservative Prime Minister, Edward Heath, disclosed that during his term of office (1970–1974) he had on various occasions modified Government policy in the light of the present Queen's advice, although he gave no specific examples. The Prime Minister must keep the Queen adequately informed of the government's decisions and actions.

The Queen receives Cabinet and State papers, which she apparently spends a great deal of time reading and studying.

Also, it is suggested, conventions only operate clearly to limit the Queen's prerogative powers when political conditions are stable. The Queen has residuary discretions. Should there be the necessity to do so, the Queen could exercise her prerogative on her own initiative. The following are some examples of occasions when the monarch might need to act in this way:

a) if after a General Election there was a 'hung' Parliament, ie one where no party had a clear majority and the political leaders were unable to reach any agreement for a coalition then, in the last resort the monarch might have to decide whom to summon to form a Government. This is with the first past the post system, an unlikely occurrence;

b) if a Government was defeated on a vote of confidence in the Commons but broke convention and did not resign the Queen might dismiss the Prime Minister to enable a General Election to be held. In 1975 in Australia the Labour Government failed to secure support for its financial policies in the Senate and proposed to call an election to the senate but not a full General Election. The Governor General, who acts on behalf of the monarch, dismissed the Prime Minister, Gough Whitlam, and replaced him by a caretaker Prime Minister who called a General Election for both Houses of the Legislature;

c) if a Prime Minister abused the position by calling for a second General Election immediately having just been defeated at a first then the Queen might refuse to dissolve Parliament as she has a residuary right to protect the national interest in this way.

13.5 Statutes

The two major results of the Glorious Revolution were:

a) the Crown's prerogative powers were to be exercised in a constitutional way (discussed above); and

b) they could be removed, or suspended, by Parliament, ie by statute law.

The Crown's powers are subordinate to the power of Parliament to restrict them: see Articles 1, 2 and 4 of the Bill of Rights 1689.

Parliament, on the other hand, cannot create new prerogative powers, as these derive from common law.

Parliament can expressly remove a prerogative power (ie by expressly stating that it no longer exists), but it can also impliedly suspend a prerogative by passing a statute which creates a scheme which covers the same area as a prerogative. For example:

In *Attorney-General* v *De Keyser's Royal Hotel* (1920) House of Lords, an hotel was requisitioned by the Crown during World War I to provide air force administrative accommodation. The owners sought compensation, claiming that the requisitioning had been effected under the provisions of the Defence of the Realm Act 1914 and regulations made thereunder. But the Crown alleged that it had acted under prerogative powers and that no compensation was payable.

It was held that in fact the Crown had acted under the statutory powers, not under the prerogative; while the statute was in force, as it covered the same ground as a prerogative, the prerogative was suspended and could not be used.

Lord Dunedin said:

> 'Those powers which the executive exercises without parliamentary authority are comprised under the comprehensive term of the prerogative. Where, however, Parliament has intervened and has provided by statute for powers, previously within the prerogative, being exercised in a particular manner and subject to the limitations and provisions contained in the statute, they can only be so exercised. Otherwise, what use would there be in imposing limitations if the Crown could at its pleasure disregard them and fall back on prerogative? It is quite obvious that it would be useless and meaningless for the legislature to impose restrictions and limitations upon and to attach conditions to the exercise by the Crown of the powers conferred by a statute, if the Crown were free at its pleasure to disregard these provisions and by virtue of its prerogative, do the very thing the statutes empowered it to do. One cannot in the construction of a statute attribute to the legislature (in the absence of compelling words) an intention so absurd ... when such a statute expressing the will and intention of the King and of the three estates of the realm is passed, it abridges the Royal Prerogative while it is in force to this extent; that the Crown can only do the particular thing under and in accordance with the statutory provisions and that its prerogative power to do that thing is in abeyance. Whichever mode of expression be used, the result intended to be indicated is, I think, the same, namely that after the statute has been passed and while it is in force, the thing it empowers the Crown to do can thenceforth only be done by and under the statute and subject to all limitations and restrictions and conditions by it imposed, however unrestricted the Royal Prerogative may theretofore have been ...'

Therefore, statutes can expressly or impliedly restrict prerogative powers. However, in some cases Parliament may decide to set up a statutory scheme which covers the same area as a prerogative and yet expressly preserve the prerogative power. This was done, for example, by the Immigration Act 1971 which set up a statutory scheme for the control of immigration, yet preserved the Crown's common law power to exclude aliens.

13.6 When do statutes apply to the Crown?

When will statutory provisions bind the Crown?

The established rule is that a statute only binds the Crown when the statute expressly states that it does, or when the purpose of the statute would be 'wholly frustrated' if the Crown was not bound, ie the Crown is bound by 'necessary implication'.

In *Province of Bombay* v *Bombay Municipal Corporation* (1947) Privy Council, Lord Du Parcq said:

> 'If it can be affirmed that, at the time when the statute was passed and received the royal sanction, it was apparent from its terms that its beneficient purpose must be wholly frustrated unless the Crown were bound, then it may be inferred that the Crown has agreed to be bound. Their Lordships will add that when the court is asked to draw this inference, it must always be remembered that, if it be the

intention of that legislature that the Crown shall be bound, nothing is easier than to say so in plain words ...'

13.7 The courts

In 1984 there was a major development in the law when in the *GCHQ* case the House of Lords extended the control of the courts over exercises of prerogative powers.

In order fully to understand the importance of the decision the pre 1984 position was as follows.

When a case which involved an alleged exercise of prerogative power by the Crown came before the courts, the courts could determine:

a) whether the claimed prerogative existed at law and how far it extended;

b) whether it had been limited by statute and if so, in what way.

> 'The King has no prerogative but that which the law of the land allows him.'
>
> *Case of Proclamations (1610).*

c) whether there was any requirement that the Crown pay compensation after the exercise of a prerogative:

In *Burmah Oil* v *Lord Advocate* (1965) House of Lords, British troops operating in Burmah during World War II, destroyed some oil installations near Rangoon, to ensure that the installations did not fall into the hands of the advancing Japanese army. The destruction was carried out in the exercise of prerogative powers exercisable in time of war, but the installations were not destroyed in battle. After the War, the owners of the installation claimed compensation for the destruction.

It was held that as a general rule compensation had to be paid by the Crown when property was destroyed in times of war in the exercise of prerogative powers. There was an exception to this general rule for 'battle damage', but the destruction in this case did not fall under that exception.

NOTE: The main effect of this decision was retrospectively annulled by the War Damage Act 1965.

Section 1(1):

> 'No person shall be entitled at common law to receive from the Crown compensation in respect of damage to, or destruction of, property caused (whether before or after the passing of this Act, within or outside the United Kingdom) by acts lawfully done, or on the authority of the Crown during or in contemplation of a war in which the Sovereign was, or is, engaged.'

NOTE: The War Damage Act 1965 does not cover the taking of property for use but only refers to 'damage to, or destruction of property'. The exercise of the prerogative to take property for use involves an obligation to pay compensation.

However, the courts traditionally took the view that, although they could consider the matters listed at (a)–(c) above, they could not review the actual exercise of the prerogative: *Attorney-General* v *De Keyser's Royal Hotel* (1920) HL.

For example, in *Chandler* v *DPP* (1964) House of Lords, some members of CND planned a demonstration at a military airfield, to protest against the maintenance of nuclear weapons. They were charged with conspiring to enter a prohibited place (the airfield) for a purpose prejudicial to the safety or interests of the State. They were convicted and appealed. They argued that their purpose was not prejudicial to the interests of the State because the maintenance of nuclear weapons was itself prejudicial to such interests. The policy decision to have nuclear weapons was made in exercise of the prerogative, ie the disposition, etc of armed forces.

It was held that:

> 'It is clear that the disposition and armament of the armed forces are within the exclusive discretion of the Crown and no one can seek a legal remedy on the ground that such discretion

> has been wrongfully exercised. Anyone is entitled to urge that policy be changed, but no one is entitled to challenge it in court.'
>
> per Lord Reid.

Lord Devlin did say, though, that: 'The courts will not review the proper exercise of discretionary power *but* they will intervene to correct excess or abuse.'

In *Laker Airways* v *Department of Trade* (1977) Court of Appeal, to operate its 'Skytrain' service, Laker needed:

a) to be designated as an air carrier by the United Kingdom authorities under the provisions of the 1946 Bermuda Agreement (a treaty); and

b) a licence from the Civil Aviation Authority, which was established by the Civil Aviation Act 1971.

   Laker was given both. But then, the government changed its policy. The Secretary of State for Trade issued guidance to the Civil Aviation Authority to cancel Laker's licence. Two questions arose for the court:

a) Had the Secretary of State acted within his powers in issuing the new guidance?

b) Could the Secretary of State avoid any difficulties, by cancelling Laker's designation under the Treaty, ie by exercising a prerogative power?

It was held that, on (a) the Secretary of State had acted against the policy of the 1971 Act and, therefore, ultra vires. On (b) that the prerogative power had been fettered by statute because the 1971 Act covered the same ground (see *De Keyser's Royal Hotel*). Their Lordships also considered whether an exercise of prerogative power could be reviewed: the majority held (Roskill and Lawton LJJ) that the court could only determine whether the prerogative had been fettered by statute, it could not review how a prerogative had been exercised.

The minority (on this point) held:

> 'The prerogative is a discretionary power exercised by the executive government for the public good. The law does not interfere with the proper exercise of the discretion by the executive, but ... it can intervene if the discretion is exercised improperly or mistakenly ... its exercise can be examined by the courts just as any other discretionary power which is vested in the executive.'
>
> per Lord Denning MR.

In *Gouriet* v *UPOW* (1978) the House of Lords held that the Attorney-General's discretion in giving or in this case withholding consent to a relator action was not reviewable by the courts, as the power was part of the prerogative.

In the *GCHQ* case (1984), however, the House of Lords took a more modern view of the reviewability of the prerogative – a reflection of the importance of judicial review in general today.

In that case, the Prime Minister, acting under the prerogative, ordered that the right to join a trade union should be withdrawn from employees at GCHQ on the grounds of national security. The Council for the Civil Service Unions challenged the ban on the grounds that the Government had not consulted them prior to making the ban when on all other employment matters consultation would have taken place. The High Court decided in favour of the unions but the Court of Appeal reversed this decision. The House of Lords agreed. The Government was not bound to consult with the trade unions before making a ban because national security had been at stake and this meant that the rules of natural justice did not apply. The House went on to consider whether the courts could review the exercise of prerogative powers in a similar way to their review of powers derived from statute. They decided that there was no logical reason for differentiating their approach according to the source of the power at issue in a case. In future they would treat powers derived from the prerogative as reviewable but the Lords accepted that many prerogative powers were political in nature and not suitable for judicial interference, the subject matter was not justiciable, and therefore these prerogative powers would remain immune from judicial review. Lord Roskill gave a list of some examples of such powers, the defence of the realm, mercy, the making of treaties, the appointment of ministers, the dissolution of Parliament, the granting of honours (among others) were not amenable to the judicial process and, therefore, were not susceptible of judicial review.

In *R* v *Secretary of State for Foreign Affairs, ex parte Everett* (1987) QBD, it was held that the refusal to issue a passport was an exercise of prerogative discretion reviewable by the courts (following the majority in GCHQ).

This is a complicated area but to promote understanding it may be represented in the form of the following over-simplified diagram.

Pre-GCHQ decision 1984	
Reviewable by the courts Exercise of statutory powers	*Not reviewable by the courts* Exercise of prerogative powers
Post-GCHQ decision	
Reviewable by the courts a) exercise of statutory powers b) exercise of prerogative powers where subject matter is amenable eg grant of passports	*Not reviewable by the courts* Exercise of prerogative powers where subject matter is not justifiable, eg defence of realm, grant of honours, choice of ministers

NB: *The Crown and contempt of court*

In *M* v *Home Office* (1991) it was held that the Home Secretary was in contempt of court when he took a decision not to comply with a court order requiring him to arrange to have returned an asylum-seeker who had been unlawfully deported.

If confirmed (leave has been sought for an appeal to the Lords), this decision will mean that ministers and civil servants will be liable to the courts' jurisdiction for contempt even though acting in the discharge or furtherance of their duties on behalf of the Crown.

13.8 The prerogative and foreign affairs; Act of State

The Crown has a vast range of prerogative powers in relation to foreign affairs. For example, at common law the Crown can:

a) recognise states and governments;

b) declare war and peace;

c) negotiate and sign treaties;

d) annex and cede territories.

(By convention these powers are limited.)

Act of State

Whenever the Crown (ie normally a Minister acting on behalf of the Crown or a person acting under the authority of such a Minister) exercises a prerogative power in relation to a foreign state, or to a person who does not owe allegiance to the Crown (ie someone who is neither a British citizen nor a Commonwealth citizen, nor a friendly alien) that exercise of power can be described as an Act of State. If in a court case involving the exercise of such a power the Crown properly enters a *plea* that there has been an Act of State, then the court has no jurisdiction to decide whether the Crown has acted lawfully or unlawfully in the course of the Act of State.

That is, if a plea of Act of State is properly entered, an Act of State is a non-justifiable issue.

13.9 The principles of an Act of State

a) The court can decide whether an exercise of power is an Act of State.

In *Nissan* v *Attorney-General* (1970) House of Lords, an hotel, in Cyprus, belonging to a citizen of the United Kingdom and Colonies, was occupied by British troops. On a claim by the owner for compensation, the Crown raised a preliminary issue and alleged that the requisitioning and use of the hotel were Acts of State.

It was held that the acts were not Act of State.

> '... the courts are not bound to accept the ipse dixit (the statement) of the executive, but have the right to decide for themselves whether the act is an "act of state".'

per Lord Wilberforce.

Although the dispatch of British troops to Cyprus on a peace keeping mission had been on Act of State as it was an act of high executive policy not everything that the troops did once there could be so classified. Since the damage complained of by Nissan had occurred during a drunken brawl the actions of the soldiers could not be classified as Act of State.

b) But if the court decides that there has been an Act of State:

'An act of state is an act of sovereign power and cannot be challenged, controlled, or interfered with by municipal courts ... (they) must accept it as it is without question.'

per Fletcher Moulton LJ in *Salaman* v *Secretary of State for India* (1906).

c) An Act of State can be pleaded when there is an act against an alien, outside British territory.

In *Buron* v *Denman* (1848) the captain of a British warship set fire to buildings in West Africa outside British territory, belonging to a Spaniard, and released slaves being kept there. The captain's actions later received ministerial approval. The Spaniard sued for damages.

It was held that there had been an Act of State and, therefore, the court could not consider the case further.

d) An Act of State can be pleaded when there is an act against an enemy alien, inside British territory.

In *R* v *Bottrill, ex parte Keuchenmeister* (1947) a German national (an enemy alien) who had lived in England since 1918, but had not been naturalised, was detained under prerogative powers. An application for habeas corpus, made while Britain and Germany were still officially at war with each other, failed because it was held that the detention was an Act of State.

e) But an Act of State cannot be pleaded when there is an act against a friendly alien, inside British territory.

In *Johnstone* v *Pedlar* (1921) property was seized by the police from a United States citizen (a friendly alien) in Dublin (then part of the United Kingdom) who brought an action for the return of the property.

It was held that the seizure could not be covered by the plea of Act of State.

f) An Act of State cannot be pleaded when there is an act against a British subject, inside British territory.

In *Walker* v *Baird* (1892) the commander of a British warship acting under the authority of the government seized a lobster factory situated in Newfoundland (then within British territory) which belonged to British subjects.

It was held that the seizure was not an Act of State.

g) It is unclear whether or not an Act of State can apply to an act against a British subject outside British territory.

In *Nissan* v *Attorney-General* (1970) Lords Morris, Wilberforce and Pearson observed that in some cases falling under this category, a plea of Act of State could be successful. Lord Reid, though, stated that the plea could never be used against a British subject.

13.10 Treaties

The making (negotiating and signing) of a Treaty is a prerogative act, which the Crown acting through Ministers can exercise without the prior approval of Parliament and, therefore, cannot be challenged in the courts.

In *Blackburn* v *Attorney-General* (1971) Court of Appeal, B applied for declarations that the government would be acting in breach of the law if they signed the Treaty of Rome because they would, in doing so, be surrendering for ever a part of the supremacy of the 'Queen-in-Parliament'. It was held that the courts could not interfere with the treaty-making power of the sovereign.

But a treaty, to have any legal effect in the United Kingdom, must be implemented by an Act of Parliament: *The Parlement Belge* (1879); *Attorney-General for Canada* v *Attorney-General for Ontario* (1937).

In *Blackburn* v *Attorney-General* (1971), Lord Denning held that:

> 'Even if a treaty is signed, it is elementary that these courts take no notice of treaties as such. We take no notice of treaties until they are embodied in laws enacted by Parliament and then only to the extent that Parliament tells us.'

Therefore, the provisions of a treaty alone cannot give rise to rights enforceable in the United Kingdom courts.

In *Rustomjee* v *R* (1876) Queen's Bench Division, money was paid to the Queen by the Emperor of China, under the terms of a peace treaty, to cover claims by British subjects made against Chinese merchants. A claim was made alleging that the Crown had received this money as an agent or trustee.

It was held that the claim be rejected:

> 'In no view whatever can an individual subject have any such claim ... namely, a claim to coerce the sovereign by judicial proceedings into the payment over of a part of the indemnity received in her sovereign character from the Emperor of China.'

per Lush J.

13.11 A note on diplomatic privileges

The Diplomatic Privileges Act 1964 divides diplomatic missions into three classes and confers different degrees of immunity from the jurisdiction of the English courts on them.

Class	*Immunity*
a) Diplomatic staff and their families	Full personal immunity from criminal and civil actions
b) Administrative and technical	Full immunity from criminal and staff civil actions for their official acts, immunity from criminal actions (not civil) for acts outside the course of their duties
c) Service staff	Full immunity from criminal and civil actions for their official acts, no immunity at all for acts outside the course of their duties

These immunities can be withdrawn by Order in Council from a foreign state's diplomatic mission if the foreign state does not provide reciprocal immunities to British diplomats.

For the purposes of judicial proceedings, a certificate issued by the Foreign Secretary conclusively determines which, if any, class a person falls under. The court itself can determine, where relevant, whether or not the act was within the course of the person's duties. Commonwealth High Commissioners, etc, enjoy similar immunities.

14 THE PRIME MINISTER, CABINET, MINISTERS, THE PRIVY COUNCIL

14.1 Introduction

The primary functions of the Executive are to initiate, develop and implement governmental policies. While the term 'the Executive' covers a wide range of persons and bodies, eg the civil service, the most important members of the Executive are the Prime Minister and his/her Ministers, the most important Ministers being members of the Cabinet.

14.2 The Cabinet – introduction

The Cabinet can trace its origins to the groups of trusted advisers that discussed and developed government policies with the seventeenth century monarchs. These groups met in the King's closet ('cabinet'). In the early 1700s King George I, although he still retained some influence, began to withdraw from an effective role with his advisers, leaving them to become more and more powerful. During the reign of King George III (1760–1820) the Cabinet began to initiate policies itself without prior reference from the King. From these origins and through gradual shifts in the balance of political power between the monarch and his leading advisers/ministers, the Cabinet developed into its modern capacity as the heart of the government. Today the Cabinet discusses the most important issues of government policy, deals with the most controversial political and parliamentary matters and co-ordinates the interests of the various government departments.

14.3 The composition of the Cabinet

The size of the Cabinet varies from Prime Minister to Prime Minister. Each Prime Minister decide on exactly which ministerial posts are to be Cabinet ones, although some by convention are so important that they cannot be excluded from the Cabinet, eg the Lord Chancellor, the Chancellor of the Exchequer, the Foreign Secretary, the Home Secretary. The only statutory limitation on the Prime Minister's power of choice is that by the Ministerial and Other Salaries Act 1975 – there can only be 20 salaried Cabinet posts at any time, plus the Prime Minister and Lord Chancellor.

14.4 The Cabinet

John Major's Cabinet, as formed in 1992 following the General Election, is composed as follows:

1. Lord Chancellor
2. Chancellor of the Exchequer
3. Foreign Secretary
4. Home Secretary
5. President of the Board of Trade
6. Secretary of State for Transport
7. Secretary of State for Defence
8. Leader of the Lords
9. Leader of the Commons
10. Secretary of State for Agriculture
11. Secretary of State for the Environment
12. Secretary of State for Wales
13. Secretary of State for Social Security
14. Chancellor of the Duchy of Lancaster
15. Secretary of State for Scotland
16. Secretary of State for National Heritage
17. Secretary of State for Northern Ireland
18. Secretary of State for Education
19. Secretary of State for Health
20. Secretary of State for Employment
21. Chief Secretary to the Treasury

14.5 Non-Cabinet Ministers

Not all Ministers are Cabinet Ministers. In total, ie Cabinet and non-Cabinet, there are over 100 ministerial posts. Apart from the Cabinet Ministers, there are:

a) '*Ministers of State*', ie Ministers who do not have seats in the Cabinet. Where a government department is headed by a Secretary of State, a Minister of State acts as his assistant. Some government departments are headed by a Minister of State, not a Secretary of State.

b) '*Under Secretaries of State*' and '*Parliamentary Secretaries*', ie other non-Cabinet Ministerial posts, which rank beneath Ministers of State and which also provide assistance to the Sec of State, or Minister of State, who heads the Department.

c) Quite apart from any of the above, there are also the Law Officers of the Crown, ie the Attorney-General, the Lord Advocate, the Solicitor General, the Solicitor General for Scotland.

14.6 The Prime Minister – introduction

The Prime Minister is the most important of all the Ministers and is the leader of the government. In the eyes of the public and the press, the successes and failures of a government are mainly attributed to the particular style and quality of leadership of the Prime Minister of the day. The evolution of a clearly pre-eminent leader among the Ministers can probably be traced to Walpole (1721–42) who is commonly regarded as the first Prime Minister, but at least to the younger Pitt (1783–1801, 1804–6).

It is now necessary to consider the constitutional rules surrounding the Prime Minister and Cabinet and their relations with each other.

14.7 The Prime Minister and Cabinet: constitutional rules and roles

The individual and relative powers of the Prime Minister and Cabinet are not derived from laws, statutory or common, but from conventions. It is through conventions that the rules governing the Prime Minister and Cabinet have evolved. This is not to say that statutes do not recognise the existence of the Prime Minister and Cabinet, some do, but rather to emphasise that rules of political practice (conventions) are the source of their power, not rules of law.

a) *Constitutional rules*

Conventions establish the following rules:

i) Prime Minister is the leader of the government, and heads the Cabinet.

ii) Prime Minister also holds the office of First Lord of the Treasury and as such is the nominal head of the most powerful government department. (Since 1937 statutory provisions for the Prime Minister's salary and pension have been based on an assumption that the Prime Minister will hold this post.)

iii) Prime Minister is a member of the House of Commons (the last Prime Minister to be a member of the Lords was Lord Salisbury in 1902) because the Commons is the dominant House, the root of parliamentary power and has exclusive control over national finance.

iv) The Queen appoints as Prime Minister the leader of the largest party in the Commons.

v) Prime Minister decides which members of the Commons and Lords (all Ministers must be a member of one or other House) are to be Ministers. The Queen formally appoints them. There is an upper limit of 95 on the number of Members of Parliament who may hold a ministerial post. This is to prevent excessive patronage and control of Members of Parliament.

vi) Prime Minister decides which Ministers are to be Cabinet Ministers and what their order of precedence is.

vii) Prime Minister can require any Minister to resign and can move Ministers to other posts or to the backbenches.

viii) Prime Minister can decide on the holding of a general election (the dissolution of Parliament) without reference to the Cabinet.

ix) Prime Minister's approval, as head of the Civil Service, is required for the most senior civil service appointments.

x) Prime Minister controls the organisation of central government and, for example, can allocate and reallocate government functions among the government departments.

xi) Prime Minister nominates those who are to hold the most important Crown appointments, eg senior judges.

xii) Prime Minister has considerable powers of patronage, ie the Prime Minister decides who are to receive peerages, honours, etc. The Queen formally gives them.

xiii) Prime Minister is the channel of communication between the Cabinet and the Queen and has regular meetings with the Queen.

xiv) Prime Minister can take decisions personally, outside the Cabinet and without reference to it, or can establish a small 'inner cabinet' to take the most important decisions, eg the 'War Cabinet' used during the 1982 Falklands campaign.

xv) Prime Minister presides at meetings of the Cabinet and the most important Cabinet committees, and can control the agenda at such meetings, ie what is to be discussed, when and for how long.

xvi) Prime Minister decides when a new Cabinet committee is required, its membership and the scope of its authority to make decisions without reference to the full Cabinet.

xvii) The Cabinet Office has a special relationship with the Prime Minister.

Therefore, it can be seen that the Prime Minister in choosing his/her Ministers, in allocating Cabinet and non-cabinet posts, in presiding over the Cabinet and the government, is vested with a huge range of powers, derived from conventions which could be utilised (and sometimes are) to dominate the Cabinet. Generally speaking, the amount of domination which any Prime Minister asserts over the Cabinet depends on the particular personal and political characteristics of that Prime Minister. The Prime Minister's powers could be abused and could lead to a system of 'Prime Ministerial Government', as opposed to a system of Prime Minister and Cabinet partnership. The late Richard Crossman described our system as Prime Minister government and it has even been suggested by some writers that our system is becoming a Presidential one. But the more correct picture of the respective roles of Prime Minister and Cabinet is that the Prime Minister is merely 'first among equals'; why?

b) *The Prime Minister as 'first among equals'*

i) Prime Minister must to a certain extent live up to party expectations in making Ministerial appointments. Prime Minister depends on the support of the government party and cannot expect to receive this without some recognition of the party.

ii) Prime Minister cannot closely supervise or direct the vast range of governmental functions and, therefore, must entrust Ministers with large amounts of power.

iii) Prime Minister needs the support of the Cabinet to maintain his/her leadership and, therefore, must always try to get Cabinet backing for his ideas and policies through discussion and argument in Cabinet. If a Prime Minister persistently ignored the feelings of the Cabinet, sooner or later the Prime Minister would lose out, for while the Prime Minister has more powers than any Minister, the Cabinet *as a group* is in the long term more powerful than the Prime Minister.

iv) Prime Minister politically could not prevent the Cabinet from discussing something which its members wanted to discuss even though it is possible for major decisions to be moved to Cabinet committees rather than being taken by the full Cabinet.

NOTE: It is fair to say that the Prime Minister has greater powers than it would be politically sensible for any Prime Minister to use. The Prime Minister provides individual leadership, the Cabinet collective leadership and one cannot govern without the other. The Prime Minister may be the most authoritative Minister, but the Prime Minister's powers are *not* dictatorial.

The following material gives an indication of the different approaches adopted by Prime Ministers during the 1970s and 1980s.

Mr Heath 1970–4 – 'did not really believe in Cabinet government' (anonymous senior official).

Mr Wilson 1974–6 – 'worked very hard at Cabinet government' (anonymous senior official).

Mr Callaghan 1976–9 – used full Cabinet early on; smaller Cabinet by 1979.

Mrs Thatcher 1979–1990 regarded as moving from 'consensus' to 'conviction' politics and that this is reflected in her style of leadership, viz. placing her own supporters in Cabinet and ousting those who disagree fundamentally with her; in more general terms dominating the Cabinet system. A most interesting example of this dominance arose in January 1986 when Mr Heseltine, then Defence Secretary, stormed out of a Cabinet meeting and immediately resigned, claiming that Mrs Thatcher had continually 'gagged' discussion on a European consortium bid (which Mr Heseltine favoured) for Westland Helicopters, a British firm. He forcefully attacked Mrs Thatcher's autocratic style of leadership. Mrs Thatcher's style was again a matter of controversy at the time of the resignation of the Chancellor of the Exchequer, Nigel Lawson, in 1989. He resigned as a result of disagreement between himself and the Prime Minister over, amongst other matters, the United Kingdom's proposed membership of the European Monetary System. He could not accept the influence and interference by her economic adviser, Alan Walters. The resignation gave rise to a political storm and also resulted in the resignation of Mr Walters, and it seemed that as a result the Prime Minister would be more inclined to accept the views of other Cabinet colleagues, particularly the new Chancellor, Mr John Major, and the Foreign Secretary, Douglas Hurd, who were more pro-European.

John Major 1990 – present. Initially inherited Thatcher's choices. It was not until being returned in 1992 that Mr Major considered he had a mandate from the electorate to choose his own Cabinet. His choice while in many ways similar to Thatcher's was on a broader basis, with fewer right wingers and more 'wets'. The present Cabinet is distinguished mainly by being almost entirely composed of graduates. Only two, (including the Prime Minister himself) of the 22 are not graduates. In general, however, most of the members of the present Cabinet differ, in philosophy, very much from the Thatcher era.

Differing individual styles, then, demand an individual approach to Cabinet. Bearing in mind the reasons given above for the necessity of both Cabinet and party support, it may be true to say that the actual powers of any PM have not changed since the early twentieth century.

14.8 Cabinet committees

Cabinet committees have been a regular feature of our system of government since their successful use in World War II. Basically, Cabinet Committees exist to relieve the Cabinet of a large part of a workload which the Cabinet nominally has as its own, but which in practice it could not possibly effectively cope with. The amount and range of governmental functions are just too great for the Cabinet, as a body, to manage. Therefore, Cabinet Committees:

a) do the preparatory work on matters for discussion by the Cabinet;

b) co-ordinate the interests of, and seek to eradicate the differences between, government departments before Cabinet discussion of issues;

c) may even make some decisions instead of the Cabinet. For example, it is said that the decision to manufacture H bombs in the 1950s was taken in a Cabinet Committee and not by the full cabinet.

There are Standing Committees (approximately 20), ie Cabinet Committees that remain throughout a government's period of office.

There are certain Cabinet Committees which each government will establish to cover issues and areas that continue from government to government, eg defence, home affairs, legislative policy, the European Economic Community. Other Standing Cabinet Committees will cover areas of special importance to the particular government in office, eg the (1979–) Conservative government has a Cabinet Committee on 'disposing of state industries and assets' and it also has one on AIDS; the (1974–9) Labour government had a 'devolution' Cabinet Committee. There are also ad hoc Cabinet Committees, ie Cabinet Committees set up to deal with temporary problems and particular proposals. During a period of government there may be well over 100 such Cabinet Committees established and disbanded as various needs arise and disappear.

The most important Cabinet Committees will be chaired by the Prime Minister, who can exercise considerable powers over the composition and functions of all Cabinet Committees. Most Cabinet Committees will be 'shadowed' by committees of civil servants.

It is hard to give an accurate picture of the constitution and number of Cabinet Committees because such details are traditionally kept secret. The most significant of the details made public in 1992 are as follows:

Initial	*Functions*
EDP	Strategic issues relating to economic and domestic policies.
OPD	Defence and overseas policies.
OPDG	Review of developments in the Gulf region and co-ordination of any necessary action.
OPDN	Nuclear defence.
OPDSE	Defence and security in Europe.
OPDK	Review of implementation of the agreement with the Chinese on the future of Hong Kong and its implications.
NI	Oversee policy on Northern Ireland issues and relations with the Republic of Ireland.
EDS	Review science and technology policy.
IS	Review policy on the security and intelligence services.
EDI	Industrial, commercial and consumer issues.
EDE	Environmental policy.
EDH	Home and social policy.
EDL	Local government, including annual allocation of resources.
FLG	Preparation of Cabinet drafts of the Queen's Speeches to Parliament and proposals for Government's legislative programme.
LG	Examination of draft Bills; consideration of the parliamentary handling of Government Bills, and European Community documents.
EDC	Matters relating to Civil Service pay.

NOTE: Cabinet Committees doubtless perform tasks which, in theory, the Cabinet should. But, it is a fact that no Cabinet could work smoothly and speedily without its complex of Cabinet Committees.

14.9 Criticisms of Cabinet government

There have been recent criticisms of the way in which the system of Cabinet government operates. This is not only on the grounds that, through the use of Cabinet committees, very important decisions may be removed from the full Cabinet but also on the grounds that government policy does not fully recognise the national interest and is not made with a view to the long term benefits of the country. It is argued that this is caused because Ministers seek to enhance their individual careers by their achievements for a particular ministry and therefore fail to weigh whether the requirements for resources of a different department are more important for the national interest than are the demands of their own.

Some advocate the use of a small inner Cabinet of very senior ministers without portfolio to overcome this problem. Others consider that such Ministers would be unlikely to solve the problems since they might have insufficient understanding of the practical requirements of government departments. Perhaps the answer would lie in the strengthening of the Cabinet Office and the Prime Minister's own staff to overcome shortsightedness in government policy.

14.10 Ministers

Ministers of the Crown are members of the government party appointed by the Queen on the Prime Minister's advice to hold political offices in the government. By convention, a Minister must be a member of either the Commons or the Lords. Ministers link executive and legislative tasks and, therefore, run contrary to the theory of separation of powers. They are the most important members of the Houses of Parliament, a ruling elite chosen to head, or second, or assist in the running of government departments. The parliamentary base that Ministers have is essential for the operation of the convention of ministerial responsibility, discussed below. There are different levels of ministerial posts (see paragraphs 14.3, 14.4 and 14.5). There are no legal limits on the number of ministers that can be appointed, but the House of Commons Disqualification Act 1975 does limit the number of holders of ministerial posts in the Commons to ninety-five. Therefore, there will be, in each government, ministers drawn from the Lords. Sometimes very senior Cabinet Ministers will be Lords, eg Lord Carrington, Foreign Secretary (1979–82) and, of course, the Lord Chancellor must be a Lord. There are some Ministers who could not conceivably be Lords, eg the Chancellor of the Exchequer.

a) The Ministerial and Other Salaries Act 1975 established maximum salaries for ministers, but these are variable by Order in Council approved by the Commons.

b) *Ministers as heads of departments*:

   i) Initiate and select policies;

   ii) Organise, motivate and control their departments;

   iii) Fight for their department's interests for parliamentary time and for Treasury money.

14.11 Government departments

Central government departments are financed by Exchequer funds, staffed by civil servants and are headed by Ministers responsible to Parliament. Departmental responsibilities may be allocated and reallocated by the Member of Parliament. The Ministers of the Crown Act 1975 gives a formal power, by Order in Council, to transfer ministerial functions and dissolve and establish government departments. This was used in 1982 to dissolve the Civil Service Department and to redistribute its functions. The allocation of functions between the various government departments is not a matter of established rules, each government will experiment to a certain extent. Some have in the past fused departments to form large 'super' departments, others have split up and hived off departments into smaller ones. The allocation of functions is a continuing and evolutionary process.

14.12 List of government departments

Central government is currently based on sixteen major departments. There are also the same number of minor departments or sub-departments.

Major Departments

Ministry of Agriculture, Fisheries and Food
Ministry of Defence
Department of Education
Department of Employment

Department of the Environment
Foreign and Commonwealth Office
Department of Health
Department for National Heritage
Home Office
Northern Ireland Office
Scottish Office
Department of Social Security
Department of Trade and Industry
Department of Transport
Treasury
Welsh Office

Minor Departments

Board of Inland Revenue
Central Office of Information
Department of National Savings
Export Credits Guarantee Department
HM Customs and Excise Department
HM Household
HM Stationery Office
Law Officers' Department
Lord Advocate's Department
* Lord Chancellor's Department
Office of Arts and Libraries
Office of the Minister for the Civil Service
Overseas Development Administration
Parliamentary Counsel's Office
Paymaster General's Office
* Privy Council Office

Of these minor departments and sub-departments only those marked * have direct Cabinet representation.

14.13 Collective ministerial responsibility

a) *Introduction*

Constitutionally, the most important role of a Minister is to be responsible to Parliament. This responsibility has two aspects; collective and individual, which are considered separately in the following text. Ministerial responsibility is a matter of convention.

b) *Collective ministerial responsibility*

i) *A definition*

> 'For all that passes in Cabinet, every member of it who does not resign is absolutely and irretrievably responsible and has no right afterwards to say that he agreed in one case to a compromise, while in another he was persuaded by his colleagues.'
>
> Lord Salisbury (1878).

ii) *The first aspect* of the convention of collective ministeral responsibility is that the Cabinet and, to a less well defined extent, the Ministers, should present a front of unanimity, of agreement and accord, to the sovereign, to the public, but most of all to Parliament.

iii) *The second aspect* and the constitutional reason why the Cabinet should 'speak with one voice' is that the Cabinet is collectively responsible, ie accountable and answerable, to Parliament for its decisions and policies. During a Cabinet meeting, Ministers may well argue among themselves, even bitterly, but once the Cabinet has reached a decision all its members and all Ministers, are constitutionally bound to accept that decision, to abide by it and to show support for it outside the Cabinet. If a Minister cannot bring himself to accept the Cabinet's line on an issue, he will have to resign before he will be able to speak his mind and explain his views. Should a Minister not resign in such a case, he is bound by the convention of public unanimity. If a serving Minister speaks out against the Cabinet line, the political consequence may well be loss of office or, at the very least, severe censure from the Prime Minister.

iv) *The purpose* of collective ministeral responsibility is to ensure that the Cabinet as a group is responsible to Parliament. The most serious means of enforcing this convention that the Commons has is the vote of no confidence. If a government, ie the Cabinet, loses the 'confidence' (the support of a majority) of the Commons, it has to resign, by convention, from the office for a general election to be held. If the Commons so disapproves of the government's decisions and policies, it can hold the Cabinet responsible for them and get rid of the government, by carrying a vote of no confidence. There is no exact definition of a 'vote of no confidence', governments can lose votes on crucial issues in Parliament and not be expected to resign. It seems that a vote will be one 'of confidence' either:

   when the government explicitly states that a vote is to be a vote of confidence; or

   when the Opposition move a vote of no confidence; or

   when certain fundamental parts of a government's programme are voted on, eg the Budget, Supply, such votes being traditionally regarded as matters of confidence.

   In any of these cases, if a majority of Members of Parliament vote against the government, then it knows it has lost the confidence of the Commons and has to resign.

v) *The essence* of collective ministeral responsibility is that the Cabinet must maintain an outward appearance of unity, so that it is liable, as a united body, to fall from office on a vote of no confidence. But, in practice, collective ministeral responsibility is rarely enforced in such a way. Governments almost invariably have a majority of Members of Parliament in the Commons and on a vote of no confidence will expect and be able to ensure that all its members vote for the party line. Members of Parliament are expected to be politically loyal and Members of Parliament in a governing party generally do not want to force their party to a general election.

   Governments do not, as a rule, lose votes of confidence. This is verified by the fact that since 1924 only two governments have lost such votes in the Commons:

   1924: MacDonald's Labour government

   1979: Callaghan's Labour government

   and on both these occasions, the government was a minority government, ie it did not have a majority of Members of Parliament over the combined opposition parties. Minority governments are very unusual, normally a government has a clear majority in the Commons, so that there is very little danger that a vote of no confidence could be passed.

vi) Occasionally, collective ministeral responsibility is temporarily waived:

1932: Coalition 'National' government, 'agreement to differ' on tariffs, Ministers free to speak their minds against the majority Cabinet line, inside and outside Parliament. The dissenting Ministers resigned after eight months.

1975: Minority Labour government, majority of Cabinet favoured continued membership of European Economic Community, minority allowed to speak against this, but only outside Parliament and during the European Economic Community referendum campaign

NOTE: waiver for one topic only.

1978: Minority Labour government, Ministers free to vote according to own views on the second reading of the European Assembly Elections Bill 1977. NOTE: waiver for one topic only.

> '... the doctrine (collective ministeral responsibility) should apply except in cases where I announce that it does not.'
>
> Prime Minister Callaghan.

The purpose of the waiver, on each occasion, was to enable the government to get through times of difficulty.

NOTE: On both of the recent occasions, 1975 and 1978, the government was a minority one. These waivers do not indicate that collective ministeral responsibility is weakening. Indeed had the convention of collective ministeral responsibility been weakening it is unlikely that such waivers would have been considered necessary. The continued importance of collective ministeral responsibility is indicated by the resignation of the Defence Minister, Michael Heseltine, in January 1986 during the Westland Affair. Government policy was to remain neutral over two rival rescue bids for Westland Helicopters, the only British helicopter company which was important for defence reasons, but which was suffering financial difficulties. Mr Heseltine saw clear advantages in the bid from the European consortium and could not support Government policy. Rather than be forced to follow a policy of neutrality he resigned and made his views plain from the backbenches.

14.14 Individual ministerial responsibility

a) *Definition*

The convention of individual ministeral responsibility is that: Ministers are responsible, ie accountable, answerable, to Parliament for matters within their departmental areas of power.

b) *Preliminary note*

Ministers are legally responsible for acts which they order or authorise in that they can be sued for civil wrongs committed in the course of such acts. Apart from this, Ministers are politically responsible by convention to Parliament for their departments.

Individual ministeral responsibility can be enforced in various ways by Parliament. The most serious means is the vote of *censure*. If a vote of censure of a Minister is carried in the Commons then, by convention, he has to *resign*. (The Opposition can also seek to show disapproval of a Minister by tabling a motion that the Minister's salary be reduced.) If either of these types of vote are tabled, the government will generally rally around the Minister concerned and will use its majority in Parliament (assuming it has one) to ensure that the vote does not go against the Minister.

Individual ministeral responsibility is based on various unwritten and hard to define expectations that a Minister will do the 'honourable thing' and resign voluntarily in certain situations. For example, if a Minister has committed some personal act of misconduct, he will be expected to resign (eg Lord Lambton's associations with call girls in the early 1970s). Or if a Minister's department has committed some act of maladministration then, in some cases a resignation will be expected. This latter part of individual ministeral responsibility is very vague and it seems that whether a Minister resigns after departmental maladministration has come to light may well depend on the personal characteristics of the Minister concerned, the publicity accorded to the mistake by the media and the attitude of Prime Minister and Government Ministers. Contrast the 1954 Crichel Down matter – resignation – and the 1964 Ferranti matter – no resignation.) In 1982 an example of voluntary resignation to mark apparent departmental blunders occurred when Lord Carrington resigned as Foreign Secretary over the issue of Foreign Office handling of the events leading up to the Falklands' campaign.

During the Westland Affair 1985–6, Mr Brittan, then Trade and Industry Secretary, was ultimately forced to resign after it was revealed that his department was responsible for the 'leaking' of a confidential letter from the Solicitor General – Sir Patrick Mayhew – to Mr Heseltine, the then Minister of Defence. The leak was designed to inform shareholders that there were serious anomalies in Mr Heseltine's calculations over the European bid for Westland. The leak was an attempt to deal a blow to Mr Heseltine's support for the European bid, but Mr Brittan's failure over several weeks to disclose that he had authorised the leak showed political misjudgement and the underhand nature of the action together with a highly publicised row several weeks earlier (also in the context of the Westland Affair) involving allegations of breaches of collective ministeral responsibility by Mr Brittan and attempts to mislead the Commons gave rise to renewed calls for his resignation not only from the Opposition and certain members of the public but also from the government's own backbenchers. It was a vote of the Conservative backbenchers 1922 Committee showing that Mr Brittan had lost their support which finally led to the resignation despite the Prime Minister's and Cabinet's continued declared support for the Minister.

The most recent example of an individual ministeral responsibility resignation is that of Mrs Edwina Currie, Minister for Health in December 1988. Mrs Currie eventually resigned after a public outcry from farmers' groups and calls for her resignation not only from Opposition Members of Parliament but from Conservative backbench Members of Parliament after she had made controversial remarks which she refused to withdraw and which seemed to suggest that most eggs and poultry produced in the United Kingdom were contaminated by salmonella bacteria. These remarks led to an enormous drop in demand for eggs with the result that many eggs had to be destroyed and birds killed bringing financial ruin to certain producers. Under the pressure of criticism the government introduced a compensation scheme for those forced to destroy eggs or birds which, it was estimated, could cost the taxpayer some £19 million. Mrs Currie's remarks had therefore given rise to a large cost to the government and she could not sustain her position. But had the unfortunate Mrs Currie made her remarks on a day when there was some other matter of great public significance occurring perhaps her remarks would have attracted less media attention and less public reaction and the whole episode would have been avoided.

Few departmental decisions will be made by Ministers personally. Individual ministeral responsibility requires Ministers to be answerable for their civil servants' acts and decisions. One result of this is that civil servants remain anonymous, protected from the public's gaze by the fact that their Minister takes political responsibility for their acts. Individual ministeral responsibility is meant to ensure that civil servants remain impartial and candid in their advice and discussions. The civil service anonymity aspect of individual ministeral responsibility has been eroded to a limited extent by the investigative powers of the Ombudsman and Select Committees which are sometimes keen to trace blame to the civil servant responsible. But, it is very rare for a civil servant to be openly and publicly blamed; one such exceptional case was: the 1971–2 Vehicle and General Insurance Co investigation, in which a government appointed tribunal of inquiry blamed one named civil servant for negligent lack of action. The case involved the Department of Trade which had powers to supervise and control insurance companies. These powers were not exercised in relation to one company, which collapsed leaving a million policy holders uninsured.

If a Minister does not resign after departmental maladministration has come to light, the Prime Minister may, at a later date, simply reshuffle him to a different post. A very important factor will be the mood of the government party in Parliament.

The convention of individual ministeral responsibility is enforced on a day-to-day basis through the asking of parliamentary questions, through the fact that Ministers can be asked questions in Parliament, which they generally will be expected to answer, on matters within their departmental responsibilities. Through questions, Members of Parliament can put Ministers on the spot, can show parliamentary discontent, etc and to a limited extent control or check the exercise of Ministerial power. At question time, Ministers are literally answerable to Parliament and must pay some attention to the complaints of ordinary Members of Parliament. Individual ministeral responsibility ensures that, in theory, Ministerial power derived from Parliament is subject to some degree of control by Parliament.

14.15 Ministerial responsibility and the courts

The courts have given some legal recognition to the existence of the convention of ministerial responsibility, eg the courts have decided that, in law, a civil servant when exercising his Minister's powers acts as the alter ego (the other self) of the Minister.

In *Carltona Ltd* v *Commissioners of Works* (1943) Court of Appeal, the Defence Regulations 1939 gave 'competent authorities' the power to requisition property. The First Commissioner of Works was a 'competent authority'. C's factory was requisitioned under the Regulations, but C challenged the order on the ground that it had not been made by the Commissioner, but by a departmental official on headed Ministry paper.

The challenge failed. It was held that:

> 'In the administration of government in this country, the functions which are given to ministers (and constitutionally properly given to ministers because they are constitutionally responsible) are functions so multifarious that no minister could ever personally attend to them ... The duties imposed upon ministers and the powers given to ministers are normally exercised under the authority of the ministers by responsible officials of the department. Public business could not be carried on if that were not the case. Constitutionally, the decision of such an official is, of course, the decision of the minister. The minister is responsible. It is he who must answer before Parliament for anything that his officials have done under his authority and, if for an important matter he selected an official of such junior standing that he could not be expected competently to perform the work, the minister would have to answer for that in Parliament. The whole system of departmental organisation and administration is based on the view that ministers, being responsible to Parliament, will see that important duties are committed to experienced officials. If they do not do that, Parliament is the place where complaint must be made against them.'
>
> per Lord Greene MR.

(This case also illustrates how the courts will sometimes use the existence of a convention as a factor in deciding not to grant a legal remedy in a case.)

14.16 Cabinet secrecy

The Cabinet decision-making process is traditionally very secret. One reason is that secrecy ensures that particular Cabinet Ministers who dissented from a Cabinet decision will not be made known to the public and Parliament. This maintains collective ministeral responsibility, ie the apparent unity of the Cabinet. There are legal provisions which maintain this secrecy, eg Crown Privilege, the Official Secrets Act and the rules under which the Ombudsman acts. In practice, a breach of this secrecy if a Minister is involved, may lead to political difficulties for him. But, while a serving Minister would feel constrained from disclosing Cabinet discussions because of the risk of losing office or of receiving political criticism, former Cabinet Ministers are in a different position. If a former Cabinet Minister decides to publish such material, can he be legally restrained?

In *Attorney-General* v *Jonathan Cape Ltd* (1976) High Court, the Attorney-General sought an injunction to prevent the publication of the political diaries of Richard Crossman, a former Cabinet Minister, after his death.

It was held that the court could issue an injunction to prevent the publication of such material, because it had been received in confidence and publication would break that confidence. But the court should only act where the material still retained its confidential nature. Lapse of time could lead to the loss of confidentiality. In this case, nearly ten years had elapsed since the events described in the first diaries and, therefore, the material was 'stale' and publication of it should not be restrained. The court also referred to the convention of collective ministeral responsibility and stated that the maintenance of the convention was in the public interest.

(NOTE: if an injunction had been issued, it would have been to enforce the law of confidence, not the convention of collective ministeral responsibility itself.)

This decision showed that the law could not be relied on completely to restrict ex-Ministers disclosing Cabinet discussions and so the government decided to rely on guidelines based on political honour instead. These were formulated by the Radcliffe Report (1976, Report on the Committee of Privy Councillors on Ministerial Memoirs) as follows:

a) In cases of secret information, eg on national security, international relations, etc, a Minister must abide by the decision of the Secretary to the Cabinet (see below) as to whether publication is to be allowed.

b) Other confidential material cannot be published within 15 years, except with the approval of the Secretary.

14.17 The Cabinet Office

The Cabinet Office was introduced during World War I when a Secretary to the Cabinet was first appointed, with officials to assist him. The tasks of the Secretary and his Cabinet Office are to:

a) record decisions taken at Cabinet and Cabinet Committee meetings. Agreements recorded, dissent is not attributed to particular Ministers;

b) circulate this record of decisions to Ministers;

c) circulate the minutes and agenda of such meetings;

d) circulate working papers before such meetings.

The Cabinet Office is headed by one of the top civil servants, the Permanent Secretary to the Cabinet Office (the 'Cabinet Secretary') and staffed by approximately 100 civil servants. It is responsible primarily to the Prime Minister and its tasks have one main aim, to achieve inter-departmental co-ordination. In 1970, a 'think tank', the Central Policy Review Staff, was established within the Cabinet Office to produce in depth studies of difficult problems. This body was abolished in 1982.

14.18 The Privy Council

a) *Privy Councillors* were at one time the most important of the monarch's advisers, but that role was lost to the Cabinet. The Privy Council diminished in importance as the Cabinet developed its powers. Today, there are 300 or so Privy Councillors. Membership is made up of:

    i) certain politicians, including all Cabinet Ministers; and former Cabinet Ministers

    ii) senior judges;

    iii) noblemen;

    iv) Archbishops;

    v) Commonwealth leaders;

vi) and other 'eminent persons'.

Appointment is an honour conferred by the Queen in accordance with ministerial advice.

b) *The main function of the Privy Council is to approve Orders in Council,* which when made under powers given by statute are a type of statutory instrument. Orders in Council are used for a great number of governmental actions, but note:

i) they are drafted by government departments in advance;

ii) the Privy Council only formally approves them, no discussion of them takes place;

iii) when carrying out this formal function (and other similar ones) the Privy Council will usually consist of a meeting of just four Privy Councillors, usually Ministers, in the Queen's presence.

The Privy Council does have standing and ad hoc Committees of its members. One notable Committee is the Judicial Committee of the Privy Council, which is usually made up of five Law Lords, sometimes with senior Commonwealth judges and which hears appeals from Colonies and those Commonwealth countries which still recognise the Judicial Committee as the court of final appeal. The Judicial Committee does not decide cases, but advises the Crown, which implements the advice by Order in Council.

15 THE CIVIL SERVICE

15.1 Introduction

The Civil Service consists of the officials who administer the central government departments. The Fulton Report (1968) defined civil servants as:

	Note
'Servants of the Crown, other than holders of political or judicial	This excludes Ministers
offices, who are employed in a civil capacity	This excludes the Army
and whose remuneration is paid wholly and directly out of money voted by Parliament.'	This excludes local government officials, the police, nationalised industry officials.

15.2 Professionalism

a) *Northcote-Trevelyan Report 1854*

The basic principles of a modern Civil Service were set out in the Northcote-Trevelyan Report (1854) which recommended that civil servantervants should be recruited from:

> 'Young men above par, superior in talents or in diligence to the mass ... the flower of the youth, the most acute, the most industrious, the most ambitious.'

Instead of from:

> 'The unambitious, the indolent (lazy) and incapable.'

which the Report found the Civil Service was then comprised.

The Report recommended:

i) recruitment by competitive examination;

ii) a hierarchy based on intellectual capability;

iii) promotion by merit, rather than seniority.

These principles became the guiding principles for the Civil Service, but the Civil Service later became hampered in its efficiency by:

i) its very detailed internal 'class system' under which some 1,400 different classes of civil servant existed, each with its own pay and career structure;

ii) having too many 'generalists' and 'all-rounders' and not enough specialists;

iii) having too few civil servant with managerial skills.

b) *The Fulton Report 1968*

To remedy the defects noted above, the Fulton Report of 1968 recommended:

i) the creation of a Civil Service Department to take over from the Treasury responsibility for Civil Service organisation, recruitment, management, pay, etc;

ii) the development of greater professionalism, more specialisation by civil servants;

iii) better training in administration and management;

iv) better career structures to enable the rapid progress of the talented and trained;

v) the abolition of the class system.

These recommendations were acted upon in particular:

i) the Civil Service Department was established with the Prime Minister as its head. NOTE: The Prime Minister is the Minister for the Civil Service;

ii) a Civil Service college was established for training civil servants;

iii) the class structure was replaced by one single class, below the most senior Civil Service posts, the 'administrative class'.

Bearing in mind Fulton's recommendations, the main aim of a modern Civil Service must be to achieve professionalism. (The Northcote-Trevelyan Report despised the amateur.) But, it remains a fact that the Civil Service nearly always seems to be under criticism. The (1979–) Conservative government is committed to cutting Civil Service numbers and controlling the Civil Service more closely. To this end, the Civil Service Department was abolished in 1981.

15.3 The abolition of the Civil Service Department 1981

In December 1981 an Order in Council (made under the Ministers of the Crown Act 1975), The Transfer of Functions Order, abolished the Civil Service Department. The functions of the Civil Service Department have been transferred to other departments as follows:

a) *Responsibility for the allocation and control of Civil Service resources*, which includes the power to make decisions on the number, pay and superannuation of civil servants, is transferred to the Treasury. The Treasury therefore is now responsible for the management and control of how much money is spent on central government manpower (civil servants). The government's reason for allocating this task to the Treasury is to enable the Treasury to combine its control of central government expenditure generally with control over how much is spent on the Civil Service in particular.

The eventual aim of the government is for financial savings (cuts) to be made in the Civil Service as a result of giving the Treasury the power of control over the finance available for the Civil Service. A new Minister of State in the Treasury has been appointed to help the Treasury's new functions.

b) *The other former functions* of the Civil Service Department remain the responsibility of the Prime Minister as Minister for the Civil Service, but these are now handled by a new department, the Management and Personnel Office, which is attached to the Cabinet Office. The Secretary to the Cabinet is the Permanent Secretary of the new department. The main function retained by the Prime Minister acting through this new office is the responsibility for the organisation, management and overall efficiency of the Civil Service. The Prime Minister is in charge of the 'efficiency unit' for the Civil Service.

Summary

The new division of functions is: (1) the Treasury controls how much money is spent on the Civil Service; and (2) the Prime Minister via the new Management and Personnel Office decides on how to improve the efficiency of the Civil Service.

NOTE: The overall management and organisation of the Civil Service is within the crown prerogative powers and the Civil Service is regulated not by legislation, but by Orders in Council and regulations. Under the 1969 Civil Service Order in Council, the Minister for the Civil Service, the Prime Minister, was authorised: 'to make regulations or give instructions for controlling the conduct of the civil service and providing for the classification, remuneration and other conditions of service' of civil servants. In other words, the Prime Minister can effectively control and shape the Civil Service to an important extent and apart from this, the most senior civil servants are appointed by the Prime Minister.

15.4 Hierarchy

Within a government department the most senior civil servant is the Permanent Secretary, whose functions are:

'He is the Minister's most immediate adviser on policy; he is the managing director of the day-to-day operations of the department; he has ultimate responsibility for questions of staff and organisation; as the Accounting Officer (in nearly every department) he also has the ultimate responsibility for all departmental expenditure.'

Fulton Report 1968.

Beneath the Permanent Secretary are departmental secretaries, then under secretaries, then assistant secretaries, all of whom will be in charge of the divisions and branches, staffed by civil servants, into which the departmental administration is split.

15.5 Features

The essential feature of the Civil Service is that within each Government Department it is subordinate to the Minister who heads it. This is a matter of constitutional importance because while the most senior civil servants are extremely important and indispensable advisers to their Ministers, only Ministers are responsible and answerable to Parliament for the decisions and administration of their departments. (See *Carltona Ltd* v *Commissioners of Works*.)

To reinforce this convention of ministerial responsibility,civil servants operate generally in conditions of anonymity and secrecy. Individual civil servants are not identified or linked with the policies and decisions made in their departments, but instead act on behalf of their Ministers. The traditional reason for this anonymity is that it enables civil servants to give impartial advice to their Ministers, away from the public's gaze. It is arguable that if civil servants did not sit in an anonymous fashion:

> 'There is the risk that individual civil servants will be regarded as supporting or opposing particular policies, or measures and their views may be thought to be at variance with those of their Minister (or a successor Minister).'
>
> from evidence given to the Fulton Committee.

If the impartiality of the Civil Service was doubted then this might give rise to the situation found in some other countries where on a change of government there is also a change of civil servants. This would be undesirable as the continuity of advice and the experience and expertise of the Civil Service would be undermined.

15.6 Tenure

To enable civil servants to serve different political masters, as governments change and Ministers of different political persuasions come and go, civil servants have in practice a very high degree of job security. In practice, a civil servant will hold office as long as he does not commit some kind of misconduct. This is not reflected in law: all civil servants hold office at the pleasure of the Crown and can be dismissed whenever the Crown wishes. This contrasts with the situation of the ordinary employee who is entitled to receive at least a minimum period of notice laid down by statute if his employer wishes to dismiss him in circumstances where there has been no very serious fault on the part of the employee. If the employer fails to give the correct notice then the employee has a right to sue him for damages for wrongful dismissal to recover salary over the notice period. Since the civil servant has no notice period he has no common law remedy of wrongful dismissal and furthermore he cannot be employed for a fixed term. (*Dunn* v *R* (1896)). But, the severity of the common law has been mitigated by statutory provisions, under which a dismissed civil servant can bring an action in an Industrial Tribunal for unfair dismissal. This is provided for by the Employment Protection (Consolidation) Act 1978 and that Act applies to the Civil Service in broadly the same way as to ordinary employees. However before unfair dismissal protection is afforded to an employee he must have served the same employer for a continuous two-year period and any complaint of unfair dismissal must be made within three months' of dismissal. If the tribunal finds the allegation of unfair dismissal proven then reinstatement or re-engagement may exceptionally be awarded but the more usual remedy is an award of compensation which is subject to a minimum limit, which varies with the age, length of service and salary of the employee. A civil servant is entitled at common law to receive payment for work which he has already done, but for which he has not been paid at the time of dismissal: *Kodeeswaran* v *Attorney-General for Ceylon* (1970).

Civil servants' salaries are not determined in detail by statutory provisions, but are through a special arbitration and conciliation body, the National 'Whitley' Council. Civil servants have inflation proofed pensions established by statutory provisions.

By a Civil Service Order in Council of 5 February 1991, which came into effect on 5 April 1991, selection to the civil service is to be entirely on merit, after fair and open competition. Though open competition has been recognised for some time (see paragraph 15.2) this reinforces in legislative form earlier 'unofficial' entry regulations.

15.7 Security procedures

a) *The purge procedure* applies to all civil servants employed in connection with work that is vital to the security of the State. Under this procedure, investigations are carried out to see whether the civil servant concerned has any connections with extremist political parties, ie Communists or Fascists. If he has, he may either be transferred to unsensitive work or dismissed. If a civil servant is provisionally found to have such connections, he will be allowed a hearing before an advisory panel 'The Three Advisors' (nicknamed the 'three wise men', they are retired civil servants) before whom the rules of natural justice do not apply. The civil servant will be given the chance to say what he wants to, but without being shown, or told of, the evidence against him. The panel will advise the Minister, who is not bound by the Panel's views in making the final decision as to the civil servant' fate.

b) *The positive vetting* procedure applies to civil servants employed on exceptionally secret work and for those being considered for promotion to more senior posts. Under this procedure, investigations are carried out to find not only extremist political views, but also 'character defects' which might make the civil servant concerned a security risk and/or unsuitable for a particular post. The vetting procedure takes up to three months and involves the civil servant filling in a form in which he is asked to disclose 'unnatural tendencies', and to list people with an intimate knowledge of his background, who are interviewed investigative officers from the Ministry of Defence (responsible for vetting). The process is repeated every five years. A hearing before the Three Advisers is not available in positive vetting cases.

c) *A Standing Security Commission*, headed by a Law Lord and made up of judges and very senior ex-civil servant, will, on the request of the Prime Minister, investigate breaches of security and advise whether changes in security arrangements are necessary.

15.8 Political activities

To maintain the appearance of civil servant impartiality, it is necessary for the more important civil servant not to be seen to be involved in party politics. The rules are:

a) *Civil servants cannot become Members of Parliament* (this is an overriding rule);

b) *Civil Service is divided into three categories* with different amounts of political freedom:

   i) *The 'restricted' category* is made up of the more senior civil servants and those civil servants involved in giving advice to Ministers and those who come into direct contact with the public. Members of this category cannot participate in national political activities, although they may, with departmental permission, take part in local political activities, subject to acting with 'moderation and discretion';

   ii) *The 'intermediate' category*, ie middle ranking civil servants who do not fall within (i) or (iii). They may, with permission, take part in national and local political activities, subject to acting with discretion to avoid causing embarrassment to their Ministers and departments;

   iii) *The 'politically free (unrestricted)' category*, ie industrial staff and non-industrial staff in minor and manipulative grades. This class, made up of the lowest ranking civil servants, can take part in national and local political activities, except while on duty or on official premises, or while wearing uniform.

NOTE: All civil servants are subject to the Official Secrets Acts. The prosecutions of Sarah Tisdall in 1984 (a junior civil servant who passed documents concerning the arrival and location of cruise missiles to *The Guardian*) and Clive Ponting in 1985 (a senior civil servant who passed official documents concerning the sinking of the 'Belgrano' near the Falklands to a Labour Member of Parliament), brought fresh concern and criticism over the wide-ranging nature of Section 2 of the Official Secrets Act 1911 and renewed calls for an Official Information Act to replace the 1911 Act s2 (see chapter 27). Section 2 of the 1911 Act was finally repealed and replaced by the Official Secrets Act 1989.

16 PUBLIC CORPORATIONS

16.1 Introduction

Public corporations are established by statute for a variety of purposes. This chapter will concentrate on those established to administer industries, ie the 'nationalised industries'. The 1945–51 Labour Government followed a vigorous policy of nationalising private industrial concerns to bring them into 'state ownership'. This policy has been followed by some governments since, depending on their political persuasions.

a) *Key nationalised industries* were:

   i) Coal (1946)

   ii) Transport, electricity (1947)

   iii) Steel (1951 and 1967)

   iv) Atomic Energy (1954)

   v) Post Office (from a government department 1969)

b) *The system generally used* is for an Act of Parliament to establish a *statutory corporation*, ie a corporation with its own legal existence which can sue and be sued, enter into contracts and acquire property in its own name (just as any other company) which is vested with the property, factories, materials, etc of the industry or group of industries concerned. In short, the Act establishes a statutory corporation to take over the industry being nationalised as a going concern. The corporation will be administered by a public board made up of members appointed by a Minister and which will have the day-to-day administration of the corporation in its hands.

   The administration of a Public Corporation is conducted outside the civil service. Public Corporations are not civil servants. A Minister will be responsible to Parliament for the most important policy decisions which a Public Corporation has to take. This gives Parliament some power to scrutinise Public Corporations. The Public Corporation will seek to raise money through charging for its goods or services. Some Public Corporations are very profitable, the profits go back into the Public Corporation for investment and also to central government revenue, but many are not and have to be heavily subsidised from central government, ie really the taxpayer.

16.2 Legal status and judicial control

A Public Corporation does not have the status of the crown and is not a crown servant or agent.

Tamlin v *Hannaford* (1950) Court of Appeal

'In the eye of the law, the corporation is its own master and is answerable as fully as any other person or corporation. It is not the Crown and has none of the immunities or privileges of the Crown. Its servants are not civil servants and its property is not Crown property ... It is, of course, a public authority and its purposes, no doubt, are public purposes, but it is not a government department nor do its powers fall within the province of government.'

per Denning LJ.

Therefore, Public Corporations are subject to control by the courts. A Public Corporation will only be able to act within the express and implied powers given to it by statute and is subject to the ultra vires doctrine. Usually though, a Public Corporation's powers and duties are expressed in such wide terms by statutes that there is little scope for this doctrine to operate effectively, ie Public Corporations are given such wide powers in such wide terms that it is difficult to set limits on them (eg *Charles Roberts and Co Ltd* v *British Railways Board* (1964)).

Sometimes statutes exclude this type of control.

A Public Corporation has its own legal personality and can enter into contracts, own property, etc, and be sued for its torts and breaches of contract. But, this might be subject to a statutory exclusion, eg the Post Office Act 1969, s29 prevents tort proceedings being brought against the Post Office.

16.3 Typical structure

The following is a model structure, individual statutory schemes will differ in some or many respects.

The relevant statute will establish a Board, the number of members will depend on the statute, eg Coal Board has 12 members. Board members and chairman will be appointed by a Minister, who will also have the power to dismiss them. The Board members will be appointed from (eg, the Gas Board, which has recently been privatised):

> '... among persons appearing to him to be qualified as having had experience of and shown capacity in, gas supply, local government, industrial, commercial or financial matters, applied science, administration or the organisation of workers.'

The Board will:

a) *Provide collective leadership* for the Public Corporation. It will be given very wide powers by the statute to enable the industry to be run. It will be placed under a statutory duty, usually expressed in very wide and loose terms, to provide the goods or services that the industry is concerned with.

b) *Board members' salaries* will be determined by the Minister.

c) *Important financial decisions*, eg capital expenditure, will require Ministerial approval. The Board's borrowing powers will be restricted. Capital investment will come from the central government. The Board will have to keep accounts which will be audited by auditors appointed or approved by the Minister and will be laid before Parliament. NOTE: The accounts of Public Corporations are not audited by the Comptroller-Auditor General, therefore they escape scrutiny by the Public Accounts Committee.

d) *The Board* will be given the power to manage the industry on a day-to-day basis, but subject to the power of the Minister to give directions on important matters.

e) *The Minister* will have the power to make the most important policy decisions and is responsible to Parliament for these. The Minister will have the power to control the Board. The Minister hires and fires the members, etc, and the Board will depend to a large extent on central government financing. The Board is accountable to the Minister. The Minister is only responsible to Parliament for the decisions that he has taken or that he is responsible for.

f) *Day-to-day administration* is vested in the Board, not the Minister and, therefore, it is not subject to detailed parliamentary control through the convention of ministerial responsibility.

16.4 Parliamentary control

Parliament can try to exercise some powers of control over the Public Corporation through:

a) its legislative powers; statutes establish Public Corporations and often the details are filled in by statutory instruments;

b) its debates; particularly on the annual report and accounts of the Public Corporation;

c) Question time; but Ministers can refuse to answer questions not within their direct responsibilities, eg day-to-day Board management decisions.

From 1956–79, the Commons had a Select Committee on the nationalised industries which examined the reports and accounts of Public Corporations and which uncovered quite a few examples of bad ministerial control, management and administration. With the introduction of the new Select Committee system, this Select Committee was abolished. There is no one Select Committee which particularly covers Public Corporations now, but the new Select Committees can set up sub-committees between themselves to consider a particular Public Corporation. If a Public Corporation receives money from Parliament then it will be subject to the scrutiny of the Treasury Committee (along with its many other tasks).

16.5 Government shareholding

In some industries, the government decided that instead of nationalising the industry concerned, it would take a holding of shares in private companies, eg British Leyland, Rolls-Royce, BP, British Sugar, etc. Depending on the size of its shareholding, the government will either participate as a minority interest or exercise control as a majority interest. The Government's shareholdings in private companies are controlled by the National Enterprise Board, which has had its powers restricted by the (1979–) Conservative government.

16.6 'Privatisation'

The (1979–) Conservative government is committed to 'privatisation' of certain nationalised industries and the reduction of State shareholdings in private companies. The policy is to pass statutes to enable part or total holdings in various Public Corporations and private companies to be 'sold off' to the public in shares. For example the British Aerospace Act 1980 (Aerospace), the Civil Aviation Act 1980 (British Airways) and the Transport Act 1980 (the National Freight Corporation).

NOTE: Government policy towards Public Corporations can vary greatly between governments of different political beliefs, eg (at time of writing) the Labour Party is considering a policy to re-nationalise 'natural monopoly' industries privatised by the Conservative government eg water or telecommunications, but to leave in private hands certain other privatised industries while exerting government control in other ways.

16.7 The Competition Act 1980

Under this Act, references can be made to the Monopolies and Mergers Commission, for the Monopolies Commission to investigate the efficiency and costs of services of nationalised industries and their possible abuse of monopoly power. Already several references have been made and it is anticipated that the Monopolies Commission's reports, if critical of a Public Corporation, will enable parliamentary pressure to be mobilised for reform and change.

17 COURTS, TRIBUNALS, COURTS MARTIAL, JUDICIAL IMMUNITY – THE EXECUTIVE AND THE MACHINERY OF JUSTICE – CONTEMPT OF COURT

17.1 Courts – introduction

In this chapter particular topics of constitutional importance in relation to courts and tribunals will be discussed. This chapter does not seek to set out in detail the English Legal System, but for reference the following plans of the civil and criminal court structure are set out:

STRUCTURE OF CIVIL COURTS

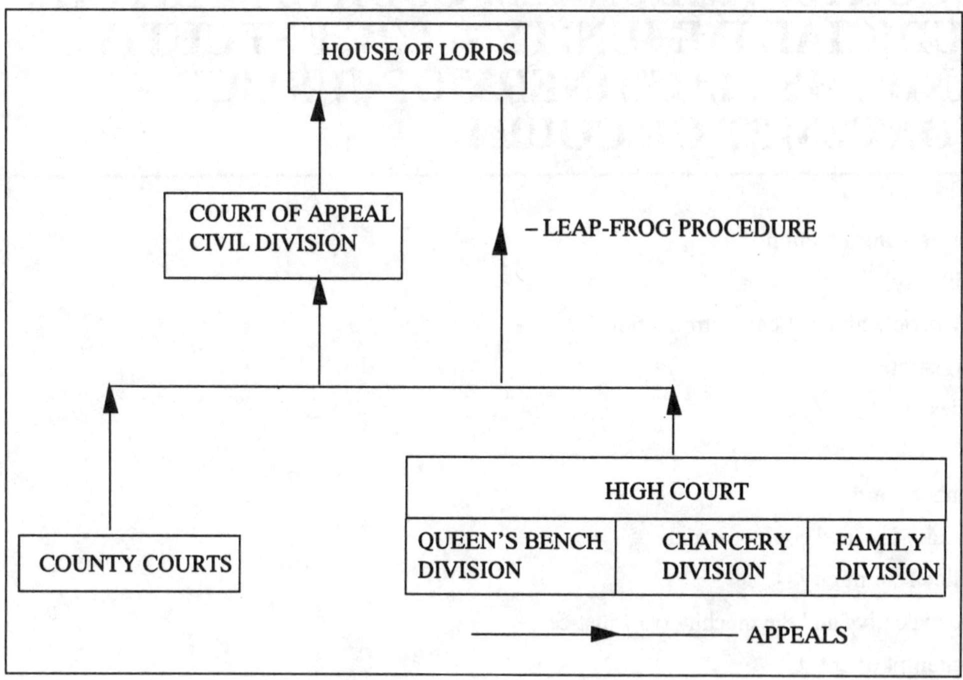

STRUCTURE OF CRIMINAL COURTS

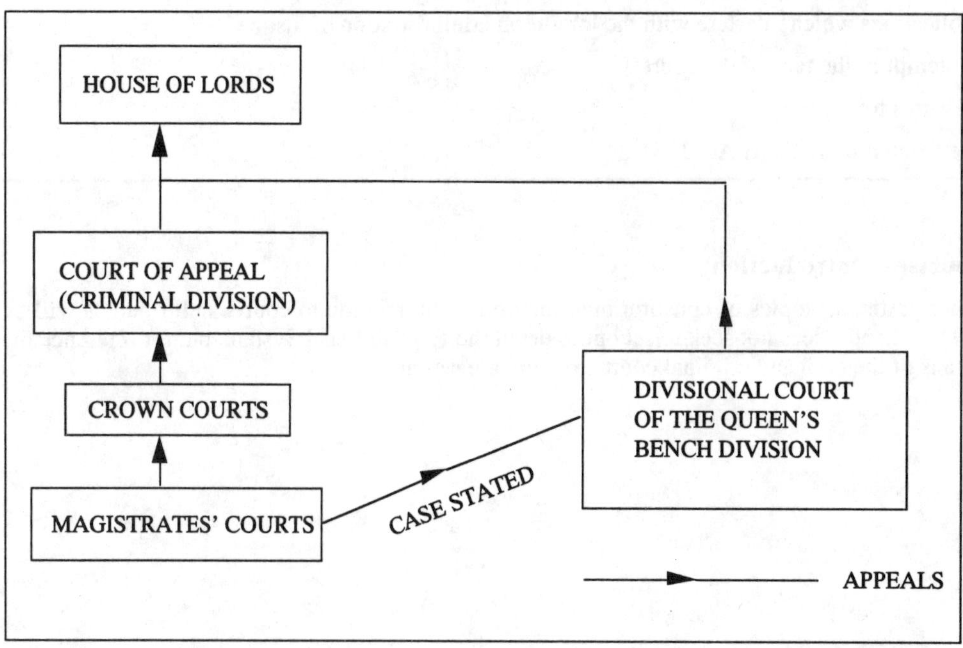

17.2 Publicity

It is a constitutional presumption, which can be rebutted by public policy or statutory provisions, that court proceedings should be open to the public, which includes the press.

Scott v *Scott* (1913) House of Lords

Lord Shaw:

> 'It is needless to quote authority on this topic from legal, philosophical, or historical writers. It moves Bentham over and over again. "In the darkness of secrecy, sinister interest and evil in every shape have full swing. Only in proportion as publicity has place can any of the checks applicable to judicial injustice operate. Where there is no publicity there is no justice." "Publicity is the very soul of justice. It is the keenest spur to exertion and the surest of all guards against improbity. It keeps the judge himself while trying under trial." "The security of securities is publicity." But amongst historians the grave and enlightened verdict of Hallam, in which he ranks the publicity of judicial proceedings even higher than the rights of Parliament as a guarantee of public security, is not likely to be forgotten...
>
> I myself should be very slow indeed (I shall speak of the exceptions hereafter) to throw any doubt upon this ...'

17.3 Lay people and justice – introduction

Ordinary people, ie non-lawyers, are involved in various different areas of the administration of justice. This chapter will consider their involvement as magistrates, jurors and members of tribunals.

17.4 Magistrates

a) *Justices of the Peace*

The office of Justice of the Peace is some 600 years old. Magistrates (Justices of the Peace, justices) are (apart from stipendiaries) appointed from lay people. At present, there are approximately 22,000 magistrates sitting in over 1,000 courts across the country.

Their chief functions are:

i) *to hold committal hearings* at which the magistrates have to decide whether there is enough evidence presented to the court to enable it to order a person to be committed (sent) to the Crown Court for trial by judge and jury for an indictable (serious) offence;

ii) *to hold trials for summary* (less serious) offences. A magistrates' court which convicts a defendant of a summary offence has limited sentencing powers, it can only impose a maximum of six months imprisonment for any one offence.

The legal system recognises that less serious offences, eg traffic offences, do not generally require the 'full dress' trial that occurs in the Crown Court, in front of a judge and jury. Therefore, many offences are summary ones which magistrates can deal with.

Magistrates do have other functions as well, some of which will be relevant later in this text, eg the issuing of arrest and search warrants to the police.

b) *Stipendiary magistrates*

There are over 50 stipendiary magistrates, ie salaried full-time magistrates who sit alone in some large towns, eg approximately 40 in London, the others in Birmingham, Manchester, Liverpool, etc. They are appointed by the Queen on the Lord Chancellor's recommendation from barristers and solicitors of at least seven years standing.

However, the vast majority of magistrates are laymen (and women). They are appointed by the Queen on the advice of the Lord Chancellor, who receives recommendations from local advisory committees of magistrates who generally put forward the names of people who have shown involvement in public affairs and/or politics, eg members of local authorities. There is a tendency for magistrates to be drawn from the middle and older age groups and, it has been alleged, from the middle classes. They are unpaid, but receive allowances for lost earnings and expenses. They sit in benches of between two and seven persons, but normally, three on a part-time basis ie a certain number of days each month. On being appointed, they receive a limited course of instruction lectures.

One major difference between trial in a magistrates' court and in the Crown Court is that lay magistrates are assisted on questions of law by a clerk. Clerks are salaried, often full-timers, appointed from barristers or solicitors of not less than five years standing. They are given many routine procedural duties, eg swearing witnesses, but they also advise magistrates on questions of law. The magistrates themselves are the judges of fact and have to apply the law to their decisions of fact. In this they can turn to their Clerk for advice on the law but a conviction will be quashed if the Clerk does more than this, eg if he is consulted on the evidence in a case – *R* v *Guildford JJ, ex parte Hardy* (1981).

17.5 Juries

'Trial by jury is the foundation of our free constitution.'

Lord Camden.

At the root of the jury system lies the principle that a man should be tried by his peers (equals). Juries, groups of laymen, have been used in the legal system for centuries, their use originates from Norman times. Originally, they were used to decide matters on their own personal knowledge or on the general belief in the area in which they lived, but today their role is substantially different. They decide disputed questions of fact on the basis only of an assessment and weighing up of the evidence presented to the court. In criminal cases, jury trials occur in the Crown Court, where indictable (serious) offences are dealt with. (Trial by jury in civil cases is rare and is generally only found in some defamation trials.) In a Crown Court trial, the judge will have exclusive jurisdiction to decide matters of law, including whether evidence is admissible or not and will decide the sentence if a defendant is convicted. The jury will decide questions of fact, ie on the evidence presented does the jury think beyond all reasonable doubt that the defendant committed the crime.

The Juries Act 1974 lays down the rules for selecting a jury.

a) *Persons eligible* for jury service are:

   i) Those aged 18–65, on the electoral roll, who have been ordinarily resident in the United Kingdom for at least five years since the age of thirteen.

b) *Those ineligible* are:

   i) members of the judiciary and others concerned with the administration of justice, eg barristers and solicitors;

   ii) the clergy;

   iii) the mentally ill.

c) *Those disqualified* from service are:

   i) persons who have been sentenced to life or five years or more imprisonment;

   ii) anyone who has served a sentence of three months or more in prison during the previous ten years.

d) *Those entitled as of right to be excused* are:

   i) Members of Parliament

   ii) members of the armed forces;

iii) members of the medical or similar professions.

e) *Those entitled to be excused as a matter of administrative discretion* are:

  i) persons who have served on a jury in the last two years;

  ii) persons with some other good reason for being excused.

f) *Composition of a jury*

Jurors are summoned at random by Crown Court officials. Those summoned to attend on a particular day form a Jury Panel. Both the prosecution and defence are entitled to inspect the list of members of the Panel which will not include details of occupation. From the Panel, 12 jurors will be selected at random using ballot cards, to form the jury for a trial.

As each juror takes the oath, he can be challenged *for cause*: ie reasons given. Both the prosecution and defence can challenge jurors without limit alleging that, eg they are disqualified, or biased. If a juror is successfully challenged, then he cannot sit and another of the Panel will sit instead.

NOTE: *Peremptory challenge* of jurors: ie with no reasons given was abolished by s18 Criminal Justice Act 1988.

In practice, before this peremptory challenge was common and barristers traditionally relied on their experience. Often jurors were challenged because a barrister felt that from their mode of dress, appearance or colour they would not be favourable to his client. This is a controversial area, eg Lord Denning's comments in his 1982 book led to his retirement. The Roskill Committee, in its 1986 Report, recommended abolition of the peremptory challenge and of trial by jury in complex fraud cases.

Challenging takes on a more sinister aspect when jury vetting is involved. Vetting takes place when police records are checked, usually on behalf of the prosecution, to check jurors' backgrounds and to provide information for challenges. This is unobjectionable when vetting turns up disqualified jurors, but it can be used in a far wider and more sensitive way, eg to find out details of jurors' political associations, etc. Vetting was declared unconstitutional by the Court of Appeal in *R* v *Sheffield Crown Court, ex parte Brownlow* (1980) (jurors should be selected at random) but in *R* v *Mason* (1980) a differently constituted Court of Appeal held that vetting was lawful to discover disqualified persons and that information could be passed to the prosecution of previous convictions even if these did not amount to disqualifying ones. In 1980 the Attorney-General issued guidelines under which vetting was approved. For the purposes of discovering disqualified persons and also police and special branch records could be checked on the specific authorisation of the Attorney-General to find out the political associations of jurors in terrorist and national security trials.

Jurors can be discharged by the judge, eg if a juror falls ill and the whole jury can be discharged if it fails to agree a verdict, or if it hears inadmissible evidence, or if there has been some misconduct.

g) *Verdicts*

At the end of hearing evidence and submissions, the judge will direct the jury, eg on the burden of proof and will remind the jury of the evidence. The jury will then retire. After this, they must be kept together, in a hotel overnight if necessary, until they decide on the verdict. What occurs in the jury room is entirely secret (s8 Contempt of Court Act 1981). Under s17 of the Jury Act 1974 a *majority* verdict is permissible, generally if ten of the jurors agree, although the judge must direct the jury to try to come to a unanimous verdict. The jury cannot return a majority verdict until they have considered for 2 hours 10 minutes. Generally, the verdicts open to a jury are: guilty; not guilty; or guilty of a lesser offence.

h) *Pros and cons of the jury system*

  i) *Arguments in favour* of the jury system:

  it is desirable to have ordinary people to decide matters of facts;

ordinary people can bring common sense to the operation of the law;

entrusting decisions to jurors selected at random protects liberty.

ii) *Against*:

jurors are sometimes ignorant, even stupid, often fail properly to understand the issues, the evidence, the judge's directions;

jury trial is expensive and slow;

the jury does not give reasons for its verdicts, and jury deliberations are secret, this makes it difficult to appeal.

17.6 Tribunals

Laymen often sit in administrative tribunals, but when they do it is often because of some specialised knowledge, eg on an industrial tribunal a trade unionist and a businessman will sit with a legally qualified chairman. A vast number of tribunals have grown up under the Welfare State, eg in the fields of:

a) Immigration

b) Employment

c) Mental Health

d) National Insurance

e) Rating

f) Rent

g) Tax

h) Supplementary Benefits, etc.

They administer various welfare schemes established by numerous statutes and deal with large numbers of cases, well over 100,000 a year. The principles behind entrusting decisions of certain types of cases to tribunals, rather than the ordinary courts of law, are that tribunals should provide simpler, speedier, cheaper, more specialised and more accessible justice to the public.

Members are appointed by the Lord Chancellor, or by some other Minister, depending on the statute in question, from people outside government service. This is to ensure that tribunals are independent of the government and its departments. Sometimes, the chairman will choose the other members. A typical tribunal will have a legally qualified chairman with two lay members who represent different interests. So many tribunals were set up in a great surge of social legislation after World War II, that concern grew at the standard of justice administered in them. This led to the appointment of the Franks Committee which reported in 1957. It identified as the fundamental aims of administrative tribunals: openness, fairness and impartiality (ie freedom from the influence of the government department associated with the scheme a tribunal is connected with).

In response the Tribunals and Inquiries Act 1958 (amended in 1971) was passed. The Act set up the *Council on Tribunals* to act as an independent watchdog to review the personnel and working of tribunals and to report to the Lord Chancellor. The Council's work has led to much improved procedural rules for tribunals, eg there is now generally a right to legal representation at tribunal hearings. The Act also established a right of appeal to the High Court from many tribunals and, very importantly, requires tribunals to give reasons for their decisions.

The Council on Tribunals recently published a report: 'Model Rules of Procedure for Tribunals' (1991) Cmnd 1434. It is designed to provide a comprehensive collection of model rules, covering:

- enacting formula;
- appeals/applications to tribunals;
- the respondent and third parties;
- pre-hearing procedures and powers;
- costs, expenses and interest;
- appeals from tribunals;
- composition and general powers of tribunals;
- illustrative basic rules for conducting hearings.

It is not intended to be a statutory code, rather a series of illustrative model rules to be selected and adapted as appropriate.

17.7 County courts

A few words on county courts are relevant here. The vast majority of courts cases brought by ordinary people involve small claims. How does the legal system deal with these? The modern County Court system was first established in 1846 to deal especially with claims involving small sums of money, something which the legal system desperately needed. At present England and Wales is divided into 400 districts, each with its own county court. They can hear claims of up to a £5,000 limit in most cases. They are presided over by circuit judges who are appointed by the Queen on the Lord Chancellor's recommendation, from barristers of at least ten years standing. County court *registrars* are appointed from solicitors of at least seven years standing and apart from having various administrative functions (they act as Clerks to the County Courts), they can decide cases involving relatively small sums (up to £500) or, with the consent of all the parties, any case. The Review Body on Civil Justice has recently presented a report to the government proposing major reforms in the civil courts. This would, inter alia, involve the county courts in an unlimited financial jurisdiction and increase their small claims jurisdiction to £1,000.

It is fair to say that these courts, in dealing with huge numbers of small claims each year, provide an essential service to the ordinary public.

17.8 Military law and courts martial

a) Military law (which must be distinguished from martial law) is a special internal code of law which applies to members and reservists of the armed forces and their families if resident with them outside the United Kingdom. Military law is found in statutes and in Queen's Regulations issued by the defence authorities and is administered by Courts Martial.

   The primary source of it is the Army Act 1955 which created various special offences for the armed forces, eg mutiny, insubordination, disobedience, desertion, absence without leave and conduct prejudicial to the good order of the armed forces and military discipline. Under s70 it is an offence for anyone subject to military law to commit in the United Kingdom or elsewhere an offence which if committed in England would be punishable under English criminal law.

   Dicey described soldiers as 'civilians in uniform' and s70 illustrates this: members of the armed forces are subject to the ordinary criminal law, as well as the special provisions of the Act. Certain serious offences under the ordinary criminal law, eg murder, manslaughter, rape, if committed by a member of the armed forces, have to be tried by the ordinary courts of law and not by courts martial. But, most cases concerning soldiers, etc can be, but not necessarily are, dealt with by courts martial and commanding officers. An ordinary court cannot try a soldier, etc for an offence substantially the same as a military offence for which he has already been tried by a Commanding Officer or a Court Martial. Under the Army Act, Commanding Officers have the power to deal summarily with many charges and can impose up to 60 days detention, but the more serious charges are referred to trial by a Court Martial.

b) *Courts martial*

Such courts are entirely made up of serving officers, who in more important cases are assisted by an independent and legally qualified Judge Advocate on matters of law and evidence. Findings of guilt and sentences imposed by such courts are subject to confirmation by higher military authorities. The Judge Advocate General, appointed by the Queen on the Lord Chancellor's recommendation, a barrister of at least ten years standing, reviews all court-martial decisions to determine whether there have been miscarriages of justice.

Appeals lie to the Court Martial Appeal Court, which is made up from ordinary judges (the LCJ, Court of Appeal and High Court judges) and not military personnel. From this court, a further appeal lies to the House of Lords.

c) *Conflicts of duty*

Under s34 of the Act, a soldier is only liable for disobedience if orders given to him are lawful and he disobeys them. It would follow that in principle, a soldier should not be able to use obedience to an unlawful order as a defence to a prosecution brought against him for his actions.

In R v *Smith* (1900) Special Court, S, a soldier, during the Boer War, shot and killed a farm servant on the orders of his captain. S was charged with murder. The case was heard by a special court and S pleaded that he had acted under the orders of a superior officer.
S was found not guilty because the order given to him was not so plainly illegal that S would have been justified in refusing to obey it and, therefore, S was protected when carrying out the order.

> 'A soldier is responsible by military and civil law and it is monstrous to suppose that a soldier would be protected where the order is grossly illegal. The court cannot, therefore, decide that a soldier is bound to obey an order that may be given him.'

But

> 'I think it is a safe rule to lay down that if a soldier honestly believes he is doing his duty in obeying the commands of his superior and if the orders are not so manifestly illegal that he must or ought to have known that they were unlawful, the private soldier would be protected by the orders of his superior officer.'
>
> per Solomon JP.

17.9 Judicial immunity

The common law prevents any action being brought against judges, jurors, counsel, witnesses and parties in respect of acts done or words spoken by them in the course of judicial proceedings.

a) *Judges*

In *Sirros* v *Moore* (1975) Court of Appeal, a Crown Court judge ordered the detention of S after following a completely inappropriate procedure (S had left the court at the end of his case, the judge got up and shouted 'stop him' whereupon police officers caught S and put him in the court's cells). S was granted habeas corpus and later brought an action for false imprisonment against, among others, the judge. S's case was dismissed. The principles applicable to judges of the superior courts are well set out in Lord Denning's judgment. He also set out what he believed to be the principles applicable to inferior courts but these remarks have since been disapproved in the House of Lords:

'*The liability of the judge*

'1. *Acts within jurisdiction*

> ... no action is maintainable against a judge for anything said or done by him in the exercise of a jurisdiction which belongs to him. The words which he speaks are protected by an

absolute privilege. The orders which he gives and the sentences which he imposes cannot be made the subject of civil proceedings against him. No matter that the judge was under some gross error or ignorance, or was actuated by envy, hatred and malice and all uncharitableness, he is not liable to an action ... Of course, if the judge has accepted bribes or been in the least degree corrupt, or has perverted the course of justice, he can be punished in the criminal courts. That apart, however, a judge is not liable to an action for damages. The reason is not because the judge has any privilege to make mistakes or to do wrong. It is so that he should be able to do his duty with complete independence and free from fear.

2. *Acts without jurisdiction*

i) *Inferior courts* (see overleaf)

So far as inferior courts are concerned, it was established for centuries that a judge of an inferior court was only immune from liability when he was exercising – albeit wrongly – a jurisdiction which belonged to him. It did not exist when he went outside his jurisdiction. Then he was liable to an action for damages ...

ii) The superior courts

But the superior courts were never so strict against one of themselves. There is no case in our books where a judge of a superior court has ever been held liable in damages. Even though a judge of a superior court has gone outside his jurisdiction he is not liable ...

... a judge of a superior court is protected when he is acting in the bona fide exercise of his office and under the belief that he has jurisdiction, though he may be mistaken in that behalf and may not in truth have any jurisdiction.

iii) *The modern courts*

In the old days, as I have said, there was a sharp distinction between the inferior courts and the superior courts. Whatever may have been the reason for this distinction, it is no longer valid ... Every judge of the courts of this land – from the highest to the lowest – should be protected to the same degree ...

... So long as he does his work in the honest belief that it is within his jurisdiction, then he is not liable to an action ...

... This principle should cover the justices of the peace also.

iv) *The crown court*

Today we are concerned with judges of a new kind. The judges of the Crown Court ... should, in principle, have the same immunity as all other judges, high or low ... Not liable for acts done by them in a judicial capacity. Only liable for acting in bad faith, knowing they have no jurisdiction to do it.'

Although it is difficult to fault Lord Denning's reasoning in *Sirros* v *Moore* the House of Lords disagreed that it represented the law in respect of the inferior courts in *Re McC* (1984). In this case a minor was imprisoned after a hearing without being reminded of his right to legal representation, although he had been fully informed at an earlier hearing. He was successful in claiming damages against the magistrates concerned and the House of Lords took the view that the historic difference in treatment between judges of the inferior courts who acted bona fide but outside jurisdiction and that of the superior court judges should remain.

b) *Jurors*

In *Bushell's Case* (1670) Court of Common Pleas, a jury acquitted defendants of charges of unlawful and tumultuous assembly. The Recorder of the court had directed the jury to convict and when the jury disobeyed this, the Recorder fined each juror 40 marks. They did not pay. The Recorder committed them to prison and they successfully applied for habeas corpus.

It was held that no judge had any right to fine or imprison a jury for discharging his directions, every case depended on its facts and the jury was the sole judge of the facts.

c) *Counsel, parties, witnesses*

In *Munster* v *Lamb* (1883) Court of Appeal, an action was brought by M against L, a solicitor, concerning words spoken by L about M during the course of L defending a client in a court case.

It was held that no such action against an advocate could lie.

Brett MR held that the same principles applied to 'judges, advocates, parties and witnesses', they were privileged against actions ...

> '... the question of malice cannot be raised, the question of bona fides cannot be raised, the question of relevancy cannot be raised; the only question which can be raised is whether what was said was said in the course of the administration of the law; and if that be so, then the action must be stopped, since for words so uttered neither civil action nor criminal prosecution can be maintained ...'

NOTE: In *Rondel* v *Worsley* (1969) the House of Lords held that a barrister was immune from being sued in negligence for the manner in which he conducted and managed a case in court (ie at trial).

In *Saif Ali* v *Sydney Mitchell & Co* (1980) the House of Lords held that a barrister's immunity from being sued in negligence was not confined to his actions in court, it also extended to cover any pre-trial work which was so closely connected with the conduct of the case in court, that it could fairly be described as involving decisions as to how the case was to be conducted in court. (Any work which does not fall within these rules can found an action in negligence.) Solicitors are covered by the same principles when acting as advocates in court.

To illustrate; it was held in *Saif Ali* that a barrister's advice as to who should be sued and his drafting of the documents which commenced a civil action (the writ and statement of claim) based on that advice, were not covered by the immunity.

17.10 The executive and the machinery of justice

a) *The monarch*

The monarch has no right to try any cases; it was decided in *Prohibitions Del Roy* (1607)

> 'that the King in his own person cannot adjudge any case ... (these) ought to be determined and adjudged in some Court of Justice according to the law and custom of England.'

The courts though are the Queen's courts and various Ministers have responsibilities connected with the administration of justice, but there is no one 'Minister of Justice'. The responsible Ministers are as follows:

b) *The Lord High Chancellor*

The office of Lord Chancellor dates back to the eleventh century. The office developed its great powers due to the Lord Chancellor's early position as head of the royal secretariat (Chancery). The Lord Chancellor's legal pre-eminence derived from the office's responsibility for: the issuing of writs to prospective litigants and for: the creation and development of the principles of Equity.

The Lord Chancellor is:

i) appointed by the Queen acting on the Prime Minister's advice;

ii) a political appointment (the Lord Chancellor changes as governments change);

iii) the leading subject after members of the Royal Family and the Archbishop of Canterbury:

iv) the keeper of the Great Seal;

v) the head of the judiciary; he presides over the House of Lords and the Chancery Division of the High Court; he appoints magistrates and advises the Prime Minister (who advises the Crown) on the appointment of circuit, High Court and senior judges;

vi) a Cabinet minister;

vii) the 'Speaker' of the Lords (but note that his office does not involve the same impartiality as that of the Speaker. Lord Chancellor may as member of Government make political speeches);

viii) responsible for reform of the civil law (advised by the Law Commission);

ix) appoints the chairmen and members of many tribunals;

x) responsible for the legal aid scheme;

xi) responsible for the Land Registry and the Public Records Office.

c) *The Home Secretary*

The Home Secretary is:

i) appointed by the Queen acting in accordance with the Prime Minister's advice;

ii) the Minister responsible for law and order;

iii) He: advises the Queen on the exercise of the prerogative of mercy and pardon;

iv) is the police authority for the Metropolis of London; supervises local police authorities; is responsible for the prison service; is responsible for reform of the criminal law (advised by the Criminal Law Review Commission).

d) *The Law Officers of the Crown*

i) *The Attorney-General* is a Minister appointed by the Queen on the Prime Minister's advice. He represents the Crown in the courts and is the Crown's principal legal adviser outside the Cabinet. Constitutionally, he is the guardian of the public interest and can, therefore, institute civil actions to enforce public rights, eg relator actions. The Attorney-General has an array of powers in relation to criminal trials:

he can enter a nolle prosequi to stop a trial on indictment;

his leave is required before certain prosecutions can be brought, eg under the Official Secrets Act, the Contempt of Court Act;

he can institute criminal proceedings and in important criminal trials he will lead the prosecution.

The Attorney-General is also the ex-officio leader of the Bar. The Attorney-General's important powers could be exercised in a political and partial way, subject to the influence of the Prime Minister and his ministerial colleagues. But, by convention, the Attorney-General acts independently.

Sir John Simon set out this convention during a parliamentary debate in 1925 on the *Campbell Case* when he stated:

> 'I understand the duty of the Attorney-General to be this. He should absolutely decline to receive orders from the Prime Minister, or Cabinet or anyone else, that he shall prosecute. His first duty is to see that no one is prosecuted with all the majesty of the law unless the Attorney-General, as head of the Bar, is satisfied that a case for prosecution lies against him. He should receive orders from nobody. But, that is very different from saying that the Attorney-General ought in all cases to ask nobody else's view ...'

ii) The Attorney-General is aided by the *Solicitor General*, who despite his title is a barrister who has similar duties to the Attorney-General, but is subordinate to him.

iii) Finally, the *Director of Public Prosecutions* is not a Minister. He is appointed by the Home Secretary from barristers or solicitors of at least ten years standing and is under the supervision of the Attorney-General.

The Director of Public Prosecutions prosecutes in a small number of cases, eg: involving people of standing in the community; or involving corruption.

Also: the Director of Public Prosecutions has cases referred to him by government departments and he instructs solicitors and counsel to conduct them.

The Director of Public Prosecutions advises the police on sufficiency of evidence for prosecutions and under some statutes the Director of Public Prosecutions's consent is necessary for the institution of legal proceedings. Under the

1985 Prosecution of Offences Act, the Director of Public Prosecutions becomes head of the new Crown Prosecution Service.

Under the Prosecution of Offences Act 1979 s4, the Director of Public Prosecutions 'if he thinks fit' can take over the conduct of any criminal proceedings begun by any person, including any private person. If he takes over a private prosecution, he can decide to offer no evidence, therefore effectively stopping the case and can act in whatever manner appears to him to be expedient in the public interest: *Raymond* v *Attorney-General* (1982) Court of Appeal.

17.11 Contempt of court

a) *Civil contempt*

The law of contempt is divided into criminal and civil contempt. This chapter is concerned primarily with criminal contempt. For completeness: a civil contempt occurs when a court order, eg an injunction, is disobeyed. A court can impose a sentence of imprisonment to coerce obedience to such an order.

b) *Criminal contempt*

The purpose of the law of contempt is to prevent interference with the administration of justice:

> 'The law on this subject is ... founded entirely on public policy. It is there to prevent interference with the administration of justice. Freedom of speech should not be limited to any greater extent than is necessary, but it cannot be allowed where there would be real prejudice to the administration of justice.'
>
> per Lord Reid in *Attorney-General* v *Times Newspapers Ltd* (1974).

A person found guilty of a criminal contempt can be fined or imprisoned, the object of the law being to punish. Criminal contempt can be divided into four different types:

i) publications prejudicial to a fair trial;

ii) publications which scandalise the court or a judge;

iii) publications which interfere with the long-term administration of justice;

iv) contempt in the face of the court.

Illustrations of each will now be given, then the Contempt of Court Act 1981 will be considered.

17.12 Publications prejudicial to a fair trail

If, for example, a newspaper publishes an article which in some way prejudges the issues in a forthcoming civil or criminal trial, then the newspaper will have committed a criminal contempt. The clearest possible illustration of this occurred in:

a) *Attorney-General* v *Times Newspapers* (1974) House of Lords

Distillers manufactured and marketed a drug, thalidomide, which pregnant women took and which led to many children being born with gross deformities. Several actions were commenced by parents against D alleging that D had been negligent in testing, manufacturing and marketing the drug. While negotiations were taking place between the parties to try to reach a settlement of the actions, the *Sunday Times* proposed to publish an article containing evidence and allegations that D had been negligent in several ways in producing the drug. The *Sunday Times* submitted the article to the Attorney-General and the Attorney-General brought proceedings for an injunction to restrain the publication of the article on the grounds that it constituted a criminal contempt.

It was held that the article was a criminal contempt and, therefore, an injunction was issued, because the article clearly prejudged the issues that were central to the actions brought by the parents against D. The Lords expressed dread of 'trial by newspaper' as it was for the courts, not newspapers, to determine issues brought before the courts by litigants.

Lord Reid held that as:

> 'a general rule it is not permissible to prejudge issues in pending cases.'

Lord Diplock held that, once a case was submitted to a court, litigants should be able to rely on there being no usurpation by any other person, eg a newspaper, of the functions of the court.

NOTE: This case no longer represents the law after the Contempt of Court Act 1981 and the judgments of the Law Lords were severely criticised in the European Court of Human Rights (see below).

b) *R* v *Bolam, ex parte Haigh* (1949)

H was charged with murder ('acid bath'). The *Daily Mirror* published an article describing H as a 'vampire' and stated that he had committed other murders.

It was held that this was clearly prejudicial to the fairness of H's trial and that a criminal contempt had been committed. The editor of the *Daily Mirror* was sentenced to three months' imprisonment; the *Daily Mirror* proprietors were fined £10,000.

This case illustrates that the courts can use the law of criminal contempt to ensure that juries sitting in criminal trials do not have their minds affected in advance by allegations in newspaper articles which they might read. The law seeks to protect the impartiality of jurors. A juror should come to a decision on the evidence presented in court, not on allegations in newspapers.

A useful summary of this type of criminal contempt was given by Lord Goddard CJ in *R* v *Evening Standard* (1954) High Court:

> '... the essence of the jurisdiction is that reports, if they contain comments on cases before they are tried, or alleged histories of the prisoner who is on trial and all misreports are matters which tend to interfere with the due course of justice. (This is) the foundation of the jurisdiction.'

17.13 Publications which scandalise the court or a judge

It is criminal contempt to publish scurrilous personal abuse of a judge or the way that a judge has conducted a case, even though the proceedings have terminated.

In *R* v *Gray* (1900) High Court, G wrote an article, published in the *Birmingham Daily Argus*, which criticised the way that Mr J Darling had decided a case and which described him as, among other things, an 'impudent little man in horsehair, a microcosm of conceit and empty-headedness.'

It was held that this constituted 'personal scurrilous abuse of a judge *as* a judge' and was criminal contempt. G was fined £100.

It is not criminal contempt though to publish reasonable and reasoned argument that a case has been wrongly decided, *Ambard* v *Attorney-General Trinidad and Tobago* (1936). In *R* v *Metropolitan Police Commissioner, ex parte Blackburn (No 2)* (1968) Salmon LJ held that:

> 'It is the inalienable right of everyone to comment fairly upon any matter of public importance ... it follows that no criticism of a judgment, however vigorous, can amount to contempt providing it keeps within the limits of reasonable courtesy and good faith.'

17.14 Publications which interfere with the long-term administration of justice

This class of criminal contempt covers publications with might in some way prejudice the future administration of justice, eg, in *Attorney-General* v *Times Newspapers* three of the Lords held that the proposed article was not only a criminal contempt because it interfered with the Distiller actions, but also because if published, it might deter people with unpopular causes from going to court, or from defending actions in the future. 'Trial by newspaper' could lead generally to disrespect for the courts as a means of settling disputes. Lord Reid felt that the article was objectionable because:

> 'its side effects may be far reaching ... disrespect for the processes of the law could follow.'

And Lord Diplock pointed out that criminal contempt:

> '... extends ... to conduct that is calculated to inhibit suitors generally from availing themselves of their constitutional rights to have their legal rights and obligations ascertained and enforced in courts of law ...'

Also in *Attorney-General* v *New Statesman* (1981) High Court it was held that an article which disclosed jury room deliberations would constitute criminal contempt, if it could adversely affect the attitude of future jurors.

NOTE: Disclosures of the jurors' deliberations are now prevented by the Contempt of Court Act s8.

17.15 Contempt in the face of the court

This type of criminal contempt occurs when a person disrupts court proceedings, eg by throwing something at a judge (tomatoes, books, eggs, etc) or by shouting or singing in court. The most amusing illustration is *Balogh* v *St Albans Crown Court* (1975) Court of Appeal, in which B was working as a solicitor's clerk and, on becoming bored with a court case, he decided to liven proceedings up by inserting a cylinder of 'laughing gas' in the court's ventilation system. B was caught in the act and taken before a judge who was not amused at B's explanation that he meant it as a practical joke. B was sentenced to six months imprisonment. (B on being sentenced, said to the judge: 'You are a humourless automaton. Why don't you self destruct?') B appealed.

It was held that while B was guilty of criminal contempt, the 14 days that he had spent in prison so far were enough to purge him of his criminal contempt. B had also apologised.

17.16 Pressures for reform

There was a great deal of criticism of the *Sunday Times* decision in the way that it limited the freedom of the press and of the uncertainties of the law of criminal contempt. A committee was established to examine the law of criminal contempt, which published a report The Phillimore Report in 1974 and recommended many changes and reforms. The report was ignored, but further pressure for reform occurred when the European Court of Human Rights held in 1979 that the law of criminal contempt as expressed in the *Sunday Times* decision was in breach of Article 10 of the European Convention on Human Rights which guarantees freedom of expression. This meant that the United Kingdom was in breach of a treaty it had signed. Eventually, in response mostly to the European Court of Human Rights' decision, the government introduced a Bill which in part implemented Phillimore. This Bill became the 1981 Act considered below.

17.17 The Contempt of Court Act 1981

Sections 1–7 of the Act are concerned with the 'strict liability rule'.

a) *Section 1* defines the strict liability rule as:

'The rule of law whereby conduct may be treated as contempt of court as tending to interfere with the course of justice in particular legal proceedings, regardless of intent to do so.'

This rule covers the first type of criminal contempt dealt with above, publications prejudicial to a fair trial, because such publications will interfere with particular legal proceedings. The other types of criminal contempt, in so far as they are unaffected by the Act, remain in their common law state.

b) Under s2 the strict liability rule only applies to 'publications', although these are defined as including 'any speech, writing, broadcast or other communication in whatever form, which is addressed to the public at large or any section of the public'. Contempt is committed when a publication:

'... creates a substantial risk that the course of justice in the proceedings ... will be seriously impeded or prejudiced.'

That is, this is the test of criminal contempt under the Act – a substantial risk of serious prejudice.

The strict liability rule only applies to restrict publications when court proceedings are 'active' which in:

i) a criminal case is:

from arrest, or the issuing of a warrant for arrest, or the service of an indictment, or the making of a charge;

to acquittal, or sentencing, or the end of proceedings in some other way, eg if charges are dropped.

ii) a civil case is:

from the setting down of a case for trial or when the date for trial is fixed;

to the time when the case is disposed of, discontinued or withdrawn.

(Appellate proceedings are also covered under the definition of 'active' proceedings.)

NOTE: Strict liability contempt can only be committed when proceedings are 'active'.

There is considerable overlap between the Contempt of Court Act 1981 and common law contempt. In *Attorney-General* v *Hislop* (1991) where a newspaper which was one party to an action for defamation published in its columns material intended to deter the other party from proceeding with the action, it was held that this amounted to contempt both under the Act and under common law. It satisfied the tests under s2 of the 1982 Act in that it created a 'substantial risk of serious prejudice' to the defamation action and it was published with the deliberate intention of deterring Mrs Sonia Sutcliffe from pursuing her action. It gave rise moreover to a serious risk that one or more jurors might be biased. Section 6(c) of the 1981 Act specifically preserved common law liability for contempt if intention to prejudice the administration of justice can be shown. It is in fact easier to establish contempt in common law, than under statute; proceedings need not be active (although they were here), only imminent.

c) *Section 3* provides a defence of innocent publication, or distribution of, contemptuous publications. If a publisher, having taken all reasonable care, does not know that proceedings are active, then he is not guilty of criminal contempt. If a distributor, having taken all reasonable care, does not know that the publication contains contemptuous material, then he is not guilty of criminal contempt.

d) *Section 4* is a very important section for the press; under its provisions:

   i) criminal contempt cannot be committed by the publication of a fair and accurate contemporaneous report of legal proceedings;

   ii) but under s4(2):

   > '... a court may, where it appears to be necessary for avoiding a substantial risk of prejudice to the administration of justice in ... proceedings ... order that the publication of any report of the proceedings ... be postponed for such period as the court thinks necessary for that purpose.'

   Under this subsection, a court can *ban* press reports. This banning power is a very controversial feature of the Act and received judicial scrutiny in *R* v *Horsham JJ, ex parte Farquharson* (1982). In this case, four men were brought before magistrates at Horsham, on charges of gun-running, for a committal hearing. The magistrates made an order under s4(2) which imposed a blanket ban on any reporting of the proceedings. Farquharson, a journalist and the National Union of Journalists applied to the High Court for judicial review of the order. The High Court reviewed the order, considered it to be too wide in its terms and remitted the matter to the magistrates for reconsideration.

   The Court of Appeal upheld the High Court's decision and per Shaw and Ackner LJJ (Lord Denning dissenting) a breach of an order made under s4(2) was automatically a contempt of court.

   In December 1982, Lord Lane CJ issued a Practice Direction on contempt reporting restrictions, stating that any order made must contain its precise scope, any time limit laid down, and the purpose behind the order, and that permanent records of such orders be kept.

e) *Section 5* is another very important provision for press freedom. Under its provisions: publication of a discussion of public affairs or other matters of general public interest is *not* criminal contempt *if*, merely *incidental* to the discussion, it impedes or prejudices legal proceedings. That is, there is a 'discussion of public affairs' defence to strict liability contempt.

   This crucial section was considered and applied in: *Attorney-General* v *English* (1983) House of Lords. In October 1981 Dr Arthur was on trial charged with murdering a three day old mongoloid baby by administering a drug which led to starvation. During the trial, a by-election was held in Croydon NW and one of the candidates was Mrs Carr, a woman who had been born without arms and who campaigned as an independent 'Pro-life' candidate. As part of her election campaign, she stated that the killing of new-born handicapped babies in hospitals had to be stopped. Dr A's trial attracted great publicity. During the trial, the *Daily Mail* published an article by Malcolm Muggeridge supporting C's campaign. The article did not mention A's trial but, among other passages, it expressed the view that if C had been born today, handicapped

   > 'someone would surely recommend letting her die of starvation or otherwise disposing of her.'

   The Attorney-General brought proceedings for criminal contempt against the editor and publishers of the *Daily Mail* alleging that the publication of the article during A's trial caused a substantial risk of seriously prejudicing that trial. The *Daily Mail* argued that the article fell within the s5 defence.

   The House of Lords held that:

   Firstly it had to be determined whether the article contained material that caused a substantial risk of seriously prejudicing Dr A's trial. It was held that it did. The 1981 Act sought to exclude liability for articles which only remotely caused risk etc, but the *Daily Mail* article which suggested that it was common practice among paediatricians to do that which A was charged with having done, created a substantial risk. As the article was published during A's trial, it put the jury's verdict at risk; the jury might have been influenced by reading it, and, therefore, the article seriously impeded or prejudiced A's trial. Thus, the article was prima facie a criminal contempt under s2.

But secondly, was the s5 defence made out? The article was a discussion of public affairs, ie C's candidature and of a matter of general public importance, ie the moral justification of allowing handicapped babies to die and of mercy killing. It was for the Attorney-General to prove that the contemptuous material in the article was not merely incidental to this discussion. The test was whether:

> 'the risk created by the words chosen by the author was merely incidental to the discussion (that is) no more than an incidental consequence of expounding its main theme.'
>
> per Lord Diplock.

Applying this test, it was held that the risk of the article prejudicing A's trial:

> 'seemed to be properly described in ordinary English as merely incidental to any meaningful discussion of Mrs Carr's election policy or ... of the wider matters of general public interest involved in the controversy as to the justification of mercy killing.'
>
> per Lord Diplock.

The article therefore fell within s5 and was *not* a criminal contempt. Section 5 was designed to prevent the gagging of bona fide public discussion in the press of controversial matters of general public interest merely because there were legal proceedings going on at the same time which involved some aspect of the same controversial matter.

This decision is a great victory for press freedom. The s5 defence may prove to be a vital protection for the press.

NOTE: The Lords distinguished the *Sunday Times* case, in which the whole subject of the discussion was the court actions against Distillers and therefore, the risk of prejudice was not merely incidental.

(PS: A was acquitted. C was not elected.)

f) Note that under s6 it is stated that the previous provisions do *not* apply to *deliberate* criminal contempt. If a person deliberately intends to impede etc the administration of justice, he cannot claim the benefit of the above defences. See *Attorney-General* v *Sport Newspapers Ltd* (1991) as to intention.

g) Under s7 the consent of the Attorney-General, or a court, is required for the institution of proceedings for strict liability criminal contempt.

h) *Other provisions of interest*

   i) *Section 8* criminal contempt to obtain, disclose or solicit the deliberations of a jury;

   ii) *Section 9* prevents the tape-recording of court proceedings without the leave of the court;

   iii) *Section 10* states that it is not criminal contempt for a person (eg a journalist) to refuse to disclose the source of published information, unless 'disclosure is necessary in the interests of justice or national security or for the prevention of disorder or crime'; The House of Lords in *Secretary of State for Defence* v *Guardian Newspapers* (1984) granted the Crown's request for the return of certain of the documents passed to *The Guardian* by Sarah Tisdall re cruise missiles 'in the interests of national security'.

   iv) *Section 11* allows a court to prohibit the publication of certain matters withheld during court proceedings, eg the name of a witness;

   v) *Section 14* sets out maximum fines and terms of imprisonment for criminal contempt (two years – superior court, one month – inferior court) and requires a sentencing court to state exactly how long the term of imprisonment is to be.

(Before s14, a court could sentence a person to a term which was *not* defined in advance and which could extend for any length of time until the sentenced person was purged of his contempt!)

18 ADMINISTRATIVE LAW – PRINCIPLES: JUDICIAL REVIEW OF ADMINISTRATIVE ACTION

18.1 Introduction

a) *Administrative action*

Central and local government provide services for and regulate the public across a huge range of activities. A list of such activities would include, eg education, health, housing, employment, social security, town planning, transport, fuel, immigration, licensing and taxation. The State regulates and provides for us through powers given to various administrative authorities such as Ministers, central government departments, governmental agencies, local authorities, tribunals, public corporations and so on. These persons and bodies are provided by Statute with the necessary powers, either duties or discretions, to carry out their tasks. Administrative action is the exercise and application of such powers.

b) *Judicial review: an introduction to ultra vires*

The powers described above can be abused as can all powers. The primary purpose of the courts when exercising 'judicial review' is to ensure that such powers are *not* abused and to *control* the use of such powers by providing an effective remedy in cases of their misuse.

Judicial review of administrative action operates mainly through the very important concept of ultra vires. To explain:

It is a basic constitutional principle that all powers exercised by administrative authorities are granted by, or originate from, statutes. Such powers are, therefore, derived from a higher authority than the administrative authorities – Parliament. (The one exception to this description is the prerogative.)

These powers are given by Parliament in statutes on certain terms, of which there are two types:

i) *Firstly*, there are 'express terms', ie express legal limitations on the exercise of a power granted by a statute and contained in the express words of the statute itself. If a statute expressly limits how and when a power can be exercised by an administrative authority, then it follows that if an administrative authority exercises a power beyond those express limitations, it is acting beyond the powers granted to it by Parliament. Or, in Latin, 'ultra vires'.

ii) Secondly, there are 'implied terms': the limitations contained under this heading are not contained in the express words of a statute granting a power, but rather are limitations implied by the courts on administrative authoritys exercising powers. The common law assumes that when Parliament grants powers to an administrative authority, Parliament intends these powers to be exercised paying heed to certain principles.

The courts imply limitations into statutes to give effect to this assumed parliamentary intention. The courts imply that Parliament intends that power that it grants should be exercised only:

for a proper purpose;

by the person to whom the power is delegated;

after considering relevant and not irrelevant matters;

without applying any fixed or rigid policy taking account of the merits of the case;

in good faith;

reasonably;

and in accordance with the rules of natural justice.

If an administrative authority exercises a power in breach of any of these implied limitations, then it acts ultra vires.

'In what way does Parliament *expect* the public body to behave? The courts will see to it that the body comes up to the expectations implicit in the statute.'

per Lord Denning MR in *R* v *CRE, ex parte Hillingdon LBC* (1982)

Note that in order to be subject to judicial review, the body in question must be an administrative authority.

In *R* v *Wachman* (1991) it was held that a move for judicial review of the Chief Rabbi's decision on appointment to a rabbinical post must fail. His functions were religious, not statutory, and not within the court's jurisdiction to review or supervise.

c) *Some important points*

Therefore, if an administrative authority acts in breach of either express statutory or implied common law limitations on its powers, it acts beyond those powers 'ultra vires' and the High Court can grant a remedy to an applicant for judicial review (see chapter 19).

NOTE: There are different ways of describing an ultra vires exercise of power, eg it can be said that in such cases there is:

i) an excess of power; or

ii) that the administrative authority has acted *unlawfully*; or

iii) that the administrative authority has acted beyond its jurisdiction.

(*Anisminic* v *Foreign Compensation Commission* (1969))

The courts, through the ultra vires doctrine, uphold the rule of law.

'Be you ever so high the law is above you.'

NOTE: The courts will only interfere if the rules set out above have been broken. If they have not, then:

'the court must *not* interfere even though in the particular circumstances the court might have exercised the power in a different manner.'

per Griffiths LJ in *R* v *CRE, ex parte Hillingdon LBC* (1982).

d) *Subjectively worded powers*

Often statutes give administrative authority powers in very widely drafted and subjective provisions, eg that an administrative authority can exercise its powers:

i) 'if it thinks fit' or

ii) 'if it appears to them to be necessary.'

It might be thought that powers given in such terms, the words being so wide, would not be open to judicial review. How can the courts imply limitations into a power which an administrative authority can exercise when it thinks fit?

At one time, it was held that the courts could not intervene in such cases (*Liversidge* v *Anderson* (1942) but modern cases, show that judicial review operates as normal regardless of the width of the statutory language (*Secretary of State for Education* v *Tameside MBC* (1977).

18.2 Ultra vires – express limitations

To illustrate: *R* v *Hereford Local Education Authority, ex parte Jones* (1981) High Court. The Education Act 1944 gives local education authorities powers to enable them to provide a system of education. Section 61(1) states that:

> 'No fees shall be charged in respect of the education provided in any school (maintained by a local authority).'

Hereford Local Education Authority began to impose a fee for music tuition in its schools.

It was held that the imposition of these fees was ultra vires.

The statute itself expressly prohibited the charging of fees. When this was broken, the Local Education Authority acted beyond its powers.

NOTE: The common law allows administrative authority to do whatever can:

> 'Fairly be regarded as incidental to or consequential upon those things which the legislature has authorised.'

per Lord Selborne in *Attorney-General* v *Fulham Corporation* (1921).

For example, it has been held that the arrangement of insurance schemes for council house tenants and their property was incidental to the statutory powers of a local housing authority to manage its council houses: *Attorney-General* v *Crayford UDC* (1962). But that the provision of a laundry service, where customers could have their washing done for them, was not incidental to the statutory power of a local authority to provide wash houses, where people could come to do their washing themselves: *Attorney-General* v *Fulham Corporation* (1921).

18.3 Ultra vires – implied limitations

a) *That a power must always be exercised for a proper purpose* and not for an improper purpose.

Sometimes, a statute will expressly state the purpose for which a power is to be used, but if the statute does not expressly do so, courts will imply a purpose. This the courts do by interpreting the relevant statute, to find:

> 'the policy and objects of the Act'.

and then limiting the exercise of the power given by the statute by requiring it to be exercised only to:

> 'promote the policy and objects of the Act.'

If this principle is broken, the administrative authority acts ultra vires as in, *Padfield* v *Minister of Agriculture* (1968) House of Lords. The Agricultural Marketing Act 1958 empowered the Minister to refer complaints made by milk producers to a committee of investigation, separate and distinct from the Milk Marketing Board on which all regional milk producers were represented. If the committee so recommended, the Minister could override the Milk Marketing Board. One regional producer, in a minority on the Milk Marketing Board and, therefore, unable to get it to act, wanted the Minister to refer a complaint over pricing to a committee of investigation. But, the Minister refused to do so, on the ground that the producer should be satisfied with the 'normal democratic machinery' of the Milk Marketing Board.

It was held that the policy and objects of the Act, which the court found *implicit* in the Act, was that the Minister could refer complaints to a committee to remedy defects in the normal democratic machinery of the Milk Marketing Board. It was contrary to this scheme and object and an exercise of power for an improper purpose, to refuse to refer the complaint for the reason that the Minister had given. The Minister had acted ultra vires.

The Lords implied a purpose into the Act, when a power given to the Minister was exercised in a way which could not promote this implied purpose, the Minister acted ultra vires.

In *Congreve* v *Home Office* (1976) Court of Appeal, the Wireless Telegraphy Act 1949 gave the Home Secretary the power to revoke tv licences. The Home Office announced that the television licence fee would increase from a certain date in the near future. Many licence holders, to save money, bought new licences at the cheaper rate, ie before the fee increase, even though their old licences had not expired. The Home Secretary, in an attempt to prevent this, used his power under the Act and revoked new licences taken out in such a way.

It was held that implicit in the Act was a requirement, a purpose, that the power to revoke licences should only be used 'for good cause'. The exercise of power in this case, which effectively was an attempt to raise extra taxation, did not promote that purpose and was, therefore, ultra vires. The revocations were a misuse of the power conferred on the Home Secretary.

b) *That a power must be exercised by the person to whom it is delegated and not by another.*

If a statute provides that a particular person or body should decide a matter then it is that person or body only which is authorised to make the decision and if another reaches the decision it may be set aside as ultra vires. In *Allingham* v *Ministry of Agriculture* (1948) local councils were authorised to direct farmers as to the growing of particular crops within their areas and when the executive officer of a district purported to make such a decision on behalf of the local committee his decision was set aside as unlawful. In *Ellis* v *Dubowski* (1921) a local council which agreed always to append to films the certification given by the British Board of Film Censors had its decision set aside for similar reasons.

NOTE: There are wide powers given by statute to allow local authorities to delegate their powers to committees, sub committees and officers and since the statute authorises the delegation there is no offence against the rule. This rule does not in any way affect the idea that a civil servant is the alter ego of the Minister and may act on his behalf.

c) *That a power must be exercised after taking into account all relevant considerations* and not after taking into account irrelevant ones.

The courts in interpreting empowering statutes will imply into them certain relevant matters which should be considered before the power given is exercised by an administrative authority; and certain irrelevant matters which should not be so considered. If this principle is broken, the administrative authority has acted ultra vires.

Exactly what constitutes relevant/irrelevant matters will depend on the exact statutory scheme involved.

To illustrate:

In cases involving local authorities spending money raised from ratepayers, the courts imply into a statute empowering expenditure the limitation that the local authority must take into account the interests of the ratepayers before exercising its powers as in *Roberts* v *Hopwood* (1925) House of Lords, where Poplar BC, empowered by an Act to pay its employees 'such wages as (the council) may think fit', decided to follow a policy of paying its employees a model wage, higher than the national average and of paying the same wage to male and female employees. (NOTE: This was 1925, many years before equal pay became an accepted and desirable aim.)

It was held that:

i) the council had taken into account irrelevant considerations in exercising its power to pay wages. These irrelevant considerations were the Council's policy of paying model and equal wages;

ii) it had failed to take into account relevant considerations, ie existing market conditions for labour and the interests of the ratepayers in minimising expenditure from the rate fund.

Notice how despite the width of the power to pay wages, the court implied limitations into the Act. See too *Bromley LBC* v *Greater London Council* (1983).

d) *That a power must be exercised without applying fixed rigid policies but taking into account the merits of the case.*

Although a decision-making body needs to develop certain general policies to assist it in carrying out its tasks it must nevertheless always keep in mind the possibility that an exception should be made to its policy if the circumstances make that appropriate. This attitude was confirmed in *R* v *Secretary of State for the Home Department, ex parte Findlay* (1984).

e) *That a power must be exercised in good faith* and not in bad faith.

The courts will always imply this limitation. A power is exercised in bad faith and therefore ultra vires if it is exercised:

i) dishonestly, or

ii) fraudulently, or

iii) maliciously.

Cases in which bad faith is proved are very rare. One Canadian example is *Roncarelli* v *Duplessis* (1959) Supreme Court of Canada, where a drinks licence was cancelled because the licensee had a practice of providing bail for an apparently troublesome group of people, Jehovah's Witnesses.

It was held that the cancellation was ultra vires because it had been done to try to deter the licensee from providing bail, this was clearly an exercise of power in bad faith. (Also, an exercise of power for an improper purpose.)

f) *That a power must be exercised reasonably* and not unreasonably. In administrative law, the term 'reasonableness' has become a term of legal art. It is ultra vires to exercise a power 'unreasonably'; but what is meant by 'unreasonably' in this context?

In *Associated Provincial Picture Houses Ltd* v *Wednesbury Corporation* (1948) (the classic authority) Lord Greene MR said that the courts can interfere:

> 'If a decision on a matter is so unreasonable that no reasonable authority could ever have come to it.'

This covers cases where the court is satisfied that:

> 'no reasonable person charged with the body's responsibilities under the statute could have exercised its power in the way that it did.'
>
> per Lord Scarman in *UKAPE* v *ACAS* (1981).

But, note reasonable people can hold different opinions on a matter and yet still both be reasonable.

> 'It is one thing to say to a person "I think you are wrong". It is quite another thing to say to him "you are being unreasonable". No one can properly be labelled as being unreasonable

unless he is not only wrong, but *unreasonably wrong,* so wrong that no reasonable person could sensibly take that view.'

per Lord Denning MR in *Secretary of State for Education* v *Tameside MBC* (1977).

In practice, there are some cases where an administrative authority obviously acts unreasonably, as with *Backhouse* v *Lambeth LBC* (1972).

In this case, local housing authorities were required by statute to increase council house rents to raise a particular overall quota of extra rent money. Lambeth LBC decided to try to evade the desired effect of the statutory provisions, by increasing the rent on one (vacant) house from £7 to £18,000 a week, which represented the whole of the quota required for Lambeth.

It was held that this exercise of power was clearly unreasonable and, therefore, ultra vires.

But in some other cases, a finding of unreasonable exercise of power is made where the facts do *not* show such obviously absurd misuse of power. In *Hall & Co* v *Shoreham UDC* (1964) Court of Appeal, the council had the power, given to it by statute, to grant planning permission 'subject to such conditions as it thinks fit'. The council granted planning permission to Hall & Co to develop a site, but on condition that the Co provided a road along one side of the development for the public's use.

It was held that the condition was unreasonable because the council was attempting to get a private company to do something for the council without the council having to pay compensation to the company which they would otherwise have had to have paid.

Reasonableness overlaps with other concepts. In *R* v *Home Secretary, ex parte Brind* (1991) the Home Secretary had issued directives under the Broadcasting Act 1981 making certain rules as to the broadcasting of statements in support of the IRA. Journalists sought judicial review of these directives, arguing that they were ultra vires on the grounds of irrationality and proportionality. The restraints were disproportionate and some would argue that they serve no rational purpose. The House of Lords held that the directives were not ultra vires. They pointed out, however, that while the test of rationality was closely akin to reasonableness, the test of proportionality went much further. They expressed unease that the courts were effectively being asked to decide whether the Minister had struck the right political balance, an issue with which judicial review had not hitherto concerned itself.

NOTE: How unreasonableness as a head of judicial review covers everything from the clearly absurd to actions more on the borderline of unreasonableness and reasonableness. Also note that the above principles overlap with one another so that in many of the cases the court's judgment could cite breaches of several of the above rules.

18.4 Implied limitations – natural justice

That a power must be exercised in accordance with the rules of natural justice or the duty to act fairly.

a) *The first rule of natural justice: the rule against bias*

A man may not be a judge in his own cause, 'nemo judex in causa sua'. The courts imply that powers should be exercised in an impartial way, ie free from bias. The courts distinguish between different sources of bias:

i) *Direct financial (pecuniary) interest*

There is an absolute rule that if a decision-maker, entrusted with a power to make a decision by statute has a direct financial interest in the subject matter of the decision which he makes, then his decision is ultra vires. This applies however small the amount of the financial interest. The question whether or not the financial interest did in fact lead to actual bias is irrelevant. The court is concerned with the appearance of bias to the public:

> '... it is of fundamental importance that *justice* should not only be done, but should manifestly and undoubtedly be *seen to be done*.'
>
> per Lord Hewart in *R* v *Sussex JJ, ex parte McCarthy* (1924).

(NOTE: If there is a financial interest, the courts assume bias.)

To illustrate: In *R* v *Hendon RDC, ex parte Chorley* (1933) a local authority granted permission for the development of land, for a residential property to be converted into a garage and restaurant; but one of the local authority councillors had acted as the estate agent for the owner of the land in negotiations for its sale to a prospective developer.

It was held that this constituted a direct financial interest in the decision to grant permission, therefore the decision was ultra vires.

ii) *Other forms of interest*

Where any other type of interest is involved, ie a non-financial interest. The courts will only interfere with a decision if there was also either:

'a real likelihood of bias' *or*

'a reasonable suspicion of bias'.

For example, some cases involve people who take part in making a decision at different stages in the decision-making process, but whose role at an earlier stage is incompatible with his role at a later stage.

In *R* v *Barnsley MBC, ex parte Hook* (1976) Court of Appeal, H was a market trader. One evening he was seen urinating in a side street near the market. He was told off by a security officer. H replied with abusive language. The incident was reported to the market manager who decided to revoke H's market licence. H was allowed to appeal, but when the local authority's committee met to hear the case, the market manager sat with it throughout. It was argued that this was contrary to natural justice because the manager, as he had revoked the licence in the first place, was in the position of a prosecutor and should not, therefore, have sat with the committee.

It was held that there had been a breach of natural justice. The committee's decision was ultra vires.

> 'When the committee discussed the case and came to their decision the market manager was there all the time. His presence at their deliberations is enough to vitiate the proceedings. It is contrary to natural justice that one who is in the position of prosecutor should be present at the deliberations of the adjudicating committee.'
>
> per Lord Denning MR.

Other types of interest, which might lead to the courts interfering, are cases where a decision maker is personally friendly or hostile or related to someone who will be affected by the decision.

In *Metropolitan Properties Ltd* v *Lannon* (1969) Court of Appeal, a rent assessment committee determined the 'fair rent' of a flat owned by a company 'Company A'. The chairman of the committee lived in his father's flat which was rented from a company, 'Company B', which was associated with 'Company A'. The chairman had also advised his father and other tenants in fair rent cases against Company B. It was alleged that the chairman had a family interest in the decision of the rent assessment committee and that this was a breach of natural justice.

It was held that on the facts there was a sufficient appearance of bias to make it a breach of natural justice for the chairman to sit on the committee.

If there is a non-financial interest, the courts also require there to be a certain degree of appearance of bias before the courts will interfere with a decision.

In *R* v *Cambourne JJ, ex parte Pearce* (1955) High Court, Slade J said:

> 'The right test is that to disqualify a person ... *a real likelihood of bias* must be shown'.

But in *Metropolitan Properties Ltd* v *Lannon* (1969) Court of Appeal it was held, per Danckwerts and Edmund Davies LJJ, that a reasonable suspicion of bias was enough.

per Lord Denning MR, the court had to see if there were:

> 'circumstances from which a reasonable man would think it likely or probable that the (decision-maker) would, or did, favour one side unfairly at the expense of the other.'

The courts have not finally settled which of the above tests is the correct one. Both are in use.

b) *The second rule of natural justice: the fair hearing rule*: hear the other side, 'audi alteram partem'.

Generally, where this rule applies, it requires that the person to be affected by the decision should be given notice that the decision is to be made. This is to enable him to have:

an opportunity to make representations on his behalf, to try to argue against the other side, either at an oral hearing or by written submissions to the authority concerned.

(The exact requirements of this rule in any particular case will depend on the statutory scheme and all the facts of the case.)

In *Cooper* v *Wandsworth Board of Works* (1863) it was held that, despite the fact that there were no statutory provisions requiring a hearing, a builder (C) was entitled at common law to be heard by the Board, before it, as it was entitled by statute to do, ordered the demolition of one of C's buildings. The court implied the fair hearing rule:

> 'The justice of the common law will supply the omission of the legislature.'
>
> per Byles J.

In *Ridge* v *Baldwin* (1964) House of Lords, the Chief Constable of Brighton was dismissed by the local police authority (the Watch Committee) acting under its statutory powers. The Committee refused to give the Chief Constable a hearing before exercising this power. It was held by the Lords that implicit in the dismissal power were the requirements that the Chief Constable should be given: notice of the grounds against him; and a fair opportunity to present his defence to the Committee.

The principles in *Ridge* were applied in *Chief Constable for North Wales* v *Evans* (1982) HL, where a police officer on probation was dismissed by his Chief Constable without being heard.

NOTE: The application of the rules of natural justice depends not upon any distinction between judicial and administrative decisions, but more importantly upon the issues at stake. If they are serious for the individual concerned, then a court may require that the rules of natural justice should have been adhered to. Lord Reid in *Ridge* v *Baldwin*, for example, felt that decisions which affect a person's liberty, or the holding of an existing licence, or his property interests, or his integrity, or which may lead to a serious sanction being imposed, would be regarded as involving serious issues normally requiring the application of natural justice. In many respects it is easier to list the circumstances in which the rules of natural justice will *not* be applied:

i) where the decision is legislative in nature rather than judicial. Here large numbers of people are affected rather than individuals.

ii) where no decision is being taken and there is merely a fact finding inquiry (*Moran* v *Lloyds* (1983) where allegations were made about an insurance broker and he argued that the inquiry should have given him an opportunity to be fully heard about the charges. But the court concluded that although the duty to act fairly applied the plaintiff had no right to an oral hearing in these circumstances as the audi alteram partem rule did not apply to a fact finding investigation).

iii) where national security is at stake: *GCHQ* decision (1984).

iv) where the plaintiff has acted in a way so reprehensible that the court consider that the misbehaviour has ousted the rule.

v) where scarce resources are being allocated to competitors but here again there is a duty to act fairly.

Where, in accordance with these principles, the audi alteram partem rule is applicable it does not always have the same content. What the rule requires varies according to the facts of the case. Thus sometimes the rule will require that a person be allowed to present their case and cross-examine witnesses at a full oral hearing, on another occasion to give an opportunity to present a written set of submissions may be all that is required. Sometimes a person need not be allowed legal representation (*Maynard* v *Osmond* (1977) Court of Appeal) but on other occasions this may be required (*R* v *Board of Visitors of Wormwood Scrubs Prison, ex parte Tangney, Clark, Anderson* (1984)). This decision indicated that although there is no absolute right to legal representation if the circumstances are such that the charges are complicated and if found guilty a person will suffer a longer imprisonment then a Prison Board of Visitors holding a disciplinary hearing should allow legal representation. One can extract from these cases the general principle that the more serious and far reaching the effect of a decision by the decision making body the more likely the courts will require strenuous efforts to satisfy the audi alteram partem rule.

c) *The duty to act fairly*

Less serious issues may involve the application of a less onerous duty. In such cases, a modified version of the second rule of natural justice applies, which involves less exacting requirements and is far more flexible: 'the duty to act fairly'.

In *Re HK* (1967) High Court, an immigration officer refused a Pakistani boy permission to enter the UK because he did not believe the boy was under 16 years old. It was argued that the boy (and his father) were entitled to a hearing.

It was held that the officer had a duty to act fairly, but this did not require him to hold a full-scale inquiry or to adopt judicial process or procedure; all he had to do was let the immigrant know what his impression was so that the immigrant could disabuse him. This had been done, the father and son had been given ample opportunity to satisfy the officer of the boy's age.

NOTE: This duty is very flexible:

> '... the duty to act fairly cannot be set down in a series of set propositions. Each case depends on its own circumstances ... Sometimes fairness may require that the man be told the outline of the case against him ... At other times, it may not be necessary to have a hearing, or even to tell the man the case against him.'
>
> per Lord Denning MR in *Payne* v *Lord Harris* (1981).

In *R* v *Civil Service Appeal Board, ex parte Cunningham* (1991) Cunningham applied for judicial review of the Board's failure to give reasons for its decision. There was no general rule of law or statutory rule that reasons must be given by the Board. However, it was held that the rules of natural justice required that reasons be given, especially a statement as to how it had calculated the sum it awarded for unfair dismissal. The application for judicial review succeeded on the basis that the rules of natural justice had not been followed.

18.5 Conclusion

In practice, it is often hard to separate the grounds of judicial review from each other:

'all these things run into one another.'

per Lord Greene in *Wednesbury* case.

To illustrate how an administrative authority might break both express and implied limitations on its powers: *Bromley LBC* v *Greater London Council* (1983) House of Lords. The facts were that the newly elected London Greater London Council followed an election manifesto promise to reduce London Transport fares, the cuts being implemented by the London Transport Executive. To pay for this policy, the Greater London Council required the London boroughs to levy a supplementary rate. The London Borough of Bromley applied for judicial review of the Greater London Council's action.

It was held that the Greater London Council had acted ultra vires (unlawfully). The two principles on which the case turned were:

a) That on a correct interpretation of the Transport (London) Act 1969 an express limitation was placed on the powers of the Greater London Council and the LTE, they were obliged to run the transport services on business principles attempting to avoid a deficit and ensuring, as far as practicable, that outgoings were met by revenue.

   This express limitation had clearly not been complied with and, therefore, the Greater London Council's actions were ultra vires.

b) That there was also an implied limitation on the Greater London Council's powers, it owed a fiduciary duty to the ratepayers.

   > 'It is well established that a local authority owes a fiduciary duty to the ratepayers from whom it obtains moneys ... This includes a duty not to expend those moneys thriftlessly, but to deploy the full financial resources available to it to the best advantage.'
   >
   > Lord Diplock.

   The Greater London Council had broken this implied limitation by failing to balance fairly the interests of the ratepayers and the transport users and had cast an inordinate burden on the ratepayers.

   The Greater London Council later modified its subsidy policy – it was found to be acceptable: *R* v *London Transport Executive, ex parte Greater London Council* (1983) QB.

   See also, *R* v *Secretary of State for Health, ex parte US Tobacco International* (1991) in which the government banned oral snuff. The applicants were the only manufacturers of the product in the United Kingdom and had in fact built their factory in Britain with a government grant. When, three years later, regulations were introduced without any consultation or notification, the Secretary of State should have realised that the change in policy would be catastrophic for the company. There was a duty under the Consumer Protection Act 1987 s11(5)(a) to consult with the producers and give them an opportunity to know and respond to the evidence against the product. In failing to do this, the procedural requirements of the 1987 Act had not been complied with and accordingly the applicants were entitled to a writ of certiorari to quash the ban on their product.

19 ADMINISTRATIVE LAW – REMEDIES

19.1 Introduction

At the heart of administrative law lie two crucial issues. The first is to define when the actions of an administrative authority can be classified as unlawful (ultra vires). The second is to define who can challenge the actions of an administrative authority, by applying to the High Court for judicial review, when it is alleged that such actions are unlawful. What standing (locus standi) does an applicant for judicial review need to show before the High Court can consider the applicant's allegations of unlawful action by an administrative authority. The decision of the House of Lords in the case of *R* v *Inland Revenue Commissioners, ex parte National Federation of Self-employed and Small Businesses Ltd* (1982) partially answers this question.

The answer given seems to strike a balance between two different approaches to the issue of standing, one liberal, the other restrictive, but before the decision of the House of Lords can be analysed the scene must be set.

19.2 Remedies

Various remedies can be obtained from the High Court when an administrative authority is adjudged to have acted, or to be acting, unlawfully. These remedies are:

a) *Certiorari: to quash* unlawful actions;

b) *Prohibition: to prevent* the taking or continuance of such actions;

c) *Mandamus: to order* an authority to act according to the law.

These first three remedies are described as 'public law' remedies, because historically they were developed by the superior courts exclusively to control public authorities; and they are not available against any private authority.

Certiorari and prohibition are often issued together; certiorari to quash what has been done, prohibition to prevent any repetition of unlawful action.

The public law remedies are freely available against Ministers of the Crown. The remaining remedies are:

d) *Injunction: to forbid* unlawful action;

e) *Declaration: to declare* (state, determine) whether an action is unlawful.

f) *Damages*

These last three remedies are described as 'private law' remedies because they apply both to public authorities, eg local authorities, and to private persons and authorities, eg they are available in contract and tort cases, etc, involving ordinary people unconnected with the government. NOTE: Because of the Crown Proceedings Act 1947, an injunction cannot be granted against the Crown, or a Minister of the Crown, but in place of an injunction in such cases the court can issue a declaration.

(Damages are also available against public authorities in a few cases, eg where an authority has acted not only ultra vires, but also negligently.)

It is a contempt of court to break the terms of any of the above orders if issued by the High Court; but this does not apply to declarations because these merely state whether an action is lawful or not, they do not have any sanction attached to them to ensure compliance. In practice, authorities always comply with the terms of a declaration. All the remedies are discretionary, ie the court has a discretion to grant or refuse them.

In January 1978 a new Order 53 of the *Rules of the Supreme Court* was brought into effect to simplify the procedural rules for applying for the remedies (the provisions of Order 53 were enacted in statutory form in s31 of the Supreme Court Act 1981). Under Order 53, an applicant instead of having to follow separate rules of procedure according to which of the remedies was being applied for, as had to be done pre Order 53, applies to a Divisional Court of the Queen's Bench Division of the High Court for judicial review ('application for judicial review') following one set of procedural rules. The High Court can, within its discretion, grant any of the remedies or a combination of them.

The procedure involves two stages. At the first an applicant must obtain leave of the court to apply for judicial review and the court must not grant leave unless it considers that the applicant has a 'sufficient interest in the matter to which the application relates' – s31(3). Under s31(6), leave may be refused if there has been undue delay in making an application. By Order 53, applications should be made within three months unless an extension is justified. Leave is usually granted by a single judge without a hearing, after which at the second stage the application will be heard at a separate hearing at a later date when the full merits of the case will be considered.

19.3 'The public spirited citizen'

The courts had developed rules of standing for each remedy before the introduction of Order 53 and there could be found in different cases either liberal or restrictive approaches to the crucial question of standing. Perhaps the most difficult problem which the courts had to try to resolve is whether a 'public spirited citizen' who has no direct link with an allegedly unlawful action, can apply for a remedy. Can a person who is not directly affected by administrative actions, who does not find his legal rights harmed, who does not suffer some form of damage over and above the rest of the community, who does not have any direct involvement or interest, challenge the lawfulness of such actions? There are many types of unlawful administrative actions which, while they do not affect an individual person in particular, might well cause in many a sense of outrage or indignation. Can the law be enforced by such persons? The restrictive approach is not to allow such persons standing, while the liberal approach is to do so.

19.4 Lord Denning's approach

One judge above all others had faithfully developed and applied the liberal approach, that judge being Lord Denning. He tried to introduce an 'actio popularis' an action which any ordinary (public spirited) citizen could bring to control unlawful administrative actions, into administrative law by assimilating the test of standing for all the remedies available. In *R* v *Greater London Council, ex parte Blackburn* (1976), Lord Denning recast a wide statement of principle which reflects this liberal approach to standing when he said:

'I regard it as a matter of high constitutional principle that if ... a government department or public authority is transgressing the law, or is about to ..., in a way which offends or injures thousands of ... subjects, then any one of those ... can draw it to the attention of the courts ... and the courts in their discretion can grant whatever remedy is appropriate ... the discretion of the court extends to permitting an application to be made by any member of the public ... though it will refuse ... a mere busybody who is interfering in things which do not concern him.'

Lord Denning had often referred to and applied to this 'mere busybody' test and it is worthy of note that the principle so evolved applied to all the available remedies, for

'... the courts ... can grant whatever remedy is appropriate.'

19.5 'Actio popularis'?

It is therefore fair to describe the law of standing as unsettled before the introduction of Order 53. It is now possible to turn to Order 53 and consider whether its terms have been interpreted to make any difference to this unsettled area. Order 53 was designed to simplify the procedural rules for applying for the various remedies available. In rule 3(5) the test of standing for an applicant must have 'a sufficient interest in the matter to which the application relates'. Is this a new test of standing? Lord Denning ingeniously argued, in *The Discipline of the Law* that:

'As a result ... of the new procedure, it can ... be said that we have ... an actio popularis.

What is the test of "sufficient interest" ... I would suggest that ... the court will not listen to a busybody who is interfering in things which do not concern him, but it will listen to an ordinary citizen who comes asking that the law should be declared and enforced, even though he is only one of a hundred ... a thousand ... a million who are affected by it.'

19.6 National Federation - Court of Appeal

In his judgment at the Court of Appeal stage of the *National Federation* case, Lord Denning applied this proposition to determine the issue of standing which arose in that case (the House of Lords rejected his approach). The essential facts of the *National Federation* case were: a tax dodge had been devised and used by casual newspaper workers (the 'Fleet Street Casuals') whereby the Revenue had been defrauded of some £1 million lost tax a year. The dodge was extremely simple yet extremely effective, the workers did not give their real names when signing for their pay, instead they gave such fanciful names as 'Mickey Mouse of Sunset Boulevard'. Eventually, the Revenue had to enter into a 'special arrangement' with all the parties involved under which the tax evaders were allowed not to pay a certain proportion of the taxes they had not paid in the past, but were to give their real names and pay the proper amount of tax due in the future. Certain taxpayers were disgruntled at the granting of this 'amnesty' and the National Federation of Self-employed and Small Businesses (the title explains the Federation's membership) sought to challenge the legal validity of the 'special arrangement'; was it within the powers of the Revenue? The Federation obviously had no direct interest in the 'arrangement'. The Federation applied for judicial review under Order 53 seeking a declaration and an order of mandamus, but the revenue opposed the application on the ground that the Federation did not have a 'sufficient interest in the matter to which the application relates'. The Divisional Court upheld the Revenue's opposition but, on appeal, the Court of Appeal by a majority reversed that decision (Lord Denning and Ackner LJ, Lawton LJ dissenting).

The Master of the Rolls held that there was only one requirement of standing under Order 53 that being a 'sufficient interest' and that any person with a 'genuine grievance' could apply for judicial review. The test of standing was wide and while a 'mere busybody' was excluded from having standing, anyone with a 'genuine grievance' was within the test. Lord Denning felt that the Federation had such a genuine grievance as required and, therefore, had standing to make the application.

'If these self-employed and small shopkeepers cannot complain, there is no-one else who can.'

19.7 House of Lords

The Revenue appealed to the House of Lords. The reasoning of the majority can be set out and analysed as follows:

a) They held Order 53 is designed to stop technical procedural arguments and to introduce flexibility, therefore any of the remedies can be granted according to the needs of a particular case. Most importantly, under the new procedure, declarations and injunctions are merely alternative remedies to the remedies of certiorari, prohibition and mandamus and a declaration or an injunction can be granted if (but only if) certiorari, prohibition or mandamus could have been granted.

   This major procedural alteration in effect means that the test of standing for declarations is no longer to be treated as separate and stricter than the test for the other remedies, if the applicant has standing for one of those other remedies than the court can, in its discretion, grant a declaration or injunction.

b) *To determine* whether the requirement of standing under Order 53 has been satisfied by an applicant the court had to base its determination on a consideration of the relationship between the applicant and 'the matter to which the application relates'. Standing was not, therefore, a point which could be considered as an isolated preliminary point, but was inextricably wrapped up with the facts and evidence in any particular case.

   The correct approach in any case was to consider the evidence available and then to consider the position of the applicant in relation to the powers and duties of the administrative authority involved and in relation to the breach of power or duty alleged by the applicant. The statute conferring power on the authority had to be looked at; did it confer, either expressly, or by implication, on the applicant any interest sufficient to allow him to complain of the breach of the law alleged? Was the applicant within the scope or ambit of the authority's powers or duties?

   This is a rejection of the test applied by Lord Denning in the Court of Appeal.

c) *The 'correct approach'* was applied to the *National Federation* case and it was held that, on the interpretation of the relevant statute(s), it was not open to one taxpayer to seek to interfere between other taxpayers and the Revenue. The Federation were not in a position to complain of anything the Revenue did in their dealings with the 'Fleet Street Casuals' because the Revenue's duty to the casuals did not in any way encompass within its scope a duty to the Federation or its members, or any other taxpayers. The Revenue were under a duty to keep confidential the affairs of individual taxpayers and needed a discretion to ensure that they could effectively recoup unpaid tax and make suitable arrangements for the future and it would not be suitable to allow other taxpayers to intervene.

d) *In a case of widespread or exceptionally grave illegalities*, a court could intervene at the instance of other persons (that is apart from those within the scope of the authority's powers). The evidence in the case had to be considered: was there any substance to the applicant's allegations, were those allegations made out? If so and the facts revealed grave illegality, the court could grant a remedy to such other persons. But, it was held, on looking at all the evidence, that the Federation had not made out any case of unlawful action by the Revenue, let alone a case of grave proportions.

   Comment

   A safety net has been provided by the House of Lords in cases where, after considering the merits of the case, it becomes apparent that an authority has acted grossly illegally.

e) *The minority* in the case followed a different route although they also rejected the Federation's application.

   Recent decisions have indicated that the requirements of locus standi may have been relaxed. For example, in *R* v *IBA, ex parte Whitehouse* (1984), it was held that W had locus standi to challenge the IBA's decision to screen the film 'Scum' because she was a TV licence holder with an interest in the quality of TV programmes. Similarly, in *R* v *HM Treasury, ex parte Smedley* [1985] 1 All ER 589, S had locus standi, as a taxpayer, to challenge the allocation of public funds to the EEC.

19.8 Relator actions

In some cases, the citizen can ask the Attorney-General to bring a 'relator' action. The Attorney-General, representing the Crown, always has standing to bring an action against an administrative authority. If an ordinary citizen, who lacks 'sufficient interest', asks the Attorney-General to bring an action on his behalf, ie on the relation of the citizen, and the Attorney-General consents, this gets round the citizen's lack of standing. The action will be brought by the Attorney-General, who will apply for an injunction or a declaration, but the citizen will be liable for the Attorney-General's costs. If the Attorney-General refuses to consent to a relator action, can his refusal be reviewed by the courts?

In *Gouriet* v *UPOW* (1978) the Union of Post Office Workers called upon its members to take industrial action against mail for South Africa during a week of protest against apartheid. To solicit or procure interference with the proper handling of the mails is an offence under the Post Office Act 1953. Mr G, who did *not* use the postal services to or from S Africa and therefore was not threatened with any special damage over and above the rest of the community, applied to the Attorney-General for his consent to a relator action against UPOW, to restrain them from breaking the law. Attorney-General refused consent. G applied himself for an injunction and declaration.

Court of Appeal held that G could apply for the remedies in his own name – if the Attorney-General refused consent in a 'proper' case (per Lord Denning). This was a form of indirect review of Attorney General's decision. The court granted G a declaration and an interlocutory injunction.

The Attorney-General appealed to the House of Lords.

House of Lords held that the Attorney-General power to grant relators was an exercise of prerogative power on behalf of the Crown and, therefore, could not be reviewed directly or indirectly. The Court of Appeal had ignored elementary principles. If the Attorney-General refused consent, a citizen could only apply for an injunction or a declaration in his own name if he had suffered damage over and above the rest of the community (see above). G was not entitled to the remedies.

NOTE: The House of Lords completely refused to interfere with the Attorney-General's exercise of prerogative power.

19.9 The use of Order 53 and the decision in *O'Reilly* v *Mackman* (1982)

As explained in paragraph 19.2 the remedies of prohibition, certiorari and mandamus have always been used in a public law context while those of the injunction and declaration have been adapted for use in a public law context while their origins lie in private law. After the reform of Order 53 in 1978 (now consolidated in s31 Supreme Court Act 1981) any of these remedies or a combination of them may be obtained by using the one procedure of an application for judicial review under Order 53. This is the only way in which the remedies of prohibition, certiorari and mandamus can ever be obtained. However injunctions and declarations can be obtained not only by following Order 53 but also by separate private law procedures in the Queen's Bench and Chancery Divisions of the High Court. The issue after the 1978 reform was whether an applicant would still be able to challenge a public law decision of a public authority by bringing an application for an injunction or declaration by the usual private law method or whether Order 53 must be used in all circumstances to question the validity of the public law decision of a public authority. This was the point at stake in *O'Reilly* v *Mackman*.

Several prisoners wished to allege that a decision of a Prison Board of Visitors in respect of them was invalid but the three month time limit for seeking an application for judicial review under Order 53 was past. They therefore applied for declarations by writ in the Queen's Bench Division. Their applications were struck out as an abuse of the process of the court for the correct way to challenge a public law decision made by a public body was by Order 53. The reasons for insisting that the Order 53 application for judicial review should be followed were that Order 53 provides a number of safeguards for the public and that, since the 1978 reforms, the procedural rules have been relaxed so that the plaintiff is in a more favourable position. Order 53 thus provides a balanced method of redressing wrongs. The safeguards referred to in the judgments were that:

a) before bringing an application for judicial review permission must be sought from the court so frivolous claims may be swiftly dismissed;

b) security for costs may be obtained before giving a plaintiff leave to apply for judicial review, thus ensuring that if he is unsuccessful in his claim there will be monies available to defray (repay) the legal expenses of the public body;

c) there is a special list for the Order 53 cases thus ensuring a speedier trial so that public authorities are not left for lengthy periods without knowing whether their decisions can be put into effect;

d) the applicant's evidence must be given by affidavit in a full candid (frank) manner.

The plaintiff in these Order 53 cases also benefits from a reformed procedure in that since 1978 he can get discovery of documents, interrogatories, etc.

After *O'Reilly* v *Mackman* the rule is therefore that an applicant seeking to challenge the public law decision of a public authority must proceed by Order 53 or his application will be struck out. If however a plaintiff makes an application for judicial review under Order 53 and the court decided that this was not the appropriate procedure because private law issues are involved (so that the applicant should have commenced proceedings for an injunction or declaration under the ordinary private law rules) it will transfer the matter to the proper division of the High Court so that the action may proceed as though started in the proper way, provided that some element of public law had been involved so as to give rise to the confusion. An aggrieved person seeking to sue a public authority now has to decide whether the decision he is challenging should be classified as one of public law (in which case he must use Order 53) or whether private law is important in which case he may apply by writ for an injunction or declaration by the normal procedures, or even use the allegation of invalidity as his defence in an action to which he is defendant. The cases below illustrate these points.

In *Wandsworth LBC* v *Winder* (1983) HL Winder was a council tenant. The council had on two occasions raised council rents. Winder paid a part of the first increase but none of the second and the Council sought to evict Winder for non payment of rent. As his defence he pleaded that the Council's decisions to raise rents had been invalid and the case came before the Lords on the preliminary issue of whether the defence should be struck out as an abuse of the process of the court on the grounds that such an argument could only be raised by an application for judicial review under Order 53. The Lords decided that since Winder had been a Council tenant before the decisions to raise rents were taken he was therefore in the private law relationship of landlord and tenant with the Council so that he was justified in pleading as his defence that the Council had reached an ultra vires decision. In other words where there is an important pre-existing private law relationship between a person and a public body then allegations of ultra vires do *not* have to be raised by applications for judicial review. In *R* v *National Coal Board, ex parte NUM* (1986) the Coal Board's decision to close a colliery was challenged by application for judicial review but the court held that this was not the appropriate method of challenge since the matter was one of private law as this was the type of decision a private company would have to take.

19.10 Attempts to exclude judicial review

Some statutes have clauses inserted which are commonly known as ouster or privative clauses and these amount to attempts to exclude judicial review of a decision made by a public body. There are two main types of this clause:

a) *The time limit clause.* This provides that a decision of a public body must be challenged within a defined period, usually six weeks, if it is to be questioned at all. Any challenge outside the time limit will automatically fail. This type of clause has been upheld by the courts in the cases of *Smith* v *East Elloe DC* (1956) and in *R* v *Secretary of State for the Environment, ex parte Ostler* (1977). In the latter case Ostler's argument that he had been improperly treated because Department arrangements with objectors to a proposal had not been divulged to him and could not be raised outside the time limit even though Mr Ostler could not have discovered the truth within the six weeks allowed. The reason which underlies the court's attitude in these cases is one of practicality and public policy. The statutes which adopt time limit clauses are often those where large numbers of people are likely to be affected by decision making and if such decisions could be challenged over a long period it would not be in the public interest for large amounts of public money could be wasted.

b) *The Anisminic type of clauses.* This type of ouster clause normally provides that the decision of a body shall 'be final and shall not be questioned in any court of law'. The courts are jealous of their jurisdiction and their interpretation of this type of clause has been that it is effective to prevent a court reviewing a body's decision where that decision was made by a body acting within jurisdiction. But that if a public body makes an error in its decision making taking it outside it jurisdiction then the clause will be ineffective to prevent the court reviewing the decision. In *Anisminic Ltd* v *Foreign Compensation Commission* (1969) s4 of the Foreign Compensation Act 1950 provided that the Commission's decision should be final and should not be questioned in court) but Anisminic Ltd, a British company, successfully persuaded the House of Lords that it should review the decision of the Commission which had misinterpreted the law despite the presence of the clause.

The court's attitude nowadays seems to be that any tribunal or other similar lay body which reaches a decision on the basis of a mistake is acting outside its jurisdiction so that the *Anisminic* type clause will not work to prevent review; but if the decision making body is a court then a mistake it makes will only take it outside jurisdiction if it is of an extremely serious nature so that in many more cases an *Anisminic* type clause will operate to prevent review: *Re Racal Communications Ltd* (1981).

20 CROWN PROCEEDINGS

20.1 Introduction – 'Petition of Right'

Seven hundred years ago, Bracton wrote that:

> 'The King must not be under man but under God and *under the law,* because it is the law that makes the King.'

Traditionally, English law regards the Crown as being prima facie subject to the law. But, English law ran into great difficulties finding a way to enforce the law against the Crown, for the courts were the King's or Queen's courts: how could the King be sued in his own courts? This problem was partially answered by the evolution of the *'Petition of Right'*. Under this system, if a person wanted to bring an action (petition) against the Crown, the Crown could voluntarily agree (grant a fiat) to the petition being referred to the courts for a decision to be made on it. If the Crown consented to the reference, the petition would be endorsed 'let right be done', the Petition of Right system worked reasonably well in contract cases:

In the *Bankers' Case* (1699) it was held that a Petition of Right could lie against the Crown for a contract debt. Charles II agreed to repay, with interest, monies taken (borrowed) from bankers. The promise was in the form of a covenant, under the Great Seal and was expressly made binding on the King and his successors. Charles II repaid the sums for four years and then ceased to do so. The bankers did not feel it was safe to take steps to enforce the debt until the reign of William and Mary. In 1689, they commenced proceedings.

It was held that the Petition of Right procedure could be used in such cases, ie in an action based on a contract debt against the Crown.

Further it was clearly recognised in *Thomas* v *The Queen* (1874) that the Sovereign could be sued by Petition of Right for breaches of contract.

NOTE: There was, though, no machinery available to the courts to enforce their judgments against the Crown.

But in tort cases the Petition of Right did not operate at all. The courts developed a doctrine that Petition of Right could not be used in tort actions against the Crown based on the maxim that the King could do no wrong.

In *Viscount Canterbury* v *Attorney-General* (1842) workmen, employed by the Crown, were sent to burn some Exchequer records, but through their negligence managed to burn down the Houses of Parliament and Viscount Canterbury's house (the Speaker of the Commons). Viscount Canterbury brought Petition of Right against the Crown for compensation for the negligence of the workmen.

It was held that the Sovereign could not be sued by Petition of Right for negligence.

Further it was held in *Tobin* v *The Queen* (1864) that the Sovereign could not be sued by Petition of Right for any tort.

NOTE: A litigant could sue the Crown servant who had committed the tort, the immunity against action was the Crown's alone. In practice the litigant would sue the individual Crown servant and, if damages were awarded against him, the Crown itself paid. It was when this practice was disapproved of by the Lords in 1947 that sufficient impetus was given for the Crown Proceedings Act 1947 to be passed.

20.2 The Crown Proceedings Act 1947 – contract cases

The Petition of Right system was abolished by the Act. In contract cases, s1 declares that if under the pre-Act law a Petition of Right would lie against the Crown for a breach of contract, then after the Act such cases could be brought as of right and without the need for the fiat (consent) of the Crown.

Therefore, to determine whether a person can bring an action against the Crown (NOTE: The Crown itself is never a party, proceedings are brought against a government department or the Attorney General), the pre-Act law has to be looked at. If, under that law, a Petition of Right would have been available, then the litigant can sue as of right now. The Petition of Right did generally lie in contract cases, but there were limitations:

a) A Petition of Right would not lie to enforce a contract which fettered the government's future executive action.

   In *Amphitrite* v *R* (1921) the British government during World War I, had a practice of requisitioning ships of neutral countries if they entered British waters. (The government needed these ships as the British had suffered heavy losses in German U-boat campaigns.) Sweden was a neutral country. A Swedish company which wanted to send a ship to Britain, sought and attained an assurance from the British Legation that the ship would be allowed to leave after delivering cargo at a British port. The ship was sent on the strength of this promise, but was requisitioned. In a Petition of Right brought by the Company alleging that the government had broken a contractual promise.

   It was held that there was no enforceable contract and that it was

   > 'not competent for the government to *fetter* its future executive action ... (it) cannot by contract hamper its freedom of action in matters which concern the *welfare of the State*.'

   NOTE: Cases involving the welfare of the State, eg national security, war efforts, were distinguished from purely commercial contracts, which were enforceable.

b) If the Crown entered into a contract to pay (eg for services or goods) from funds provided by Parliament, then if Parliament did not provide the funds no Petition of Right could lie against the Crown.

   In *Churchward* v *R* (1865) Churchward entered into a contract with the Admiralty under which, in consideration of an annual sum to be provided by Parliament, he was to run a mail service between Dover and the continent for 11 years. In the fourth year the Admiralty terminated the contract and Parliament expressly refused to vote any more money for the payment of Churchward. Churchward brought a Petition of Right.

   It was held that the contract entered into by the Admiralty was a contract to pay if Parliament provided the funds and, therefore, when Parliament did not provide the funds, no Petition of Right could lie. The court distinguished contracts made by the Crown which included an absolute promise to pay regardless of whether Parliament provided the funds or not, for breach of such contracts a Petition of Right could lie.

   Therefore, if the Crown takes on a contractual liability to pay from monies provided by Parliament, the other party to the contract cannot bring an action if Parliament refuses the funds and, therefore, the Crown does not pay. In practice, in such cases, which are common, eg in defence expenditure contracts, the government makes an ex-gratia payment.

c) In *R* v *Lord Chancellor's Department, ex parte Nangle* (1991) it was held that civil servants did have an ordinary contract of employment with the Crown. If this is correct, a civil servant who is treated wrongfully or unfairly will have redress under normal employment law.

   It will no longer be possible for civil servants to seek judicial review on the basis that their employment is in the field of public law.

20.3 Tort cases

Section 2 of the 1947 Act makes the Crown liable for torts committed by 'Crown servants' and specifically for various other torts too, for breaches of common law duties owed by an employer to an employee and those owed by a landowner or occupier to those affected by the condition of his premises. Generally, s2 places the Crown in the same position for liability in tort as:

> 'if it were a private person of full age and capacity.'

This reverses the pre-Act position.

A 'Crown servant' is defined as:

> 'any officer of the Crown directly or indirectly appointed by the Crown paid *wholly* out of monies provided by Parliament.'

This excludes the police because they are paid partially out of local rates. (NOTE: Under the Police Act 1964 the Chief Constable of a police area can be sued for the torts of his constables.)

The Act also excludes liability for the acts of any person discharging judicial functions or exercising judicial process.

The Armed Forces

For 40 years the Act provided complete immunity from liability in tort for the Crown and the tortfeasor where the latter had caused the death of, or personal injury to, another member of the armed forces while on duty or on armed services property. This provision caused great hardship and its scope is now limited to situations of 'grave national emergency' or war by the Crown Proceedings (Armed Forces) Act 1987.

In summary, apart from certain exceptions, the Crown is now liable in tort for the actions of its servants. A classic example of an action brought under s2 is *Dorset Yacht Company* v *Home Office* (1970) House of Lords. A group of Borstal boys, who were working on an island under the control and supervision of three Borstal officers, escaped and caused damage to a yacht. The Company brought an action against the Home Office alleging negligence (ie negligent custody, etc).

It was held that the Home Office could be sued for the negligence of the officers.

NOTE: To grasp the effect of s2 compare this case with *Viscount Canterbury* v *Attorney-General* (1842).

20.4 Procedure

When the Crown is suing or being sued, the Crown itself is not a party to any action; instead a government department or the Attorney-General will be. Remedies cannot be enforced against the Crown, but are in practice complied with.

21 'CROWN PRIVILEGE' OR PUBLIC INTEREST IMMUNITY

21.1 Conflicting public interests

In a civil action it is normal procedure for the parties to disclose to each other any documents which they have in their possession which are relevant to the subject matter of the action. If necessary, disclosure can be ordered by the courts. The reason for this procedural rule is simply to enable justice to be done: *but* while, on the one hand, the administration of justice may require the fullest disclosure possible, on the other hand, in some actions there may be documents which it would be against the public interest to disclose, eg documents that contained information which might lead to harm to the nation or the machinery of government if disclosed. The courts have had to decide how and where the *balance* between these conflicting interests should be struck.

21.2 'Crown privilege'

In many cases, the government contends that governmental documents should not be disclosed, because disclosure would harm the public interest, eg a document containing a record of discussions between a Minister and his civil servants. The Crown, acting through a Minister or the Attorney-General, has the right to lodge an objection to the disclosure of any document in an action, whether or not the Crown itself is a party to the action; this right to object used to be described as a 'crown privilege'. The courts have had to resolve the question of how much weight or regard should be given to an objection made on behalf of the Crown to the disclosure of a document. Should such objection be conclusive, or should it just be a factor for the courts to consider in deciding whether to order disclosure?

21.3 *Duncan* v *Cammell, Laird & Co*

A submarine sank during trials and 99 men were lost. Actions were brought by some of their dependants, alleging that the builders of the submarine had been negligent. The plaintiffs wanted the builders to disclose documents which contained details of the submarine's design. The First Lord of the Admiralty (a Minister) entered an affidavit objecting to such disclosure on the basis that disclosure would be harmful to the public interest.

It was held that:

a) the court could not inspect the documents itself;

b) an objection, made by a Minister, was conclusive to prevent disclosure;

c) this rule applied whether the objection was on the basis of 'contents' or 'class'.

A contents claim against disclosure occurs when it is argued that a document should not be disclosed because its contents if revealed would or could harm the public interest; eg, a document might contain the details of a secret weapons development, as in *Duncan* v *Cammell, Laird & Co*.

A class claim against disclosure occurs when it is argued that a document should not be disclosed simply because it belongs to a class of documents which should not be disclosed as a whole (class) for reasons of public interest. For example, in *Duncan* v *Cammell, Laird & Co* the view was expressed that communications within government departments should be kept secret as a class because this was necessary to preserve the proper functioning of the public service. It was argued, the candour argument, that if such documents were disclosed civil servants would not be so candid (outspoken, blunt) in their discussions and, therefore, such documents, as a class, should not be disclosed. Class claims are made, regardless of the particular contents of a document, solely because a document is of a certain type. The power of conclusive objection given to Ministers by *Duncan* v *Cammell, Laird & Co* was open to abuse and class claims were often made simply to preserve a very high degree of governmental secrecy, whether or not this was really necessary. An example of the problem is *Ellis* v *Home Office* (1953) where Ellis sought to recover damages for injuries he received whilst in a prison hospital from another inmate who was mentally ill. When he sought damages the Home Office pleaded Crown privilege for the medical records of the attacker and this prevented Ellis pursuing his claim and led to public outcry at the injustice caused. Cases of this type caused the issue by government of administrative guidelines to the effect that in future witness reports of accidents, medical reports and documents necessary to a person's prosecution of the police for wrongful arrest, etc, would no longer be withheld. However it was not until *Conway v Rimmer* (1968) that the courts changed the law.

21.4 *Conway* v *Rimmer*

A police superintendent had instituted an unsuccessful prosecution, for the theft of a torch, against a probationary police officer. The officer sued the superintendent for malicious prosecution. To aid his action, the police officer wanted disclosure of reports that had been made about him; but the Home Secretary objected to disclosure on the grounds that the reports belonged to a class of documents which should not as a whole be disclosed.

It was held that:

a) *Duncan* v *Cammell, Laird & Co* should be overruled;

b) a Ministerial objection to disclosure was not to be conclusive. The courts themselves should weigh the competing interests in a case to decide where the balance between them lay and whether this favoured disclosure or not;

c) while in a contents claim the courts would rarely question a Ministerial objection, in a *class* claim a court could set aside such objection;

d) while there were certain classes which should not be disclosed, eg Cabinet minutes, in most cases where class claims were made the courts were to decide whether non-disclosure was:

> 'really necessary for the proper functioning of the public service.'
>
> per Lord Reid.

e) the courts should also take into account in the balancing of interests the probable importance of the documents to the case for which their disclosure is sought;

f) if necessary the courts could inspect the documents;

g) applying the above the Lords held, after inspecting the documents, that the reports should be disclosed.

Therefore, a Ministerial objection to disclosure was no longer to be conclusive; it was a factor to be taken into account by the court.

21.5 *R* v *Lewis JJ, ex parte Home Secretary*

This case is referred to because it marks the end of the use of the term 'crown privilege' and its replacement by the new term 'public interest immunity'. It was recognised that not only Ministers could object to disclosure, but that any interested person could do so. Lord Reid said of the term 'crown privilege':

'that expression is wrong and may be misleading. There is no question of any privilege. The real question is whether the public interest is so strong as to override the ordinary right and interest of a litigant that he shall be able to lay before a court all relevant evidence. A Minister is often the most appropriate person to assert this public interest, but it must always be open to any person interested to raise the question.'

An illustration of a non-governmental objection to disclosure which was successful occurred in *D* v *NSPCC* (1978).

21.6 *D* v *NSPCC*

The NSPCC, an independent non-governmental body, empowered by statute to institute child-care proceedings, received a complaint that Mrs D was ill-treating her children. An NSPCC Inspector called on D, but the complaint turned out to be groundless. D brought an action against the NSPCC alleging negligence in failing properly to investigate the complaint before sending the inspector. To further her action, D wanted certain documents disclosed. The NSPCC objected to the disclosure of any document which would reveal the identity of the person who had made the complaint (the informer). The NSPCC argued that it received all complaints under an express pledge that it would keep the identity of informers secret (an express pledge of confidentiality) and that disclosing the names of informers would lead to a drying up of information from the public to the NSPCC.

It was held that:

a) applying the balancing exercise (*Conway*) the court had to weigh the various arguments for and against disclosure;

b) that the confidentiality of the information was not itself enough to tip the balance against disclosure. Some other factor over and above confidentiality had to be present;

c) that extra factor in this case was the risk that the NSPCC's sources would dry up; the public had an interest in the work of the NSPCC which had to be protected. This factor tipped the balance in favour of the NSPCC's contention against disclosure.

This case illustrates how the courts will demand a convincing reason to prevent disclosure. The principle that confidentiality is not enough to do so, is now an established principle. If disclosure is necessary to dispose fairly of a case, then it will be ordered notwithstanding confidentiality.

21.7 *Burmah Oil Ltd* v *Bank of England*

Burmah Oil, in grave financial difficulties, entered into an agreement with the Bank of England, under which the Bank provided financial assistance in return for a transfer of Burmah Oil's shares in British Petroleum to the Bank. The Bank worked closely with the government in entering this deal and the shares were obtained for a very favourable price. Later, Burmah Oil brought an action against the Bank, claiming that the agreement was inequitable. (The transfer price had been £2.30 per unit, they were now worth £15.44.) The Bank refused, on government instructions, to disclose certain documents to Burmah Oil, including documents that recorded discussions between Bank officials, Ministers and senior civil servants. An objection to disclosure was entered by a Minister. (NOTE: This was a class claim.)

It was held that:

a) Where there was a contents claim, the weight of the arguments against disclosure could be easily measured. It would be rare for a court to go against a Ministerial objection in such a case; but

b) Class claims were different; the Lords examined the reasons put forward against disclosure and decided:

   i) to reject the candour argument:

      'The notion that any competent and conscientious public servant would be inhibited at all in the candour of his writings by consideration of the off-chance that they might have to be produced in litigation is grotesque.'

      per Lord Keith of Kinkel.

   ii) 'that the court had to weigh up and see where the balance lay between, all the factors for and against disclosure to reach a decision. In particular, 'the nature of the litigation and the apparent importance to it of the documents in question may demand production even of the most sensitive communications at the highest level.'

      per Lord Keith of Kinkel.

   iii) that there was a reasonable probability that the documents would lend substantial support to Burmah Oil's case and, therefore, the court itself would look at the documents to help it decide whether to order disclosure.

But

c) after looking at the documents, the Lords decided that their disclosure was not 'necessary for disposing fairly of the case'.

The Lords in *Burmah Oil* took the principle of 'discovery' further than it was expressed in *Conway*. It appeared that departmental material relating to the formulation of government policy might become subject to discovery more freely.

Such was the case in *Williams* v *Home Office (No 2)* (1981), where McNeill J ordered discovery of certain documents relating to Home Office policy on 'control units' in prisons.

However, the House of Lords in *Air Canada* v *Secretary of State for Trade* (1983) reverted to a much stricter test in deciding whether to order disclosure of Crown documents. In that case, the plaintiff, Air Canada, sought discovery of documents relating to government policy on the increase of landing charges at Heathrow Airport. The Lords refused to order discovery, the majority holding that a party seeking disclosure must show that there was a reasonable probability that the documents in question would help his case or damage his adversary's case, and not simply that they 'might'. The minority (Lords Templeman and Scarman) did not agree with this point, but did feel that it must be shown that the documents were necessary for fairly disposing of the issues (see *Burmah Oil* above).

22 THE OMBUDSMAN

22.1 Introduction

A government department or authority may act in an 'unfair' way without acting unlawfully (ultra vires). In such cases an aggrieved person cannot apply for judicial review, but the Parliamentary Commissioner for Administration (the Ombudsman) has been established to provide a non-legal 'remedy'. The Parliamentary Commissioner's function is to investigate administrative actions where it is alleged that a person has suffered injustice as a consequence of 'maladministration'. The Ombudsman idea originated in Scandinavia; in 1961 the Whyatt report recommended the introduction of such an officer in this country, this was accepted by the Labour government in 1966 and the Parliamentary Commissioner Act 1967 was enacted.

22.2 The Parliamentary Commissioner

The Parliamentary Commissioner is appointed by the Crown on the Prime Minister's advice. The earlier Parliamentary Commissioners were civil servants. More recently Parliamentary Commissioners have been selected from the ranks of lawyers. The Parliamentary Commissioner is assisted by a department staffed by approximately 50 civil servants.

22.3 Member of Parliament 'filter'

The Parliamentary Commissioner has a discretion whether to investigate a complaint and cannot be ordered by a court to do so. The Parliamentary Commissioner can only act on a complaint received from a Member of Parliament who in turn receives complaints from members of the public. This system was designed to act as a 'filter' under which the Member of Parliament was not meant to refer complaints received which were not within the Parliamentary Commissioner's authority. But, in practice, the Parliamentary Commissioner often receives complaints direct form the public The Parliamentary Commissioner introduced a rule of practice in 1978 under which he will refer any complaint sent direct to him, to an Member of Parliament with a statement of whether he is willing to investigate the complaint. The Member of Parliament can then refer it to the Parliamentary Commissioner in accordance with the requirements of the 1967 Act.

After completing his investigation, the Parliamentary Commissioner reports back to the Member of Parliament. NOTE: The Parliamentary Commissioner does not issue any remedies if he finds maladministration, he makes reports. The Parliamentary Commissioner also makes quarterly, annual and special reports to Parliament and a Select Committee monitors his work. The Parliamentary Commissioner is part of Parliament's machinery of control of the administration.

22.4 Jurisdiction

The Parliamentary Commissioner only has jurisdiction to investigate complaints against the central government although this includes Ministers as well as departments (which are listed by the Act, the list is up-dated by Orders in Council).

The following matters are expressly not within the Parliamentary Commissioner's investigative jurisdiction, under s5(3) and the third schedule of the Act:

a) local authorities (note: there are Local Commissioners to deal with these);

b) foreign affairs;

c) extradition and fugitive offenders;

d) police;

e) investigation of crime;

f) protection of state security;

g) passports;

h) legal proceedings before any court or tribunal, including disciplinary proceedings in the armed forces (but note that under the Courts and Legal Services Act 1990, there is a Legal Services Commissioner);

i) prerogative of mercy;

j) hospital service (note: there is a Health Service Commissioner to deal with this);

k) public corporations;

l) contractual and commercial transactions;

m) all civil service and armed forces personnel matters, including pay, discipline, removal;

n) grants by the Crown of honours, awards, privileges, charters.

The Parliamentary Commissioner is also expressly warned by s12(3) that he is not authorised to question the merits of any decision taken without maladministration.

Also, the Parliamentary Commissioner should not investigate a complaint if a remedy is available in the courts.

There is a time limit for complaint of twelve months from the date of the event giving rise to complaint.

22.5 Maladministration

This is not defined in the Act. In practice, it covers:

> 'bias, neglect, inattention, delay, incompetence, ineptitude, arbitrariness and so on.'

(The 1966 'Crossman catalogue' of which the most important words are 'and so on'.)

In reality, maladministration is simply anything which the Parliamentary Commissioner considers to be *bad* administration. In *R* v *Local Commissioner for Administration N and E Area England, ex parte Bradford MCC* (1979) in discussing the meaning of 'maladministration', Lord Denning referred to the Crossman catalogue, while Eveleigh LJ referred to the *Shorter Oxford English Dictionary* definition:

> 'faulty administration or ineffective or improper management of affairs.'

22.6 Investigations

The Parliamentary Commissioner:

a) conducts his investigations in private;

b) determines his own procedure;

c) has all the powers of the High Court to compel evidence;

d) obstruction of his investigations is a contempt;

e) investigations cannot be stopped by a Minister;

f) cannot be restricted in his investigations by claims based on the Official Secrets Act or Crown Privilege.

In 1979, 37 per cent of cases investigated were found to involve maladministration; the worst departments since the Parliamentary Commissioner began his tasks are the DHSS and the Inland Revenue.

22.7 Effectiveness

In practice, if the Parliamentary Commissioner finds maladministration, the department concerned may be recommended to pay compensation to the aggrieved member of the public and will (or should) take steps to change and reform the bad departmental procedure which was the subject of the Parliamentary Commissioner's criticism. Much of the Parliamentary Commissioner's success can be attributed to the ammunition which his reports provide to Parliament, which it can use to bring pressure to bear on departments to change their ways.

a) The Parliamentary Commissioner has had grand successes:

The *Sachsenhausen* report (1967–8):

The German government paid the UK £1 million to compensate UK citizens who had suffered from Nazi persecution during World War II. The Foreign Office was given the task of distributing this money; it drew up rules and under these, it refused payments to twelve people who had been detained in Sachsenhausen concentration camp. A complaint to the Parliamentary Commissioner was made. The Parliamentary Commissioner reported that the Foreign Office had a defective administrative procedure which had led to maladministration. The Foreign Secretary accepted responsibility and the Foreign Office made available an additional £25,000 to compensate the twelve.

b) But the Parliamentary Commissioner has also had grand failures:

In the *Court Line* report (1975) the Parliamentary Commissioner blamed the Secretary of State for Industry (Tony Benn) for having made misleading public assurances that the Court Line Holiday Company was financially sound, in accordance with a Cabinet decision, very shortly before the company crashed, adversely affecting a lot of members of the public. No ministerial or departmental satisfaction was given in response to the Parliamentary Commissioner's critical report.

c) *But in practice*, Parliamentary Commissioner's reports often lead to compensation and satisfactory amends being made. For example:

A series of Parliamentary Commissioner reports criticised the DHSS for not back-dating allowances due to disabled war pensioners. As a result of this, £2,500 was paid to one pensioner, £4,000 to another and some 16,000 other cases were reviewed.

d) *Continuing criticisms of the role of the Parliamentary Commissioner*

   i) The Parliamentary Commissioner has a very much more restricted jurisdiction than his counterparts in European countries. Parliamentary Commissioners have themselves expressed regret that they are not able to deal with any commercial transactions or personnel matters and many argue that the jurisdiction should be extended especially since a large proportion of the complaints received by the Parliamentary Commissioner have to be rejected on grounds of jurisdiction (70 per cent for the period between 1979–83).

ii) Although the Member of Parliament filter was introduced to prevent the Parliamentary Commissioner being swamped by complaints some argue it is no longer required. However, the advantage is that if the Parliamentary Commissioner's recommendations are not followed by government a Member of Parliament is already involved with the case and may ask Parliamentary questions.

iii) The most serious criticism is that the Parliamentary Commissioner is a watchdog with a bark, but no bite. This is because the Ombudsman, while he has powers to recommend methods of redress, is, if the recommendations are ignored, powerless to enforce them. Many therefore consider that he should be given sanctions to enable him to do this. Others would argue that this is not necessary because, for the most part, his recommendations are followed. They would also take the view that the Parliamentary Commissioner has a great variety of methods of redress, he may simply recommend an apology, or some reform in departmental procedures, these would be difficult to enforce and unsuitable for sanctions. Certain Parliamentary Commissioners have themselves taken the view that their major weapon to ensure obedience to reports is the bad publicity received when a department fails to follow a recommendation and that this is all that is necessary.

iv) The Parliamentary Commissioner should be able to initiate his own investigations rather than being required to wait for a complaint to be referred to him.

On this last point, note that the House of Commons Committee on the Parliamentary Commissioner has recommended this rule be abolished (Cmnd 129, HMSO 1991).

23 THE POLICE FORCE – ORGANISATION

23.1 Local police forces

The police are organised into local forces which are maintained by local authorities and which, apart from in London, are not under the direct control of the central government. The Metropolitan police force was established in 1829 and was put under the Home Secretary's control. Later police forces established for the boroughs were put under local control due to a nineteenth century fear of creating a central government controlled police force. There are a considerable number of regulatory powers which are vested in the central government, but it cannot give direct orders to the local forces. Now local police forces are allocated to the county authorities established by the Local Government Act 1972 and the 123 English and Welsh borough police forces which existed in 1961 have been consolidated into 43 forces. The Chief Constables of these forces are in practice largely independent of both central and local government.

23.2 Administration and appointments

Under the Police Act 1964 local authorities (after 1972, county authorities) form police committees which constitute the police authorities for each area. Two-thirds of the members of a police committee are local councillors, appointed by the county councils and one-third are magistrates, appointed by the magistrates' court committee. The police authorities have a statutory duty to secure the maintenance of an adequate and efficient police force for the area. They appoint, subject to the Home Secretary's approval, the local Chief Constable and his deputy and assistant Chief Constables. The Home Secretary has a policy of interchanging senior officers between forces, ie to be appointed a Chief Constable a senior police officer must have had at least two years experience in a senior post with another police force. The police authority can also, subject to Home Secretary approval, require the Chief Constable and his deputy and assistants to retire in the interests of efficiency. Lower ranking police officers are appointed by the Chief Constable subject to regulations issued under the Home Secretary's authority. In London, the Home Secretary is the police authority for the Metropolitan police force and on his recommendation the commander of the Metropolitan Police, the Metropolitan Police Commissioner, is appointed.

23.3 Central control and finance

Despite the essentially local character of police forces, there is a large amount of control by central government. Under the 1964 Act, the Home Secretary is under a general duty to promote the efficiency of the police and has the power to issue regulations concerning their government, administration and conditions of service. Home Secretary regulations which cover, eg police discipline, pay, hours, leave and clothing, have set down a uniform administrative code across the country for the various local police forces. The Home Secretary can require reports from Chief Constables concerning the policing in their areas and can also require a police authority to retire their Chief Constable.

The central government, in the form of grants, provides half of the money required to cover the cost of providing police services, the other half is raised by the local authorities themselves.

In return for this extensive central government financing, local forces are subject to the overview of the Inspector of Constabulary. The Inspector of Constabulary has to certify every police force as efficient and if he decides that a police force does not deserve such certification, then the central government may well withhold that police force's grant aid. This adds to the degree of central control over police forces.

NOTE: The central government cannot interfere with the daily duties of the police and there is no Minister responsible to Parliament for the actions of the police, although the Home Secretary answers for the Metropolitan police force.

23.4 Legal status of police officers

In exercising their daily duties, the police are free from the control of central and local government. Police officers do not owe their obedience as officers of the peace to anyone outside the police force and are in the command of their Chief Constable. In *Fisher* v *Oldham Corporation* (1930) an action for damages brought against a local police authority for the wrongful arrest of a man by a police officer failed. It was held that police officers when exercising their duties were not acting as the police authority's servants. Therefore, police authorities could not be vicariously liable for the actions of police officers.

Also, while a police officer was described as a 'servant of the State' in *Fisher*, a police officer is not a Crown servant under the Crown Proceedings Act 1947 (because he is not paid wholly from central government funds) which means that the Crown cannot be sued for the torts of police officers either. This lack of vicarious liability is the other aspect of the fact that police officers are not subject to central or local control in exercising their daily duties.

Under s48 of the 1964 Act, police officers are nationally the servants of the Chief Constable for the purposes of tort liability. Therefore, the Chief Constable can be sued for police officers' torts. Any damages awarded will be paid out of the local police force's funds.

Police officers have been described as 'citizens in uniform' due to the fact that many of their powers are also held by ordinary citizens, eg some powers of arrest and that if a police officer exceeds his powers, he can be sued for his torts and prosecuted for his criminal acts. Having said that, though, police officers are vested with many additional powers which ordinary citizens do not have (as will be seen in subsequent chapters).

23.5 Independence of the Chief Constable

A Chief Constable commands his police force but no one commands the Chief Constable.

In *R* v *Chief Constable Devon and Cornwall, ex parte CEGB* (1982) Court of Appeal, protestors obstructed the attempts of the CEGB to survey a site to assess its suitability for a nuclear power station. The protestors were peaceful and non-violent. CEGB sought the assistance of the Chief Constable to prevent further obstructions, but the Chief Constable refused to intervene. CEGB brought an action for a court order to require the Chief Constable to deploy his police force to remove, or assist in removing, the protestors.

It was held that police had the power to assist CEGB, but no order was issued against the Chief Constable because it was for the police at the site, not the court, to decide when and how to exercise their powers.

> '... I would not give any orders to the Chief Constable or his men. It is of the first importance that the police should decide on their own responsibility what action should be taken in any particular situation. The decision of the Chief Constable not to intervene in this case was a policy decision with which the courts should not interfere.'
>
> per Lord Denning MR.

But Chief Constables have a duty to enforce the law: *R* v *Metropolitan Police Commissioner, ex parte Blackburn* (1968) Court of Appeal. The Metropolitan Police Commissioner had a policy of not enforcing the gaming laws against clubs in London. Mandamus was sought to order Metropolitan Police Commissioner to reverse his decision and comply with his duty to enforce the law.

It was held that MPC's policy was 'unfortunate', but he had undertaken to reverse it and so no order was necessary. (Although in some cases mandamus could issue.)

Lord Denning MR said of the duty of the Metropolitan Police Commissioner:

> '... like every constable in the land he should be, and is, independent of the executive. He is not subject to the orders of the Secretary of State, save that under the Police Act the Secretary of State can call upon him to give a report or to retire in the interests of efficiency. I hold it to be the duty of the Metropolitan Police Commissioner, as it is of every Chief Constable, to enforce the law. But ... he is not the servant of anyone, save of the law itself. No Minister can tell him that he must, or must not keep observation on this place or that ... or prosecute this man or that. Nor can any police authority tell him so. The responsibility for law enforcement lies on him. He is answerable to the law alone.
>
> Although the chief officers of the police are answerable to the law, there are many fields in which they have a discretion with which the law will not interfere. For instance ... to decide whether investigations should be pursued, or an arrest made, or a prosecution brought. It must be for him to decide on the disposition of the force and the concentration of his resources. No court can or should give him directions on such a matter. He can also make policy decisions ... But there are some policy decisions with which the courts can, if necessary, interfere. Suppose a Chief Constable were to issue a directive to his men that no person should be prosecuted for stealing any goods less than £100 in value ... the court could countermand it. He would be failing in his duty to enforce the law.'

23.6 Complaints against the police

The system of complaints against the police set up under the Police Acts 1964 and 1976 has failed to quell public disquiet over the conduct of investigation of such complaints.

The Police Complaints Board set up under the 1976 Act has been replaced by a new Police Complaints Authority under the 1984 Police and Criminal Evidence Act. The object of the change is an attempt to restore public confidence in the complaints system.

Any complaints made are the concern of the chief officer of each force. Less serious complaints, ie those that would not involve a criminal or disciplinary charge, may be resolved informally. More serious complaints are to be investigated by an officer of that or another force, and a report of the case is to be sent to the Director of Public Prosecutions, who will decide whether criminal proceedings or disciplinary charges should be brought. The Police Complaints Authority has a supervisory role, and can exceptionally direct that disciplinary hearings are undertaken by the Chief Constable and two members of the Police Complaints Authority. Finally, complaints alleging misconduct leading to death or serious injury must be referred to the Police Complaints Authority immediately, and before any investigation is undertaken. It will appoint an investigating officer and will therefore oversee the investigation.

It is hoped that the Police Complaints Authority will acquire a more independent role in the conduct of investigations and that public confidence in the force will be restored. However, many commentators stress the fact that while investigation remains in the hands of the police, impartiality may not always be seen to have been attained.

24 FREEDOM OF THE PERSON – POLICE POWERS I

24.1 Arrest – introduction

The piecemeal growth of the law relating to police powers of arrest, entry, search and seizure and ancillary matters has now been reformed and consolidated in the Police and Criminal Evidence Act 1984 (hereafter PACE 1984).

If a person is unlawfully arrested or detained by the police, he can bring an action in civil law claiming damages for tort of assault and/or false imprisonment (both are trespass to the person). In such a case, the court can award punitive damages (ie to punish not just to compensate) under *Cassell & Co Ltd* v *Broome* (1972) and *Rookes* v *Barnard* (1964). For example, in *White* v *MPC* (1982) the High Court made an award of £20,000 exemplary damages to two plaintiffs for the 'oppressive, arbitrary, or unconstitutional' behaviour of the police. This was a case of grossly unlawful action by the police though.) But a defence to such actions is *lawful authority*. It is, therefore, essential to know exactly when a police constable is acting lawfully (in the execution of his duty).

If the police have acted unlawfully a criminal prosecution can also be brought against them for the crimes of assault and/or false imprisonment, the object being to punish. As above, lawful authority is a defence.

Also the lawfulness of police actions often arises in prosecutions brought by the police under s51 Police Act 1964.

Under s51(1) a prosecution can be brought against:

> 'any person who *assaults a constable in the execution of his duty.*'

Under s51(3) against:

> 'any person who resists or wilfully obstructs a constable in the execution of his duty.'

In such cases, it is important to known exactly when a police constable is acting 'in the execution of his duty' because if a police constable is not so acting then:

a) this will form a defence to a s51 prosecution:

> 'I regard it as unthinkable that a policeman may be regarded as acting in the execution of his duty when he is acting unlawfully ... regardless of whether his contravention is of the criminal ... or ... civil law.'
>
> per Lord Edmund-Davies in *Morris* v *Beardmore* (1980).

Thus, for a police constable to act in the execution of his duty, he must act lawfully;

b) a person can lawfully resist the police constable's actions (see 24.3 below); this might be an ill advised thing to do!

Police Act 1964

24.2 The elements of an offence under s51(3). Is there any legal duty to answer police questions?

In *Rice* v *Connolly* (1966) High Court, police officers patrolling an area where a number of properties had just been broken into, saw R and asked him where he was going to, where he had come from and what his name and address was. R only gave his surname and the name of his home street and refused to go to a police box for the information to be checked unless he was arrested. The police officers arrested R who was later charged with s51(3) *wilful obstruction* of the police. He was convicted and appealed.

On appeal, it was held, per Lord Parker CJ, that:

a) 'It is part of the *duties* of a police constable to take all steps which appear to him necessary for keeping property from criminal injury ... and they would further include the duty to detect crime and to bring an offender to justice.'

Therefore the police officers:

> 'at the time and throughout were acting in accordance with their duties' in seeking to question R.

b) ' "*Obstruct*" under s51(3) is the doing of any act which makes it *more difficult* for the police to carry out their duty.'

And therefore:

> 'it seems quite clear that the defendant *was* making it more difficult for the police to carry out their duties.'

c) 'The only *remaining* ingredient ... is whether the obstructing was a wilful obstruction. "*Wilful*" in this context not only means "intentional", but something which is done *without lawful excuse.* Accordingly, the sole question here is whether the defendant had a lawful excuse for refusing to answer the questions put to him.'

d) R did have a lawful excuse:

> 'It seems to me quite clear that though every citizen has a *moral* duty or a social duty to assist the police, there is *no legal* duty to that effect and indeed the whole basis of the common law is the *right of the individual* to refuse to *answer* questions put to him by persons in authority; and to refuse to accompany those in authority to any particular place; short, of course, of arrest.'

(NOTE: Though deliberately to tell a false story would be to act without a lawful excuse.)

Comment

Rice v *Connolly* is important because it defines the elements of a crime under s51(3) and decides that a person has a common law right of silence, ie that he is acting lawfully if he refuses to answer questions asked by the police.

BUT NOW by s 34-9 of Criminal Justice and Public Order Act 1994 if he fails to mention anything on which he subsequently relies, the court can draw an adverse inference.

On the elements of s51(3) note:

Dibble v *Ingleton* (1972) High Court in which a man who deliberately drunk from a bottle of whisky to render a proper breath test impossible, was found guilty of wilfully obstructing the police. It was held per Bridge J, that there was a:

> 'clear distinction between a *refusal* to act *and doing* some positive act. Where obstruction consists of a *refusal* to do the act which the police constable has asked him to do, such a refusal cannot amount to wilful obstruction *unless* the law imposes on the person some *obligation* to act in the manner required.

On the other hand, I can see *no* basis in principle or authority for saying that where the obstruction consists of a *positive* act it must be unlawful *independent* of its operation as an obstruction. The act of drinking the whisky with the subject of frustrating the procedure clearly *was* a wilful obstruction.'

Also: a person cannot be found guilty of a wilful obstruction of a police constable under s51(3) if the person reasonably believed that the police constable was not a police constable (*Ostler* v *Elliott* (1980)) although such reasonable belief is not a defence to a prosecution for a s51(1) assault (*McBride* v *Turnock* (1964)).

24.3 Do the police have any lawful authority to detain a person for questioning without arresting him?

In *Kenlin* v *Gardiner* (1967) High Court, two boys, visiting the homes of members of their school rugby team, were seen by plain-clothed pos who began to question the boys. One boy tried to run away but was held onto by a police officer. The boy, not realising that the men were police officers, hit the police officer. The boy was prosecuted under s51(1) (assault), convicted and appealed. It was held that the police officers had no lawful authority to detain a person to ask questions; primarily a person can only be detained by the police if arrested. It was unlawful for the police officers to detain the boys to question them and, therefore, the police officer who was hit was not acting in the execution of his duty.

> 'Was this officer entitled in law to take hold of the boy by the arm? ... the answer must be in the negative. What was done was *not* an *integral* step in the process of arresting, but was done in order to secure an opportunity, by detaining the boys from escape, to put to them (a) test question ... there was a technical assault by the police officer.'

per Winn LJ.

Therefore a person does not have to answer police questions (*Rice* v *Connolly*) and the police cannot detain a person (unless there is an arrest) to ask questions (*Kenlin* v *Gardiner*). It was held in *Ludlow* v *Burgess* (1971) High Court that forcibly to detain a person against his will without arresting him was:

> 'a serious interference with a citizen's liberty.'

NOTE: In *Donnelly* v *Jackman* (1970) High Court, a police officer, who wanted to ask a person walking along a street some questions, tapped him on his shoulder. The man struck the police officer and was later convicted of s51(1) assault; he appealed.

It was held that the police officer was acting in the execution of his duty when he tapped the man on his shoulder:

> 'not every *trivial interference* with a citizen's liberty amounts to a course of conduct sufficient to take the officer out of the course of his duties.'

per Talbot J.

(That is, tapping a person's shoulder to attract his attention is lawful.)

Although, of course, an attempt to prevent a person from walking away from a police officer by holding onto him, is unlawful under *Kenlin* v *Gardiner*: *Bentley* v *Brudzinski* (1982).

In *Collins* v *Wilcock* (1984), a policewoman who physically restrained a suspected prostitute by taking hold of her arm was held to have acted unlawfully.

24.4 What powers of arrest are there?

a) *Arrest with a warrant*

A number of statutes authorise the issuing of warrants for a person's arrest. The most important statutory provision is s1 Magistrates' Courts Act 1980 under which:

On information being laid, in writing and substantiated on oath, before a magistrate alleging that a person has, or is suspected of having, committed an offence, the magistrate may issue a warrant for the person's arrest. (There are similar provisions for the Crown Court to issue warrants.)

Under the Act, an arrest warrant:

i) remains in force until it is executed (used) or withdrawn;

ii) can be executed anywhere in England or Wales by anyone to whom it is directed,

iii) can be executed by a police constable notwithstanding that the police constable does not have the warrant in his possession at the time, but it must be shown (if demanded by the arrested person) as soon as practicable.

(NOTE: for other types of warrant, eg, search warrants, at common law the police constable must have the warrant with him when executing it: *R* v *Purdy* (1975).)

An arrest warrant must specify the name of the person to be arrested and the general particulars of the offence it relates to, a warrant which does not comply with these requirements is a 'general warrant' and at common law is illegal: *Leach* v *Money* (1765).

If a warrant (any type) is issued by a magistrate, or other authority, acting outside his lawful powers, a police constable executing it, in good faith, is protected: Constables Protection Act 1750.

b) *Arrest without warrant*

Powers to arrest without warrant may be described as 'on the spot' and immediate powers of arrest.

i) *Section 24 PACE 1984*

Section 24 powers apply to 'arrestable offences'; and these are defined in s24 as:

offences for which the sentence is fixed by law (for example murder – life imprisonment);

all offences which may carry a five-year prison sentence or more for a first adult offender; and

other specified offences – for example under the 1968 Theft Act; the 1911–20 Official Secrets Acts; and the Sexual Offences Act 1956.

Section 24(4)–(7) which deal with powers of arrest for arrestable offences restate the previous law. They provide different powers of arrest for the police and for other citizens, as might be expected those of the police are wider.

The 'citizens'' powers of arrest are dealt with first:

Power to arrest without warrant exercisable by 'any person' (including the police)

Section 24(4): Any person may arrest without a warrant:

anyone who is in the act of committing an arrestable offence;

anyone whom he has reasonable grounds for suspecting to be committing such an offence.

Section 24(5): Where an arrestable offence has been committed, any person may arrest without a warrant:

anyone who is guilty of the offence;

anyone whom he has reasonable grounds for suspecting to be guilty of it.

Power to arrest without warrant exercisable only by the police

Section 24(6): Where a constable has reasonable grounds for suspecting that an arrestable offence has been committed, he may arrest without a warrant anyone whom he has reasonable grounds for suspecting to be guilty of the offence.

Section 24(7): A constable may arrest without a warrant:

anyone who is about to commit an arrestable offence;

anyone whom he has reasonable grounds for suspecting to be about to commit an arrestable offence.

The easiest method of explanation for these sections is that before commission of an arrestable offence ONLY the police may arrest, whilst it is in the act of being committed either the police or a citizen may arrest, after the commission of the offence is complete either the police or the citizen may arrest (always of course subject to reasonable grounds for suspicion of the person arrested). BUT if a citizen arrests and there later turns out to have been no arrestable offence actually committed then the citizen runs the risk that damages for wrongful arrest or imprisonment may be awarded against him. This occurred in *Walters* v *WH Smith Ltd* (1914) where a store detective arrested a suspected shoplifter. The 'shoplifter', Walters, was acquitted of theft on the grounds that he had no intention to steal and he then sued the store detective's employer in tort for damages for wrongful arrest and imprisonment. He was successful in the claim because, since he had no intention to steal, no arrestable offence had in fact been committed so that the store detective (who only has the citizen's power of arrest as he is not a police officer) had acted without any power to arrest.

ii) *Section 25 PACE 1984*

This section was an innovation introduced in the PACE 84 by virtue of s25 PACE 1984, a general power of arrest is given to constables in respect of offences not falling within the definition of 'arrestable offence' under s24. This power is exercisable where an offence has been or is being committed or attempted, and is designed to cover the situation where it would be impracticable or inappropriate to rely on a later summons, such as where a constable cannot obtain the person's name or feels that he has been proferred a false name, or address, or where the police constable reasonably believes that arrest is necessary to prevent the person causing physical harm to person or property, or himself suffering physical harm or to prevent an offence against public decency or obstruction of the highway or where a child or another vulnerable person is at risk. These are the 'general arrest conditions', and if *any* of them are satisfied, then the power to arrest is exercisable.

iii) *Section 26 PACE 1984*

Under s26(2), other specific statutory powers of arrest continue in force:

For example, Offences under the Public Order Act 1936; driving a car while under the influence of drink or drugs;

At common law, any citizen can arrest without warrant where there is a breach of the peace.

iv) *Section 51 Police Act 1964*

In relation to s51(3) wilful obstruction of the police; it has been held that a police constable can only arrest a person without a warrant for this offence if the obstruction actually caused, or was likely to cause, a breach of the peace.

In *Wershof* v *Metropolitan Police Commissioner* (1978) High Court, a police constable, believing a ring in a jeweller's shop to be stolen property, asked the jeweller to give it to him. The jeweller, on the advice of his brother (a solicitor) refused to do so unless police constable gave a receipt. The police constable refused to do so and arrested, without a warrant, the jeweller's brother for wilful obstruction.

It was held that, applying the principle set out above, the arrest was unlawful (there was no likelihood of a breach of the peace).

NOTE: In relation to arrest without a warrant for s51(1) assault, the assault itself will constitute a breach of the peace and, therefore, there is a power to arrest without warrant in such cases.

24.5 What are the elements of a lawful arrest?

If the police have the power to arrest, in accordance with the rules in the last section 24.4, how should they act to make a lawful arrest? NOTE: If any of the provisions set out below are not complied with, then the detention of the 'arrested' person is unlawful (false imprisonment).

a) *Section 28 PACE 1984*

i) Section 28(1): Where a person has been arrested but is not told so, the arrest is only lawful if he is told this as soon as practicable thereafter.

ii) In cases of arrest without a warrant, the police must inform the arrested person of the true grounds/reasons for the arrest.

In cases of arrest with a warrant, the reason for the arrest will be apparent from the warrant itself.

iii) Section 28(3) An arrest is only lawful where the arrested person is told the grounds for arrest at the time of arrest or as soon as practicable thereafter.

NOTE: The provisions in ss28(1) and 28(3) apply even where the fact or ground for arrest is obvious: ss28(2) and (4). There is no requirement that a person be told he is under arrest or of the ground for arrest where he has escaped from arrest before the information could be given: s28(5).

iv) Only reasonable force can be used to make an arrest or to resist an unlawful one: s3 Criminal Law Act 1967. If unreasonable force is used, the arrest is unlawful.

In *Allen* v *Metropolitan Police Commissioner* (1980) High Court, A, a short middle-aged Jamaican, who had never been in trouble with the police before, was arrested for allegedly driving while drunk. A felt this was unfair. The police officers, rather than take a minute to explain the circumstances more fully to him, put A into an armlock and forcibly tried to push him into a police car. A resisted. One police officer radioed for assistance. Another police officer put his arm around A's neck and pushed A's arm further up his back. A police van arrived with ten police officers. A was picked up by his arms and legs, put on the floor of the van and kept there by the pos putting their feet on him. A sustained injuries and later sued for damages, alleging unlawful police action. It was held that the police had used unreasonable and unlawful force. A was awarded £1,115 damages. May J held that to decide whether unreasonable force was used, the court had to consider:

the nature of the offence for which the person was arrested;

the nature of the arrested person's reactions;

the relative physical and numerical strength of the parties involved;

the place where the arrest took place.

24.6 After arrest – normal sequence of events

a) The arrested person is questioned by the police.

b) If enough evidence comes to light through this questioning, then the arrested person will be charged with an offence.

c) Pending a trial of the arrested person for the offence with which he has been charged, he may be released on bail or remanded in custody.

d) Finally, at a later date, the trial itself will take place.

24.7 After arrest – bail

a) *Introduction*

An arrested person is bailed when he is released from custody, on the condition that he will attend either at a police station or at a court, on a specified day, at a specified time. If he fails to comply, he commits an offence, Bail Act 1976. Bail can be granted by a court before which an arrested person is brought, or, in some cases, by the police.

Under the 1976 Act, there is a presumption in favour of bail, ie the person should be granted bail *unless* there are substantial grounds to believe that the person either:

i) will fail to attend as required;

ii) will commit further offences if released;

iii) will obstruct the course of justice, eg trying to interfere with witnesses.

Before deciding to grant bail, the following matters should be considered:

i) the nature of the alleged offence;

ii) the strength of the case against the arrested person;

iii) the previous convictions of the arrested person;

iv) whether the person has failed to comply with bail requirements on previous occasions.

If a person is refused bail by the police, then when he is brought before a magistrates' court, that court can grant him bail. If the magistrates' court refuses bail, then the detained person can apply to a High Court judge in chambers for bail, under s22 Criminal Justice Act 1967.

b) *Bail – on arrest with a warrant*

Often an arrest warrant will be 'backed for bail', ie the warrant itself will direct whether bail should be given. If it is not backed for bail, then when the arrested person is brought before a magistrates' court, the court can grant him bail.

c) *Bail – on arrest without a warrant*

Section 46 PACE 1984 requires that a person be brought before a magistrates court as soon as is practicable and in any event on the day following the charge.

NOTE: Under s30 PACE 1984, anyone arrested by a constable otherwise than at a police station must be brought to a police station as soon as practicable after arrest. This is not necessary where that person's presence is required elsewhere for immediate investigation.

24.8 Habeas corpus

a) *Introduction*

If a person is unlawfully detained, eg, if the provisions of s46 are broken, the person can at a later date sue the police for damages for false imprisonment. A more immediate remedy is to apply for the writ of habeas corpus.

The function of habeus corpus procedure is to get the detainer to appear before a court to explain the lawful authority he has (if any) to detain the person concerned; the reasons given can then be considered by the court to see if the detention is lawful or unlawful.

b) *Procedure* (under Habeas Corpus Acts 1679, 1816, Administration of Justice Act 1960, Order 54 RSC):

i) An application for the writ of habeus corpus is made ex parte (ie at this stage the other side, often the police, do not have to be informed of the application) to a Divisional Court of the QBD of the High Court, or, if no court is sitting, eg at night or weekends, the application can be made to a High Court judge in chambers or even at his home.

'Such applications are given absolute priority in the fixing of the business of the court.'

per Donaldson LJ, Sherman and Apps.

ii) The application is made on affidavit, ie written evidence, only.

iii) If on the affidavit evidence the court thinks that a prima facie case of unlawful detention exists, then the court will adjourn the application and issue a summons to the detainer to appear before the court at a specified time and date, in the near future, to show the lawful cause (if any) why the person is being detained.

iv) If at the adjourned hearing the court decides, after hearing the detainer's submissions, that the detention is unlawful, it can release the detainee.

(NOTE: if a person is being held in breach of s43 MCA, the issue of a summons under (iii) will usually be enough to jolt the police into taking the person before the magistrates.)

v) If an application for habeus corpus is rejected, no other application can be made on the same grounds to any court or judge unless there is fresh evidence to support it.

vi) In a criminal case an appeal against the refusal or granting of habeus corpus can be made directly to the House of Lords.

NOTE: 'The writ of habeus corpus has not fallen into disuse but is a real and available remedy.'

per Donaldson LJ, Sherman and Apps.

Traditionally, habeus corpus is seen as the greatest common law contribution to the protection of the freedom of the person. It was on a habeus corpus application in 1772, *Somerset* v *Stewart*, that slavery was declared illegal in England.

24.9 Police powers to detain and question suspects

Prior to the PACE 1984, the Judges' Rules (1964) governed the detention and questioning of suspects. The most important of these rules was the 'rule against oppression' – ie any statement obtained by the police through oppression would be inadmissible as evidence in a court of law. Oppression meant 'something which tends to sap free will ...', for example length of questioning, periods of refreshment and characteristics of the suspect: *R* v *Prager* (1972) CA.

The Judges' Rules have been replaced by Parts IV and V of the PACE 1984.

a) *On admissibility of confessions*

Section 76 PACE 1984 provides that confessions will not be admissible (where the defence objects) unless the prosecution proves beyond reasonable doubt that the confession was not obtained by oppression (including threats or use of violence; inhuman or degrading treatment) and that nothing was done or said when it was obtained which was likely to make it unreliable.

b) Other important rules relating to detention were laid down by the PACE 1984 and Code of Practice C published under the Act. These rules were intended to improve the position of suspects and were conceded as a quid pro quo (bargaining counter) to ensure that the extended powers of stop, search and arrest given to the police by the Act would be acceptable.

The rules are many and detailed but amongst the most important are:

i) Suspects should be detained only at police stations where hygienic and suitable facilities are available, thus the Act provides for persons to be kept at designated police stations wherever possible. At such a police station a custody officer of the rank of sergeant or above will be responsible for the welfare of the arrested person and will keep a detailed custody record of the treatment of that individual. The purpose of having a custody officer is that he is an officer independent of the investigation in connection with which the arrest was made and is therefore more likely to ensure fair and proper treatment of the suspect.

ii) Where there is insufficient evidence for a charge the custody officer may authorise further detention if necessary but such detention must be reviewed after six hours and then at nine hourly intervals. Twenty four hours is the maximum detention period unless a superintendent agrees to extend the period to 36 hours and this is only allowed for serious arrestable offences. Any detention beyond 36 hours can only be obtained by application to the magistrates' court.

iii) A detained person is by s56(3) allowed to have a relative, friend or someone interested in his welfare told of the arrest unless telling the named person could cause interference with evidence of a serious arrestable offence or physical harm to others or it will alert other suspects or hinder the recovery of property. If the first named person cannot be contacted the police will try up to two alternatives.

iv) Section 58 provides a right for a person in custody to obtain legal advice at any time he wishes subject to a delaying provision if there is a serious arrestable offence and a superintendent or above authorises it. The conditions are similar to (iii) above.

v) The Code of Practice lays down provisions to ensure that arrested persons are adequately fed and provided with sufficient rest periods.

vi) The provisions relating to searches of an arrested person are dealt with in the next chapter.

vii) The Code of Practice requires arrested persons to be given detailed information on their rights in custody. At any reviews of their confirmed detention they are entitled to make representations and all these matters should be entered in the detailed custody records.

c) In April 1991 a new revised Code of Practice was introduced under the PACE 1984.

In the Code are a number of Notes for Guidance. It should be noted that these Notes do not have the same legal status as the Code provisions. Non-compliance is not an automatic breach of the police disciplinary code, nor is there a legal requirement to take the Notes into account.

The main changes introduced are:

i) Section 1(3) of the 1984 Act and the level of suspicion. In order to conduct a stop and search a police officer must now have the same level of suspicion as if he were going to effect an arrest.

ii) Those who seem incapable of giving informed consent, such as juveniles or the mentally handicapped, should not be subjected to voluntary searches.

iii) Where a search of premises is to be made increased information must be given to the owner/occupier of premises.

iv) If juveniles are being questioned an 'appropriate' adult must be present. This does not include an estranged parent. A juvenile is also entitled to legal representation and one person cannot act in both capacities.

v) Interviews can no longer occur outside a police station, save in very limited circumstances.

vi) An alternative to identity parades is provided by the new rule that video film of the suspect and at least eight other similar persons may be shown to witnesses.

24.10 Fingerprinting

A superintendent can now order fingerprinting without the need for a court order.

25 FREEDOM OF PROPERTY – POLICE POWERS II. POLICE POWERS OF ENTRY, SEARCH AND SEIZURE

25.1 General introduction

This chapter deals with the law that governs police powers to search people and property (eg a person's home), and to seize things that they find (eg evidence of a crime). NOTE: If the limitations placed on these powers are broken, then the police act unlawfully. Various torts could be committed in such cases, eg trespass to persons, premises or goods. If the police act unlawfully they can be sued; but whether the items taken unlawfully can be admitted in evidence at a trial is another question.

25.2 Stop and search

a) *Section 1 PACE 1984*

The PACE 1984 s1 now gives the police a general power to stop and search.

i) A constable may in a place to which the public have access stop and search any person or vehicle for stolen goods or 'prohibited articles' (for example, offensive weapons or articles which may be used in the course of theft or other property offences).

ii) However, no search can occur unless the police constable reasonably suspects that he will find stolen or prohibited articles. If discovered they may be seized.

iii) Before exercising the power under s1: a police constable must give the grounds for the search and his name and station, and must later record details of the search and give a copy to the person searched.

b) *Section 4 PACE 1984*

Under s4 PACE 1984, the police are empowered to set up road checks if they believe that there is or is about to be in the locality someone who:

i) has committed or witnessed a serious arrestable offence;

ii) is intending to commit such an offence; or

iii) is an escaped prisoner.

25.3 Search and seizure on arrest

a) *Section 32 PACE 1984*

A person arrested away from a police station may be searched if he is reasonably believed to have anything on him which might be evidence of an offence, or to help him escape or to present a danger to others.

b) *Section 54 PACE 1984*

A person taken to a police station may be searched to ascertain the property he has with him, and this may be retained. Clothing and personal effects may only be retained if, for example, they might be used to cause injury, damage property or interfere with evidence (compare *Lindley* v *Rutter* (1981)).

25.4 Powers of entry, search and seizure

Just as the law provides for arrests with a warrant and those without one there are provisions for entry to and search of premises with a warrant and without one.

a) *Search with a warrant*

There are very many statutory provisions allowing searches of premises with a warrant, eg under the Misuse of Drugs Act 1971, and for such a warrant an application must usually be made to the magistrates' court. The PACE 1984 is important in relation to such applications because it laid down general rules applicable to all statutory powers to search with a warrant. Sections 15 and 16 deal with this topic. Any search of premises under a warrant is unlawful unless these provisions have been complied with. In making application for a warrant a po must state:

i) the grounds for the application;

ii) the enactment under which a warrant would be issued;

iii) specify the premises to be searched; and

iv) identify the articles or persons sought.

The applicant must apply ex parte with information in writing and is required to answer, on oath, questions put to him by the magistrates or judge.

If a warrant is granted it must authorise entry on one occasion only and set out details of the applicant, the date it is made, the enactment under which it is made, the premises to be searched and what is sought. Section 16 sets out the requirements for a lawful execution. Any warrant must be executed within one month and at a reasonable hour unless it appears that otherwise the purpose of the search may be frustrated. The occupier of premises must have the situation explained to him if he is present at the time of the search and a copy of the warrant must be left with him or, if he is not there, on the premises. The extent of the search is limited to that required for the purposes for which the warrant was issued. Once executed details of what is found must be endorsed on the warrant and it must then be returned to the magistrates' court. Even if a warrant is not executed it must be returned to the court. The warrant is then kept for 12 months and the owner of the premises may inspect it if he so wishes.

The PACE 1984 added a new power to obtain a search warrant in order to assist the police in obtaining evidence they believe is available in cases of the most serious crimes. Section 8 of the Act was included to fill a loophole in the law mentioned by Lord Denning MR in *Ghani* v *Jones* (1970).

Under s8, a Justice of the Peace may issue a warrant authorising a constable to enter and search premises for material specified in the warrant which is likely to be of value as evidence relating to a serious arrestable offence. The police must give grounds for the application (s15).

NOTE (1): Warrants under s8 will only be issued if:

i) Section 8(3):

(a) it is not practicable to communicate with anyone who can grant entry to premises; or

(b) entry will not be granted unless a warrant is produced; or

(c) the purpose of the search may be frustrated or seriously prejudiced unless a constable can secure immediate entry.

ii) Section 8(2): a police constable can seize evidence specified in the warrant if found. A search warrant remains in force for only one month.

NOTE (2): This power applies only where there is a serious arrestable offence and this is defined in PACE 1984 s116. Arrestable offences are classified as serious arrestable offences in two categories:

i) Those arrestable offences which are *always* serious arrestable offences – treason, murder, manslaughter, rape, kidnapping, intercourse with a girl under 13, buggery with a boy under 16 or someone who has not consented, indecent assault which constitutes an act of gross indecency and certain other specified crimes involving firearms, causing explosions, hostage taking, hijacking and causing death by dangerous driving.

ii) other arrestable offences may be serious arrestable offences only if the commission is likely to lead to one of a list of consequences – causing serious harm to the security of the State or public order, serious interference with the administration of justice or the investigation of crime, death or serious injury to anyone, substantial financial gain or serious financial loss to any person.

However there are exceptions to the grants of warrants under s8.

Section 10, 11 and 14 PACE 1984

These are the exceptions: no warrant may be issued in respect of:

i) *Section 10* – material subject to legal privilege – for example lawyer/client.

ii) *Section 11* – excluded material:

Personal records acquired in the course of a business, profession or other office and held in confidence – generally relating to social welfare;

human tissue/tissue fluid taken for diagnosis/medical treatment and held in confidence;

journalistic material – documents, records held in obligation of confidence.

iii) *Section 14* – special procedure material – ie other forms of journalistic material and other material held in confidence or obligation of confidence and acquired in the course of a business or for the purposes of any office.

NOTE: In respect of (ii) and (iii) above, a circuit judge, on police application, can order disclosure or grant an entry and search warrant to the police.

b) *Searches without a warrant*

i) Section 17 PACE 1984

Under s17 a constable may enter and search any premises without a warrant to:

1) execute a warrant of arrest;

2) arrest a person for an arrestable offence;

3) arrest a person for an offence under: s1 Public Order Act 1936; ss6–8 or 10 Criminal Law Act 1977;

4) to recapture a person unlawfully at large;

5) to save life or limb or prevent serious damage to property.

The above powers (save (5)) are only exercisable if a constable has reasonable grounds for believing that the peron sought is on the premises and only in so far as reasonably required.

ii) Section 18 PACE 1984

1) Under s18(1) a police constable may enter and search premises occupied or controlled by a person under arrest for an arrestable offence if he has reasonable grounds for suspecting that on the premises there is evidence (other than legally privileged material) relating to that offence, or some other arrestable offence connected with or similar to that offence (compare *Jeffrey* v *Black* (1978)).

2) Section 18(2): A police constable can seize and retain the evidence.

3) Section 18(3): The power only exists as is reasonably required.

4) Section 18(4): The power must be authorised by an Inspector or above.

However,

5) Section 18(5): lays down that the power under s18 can be exercised without authorisation before taking a person to a police station if this is considered necessary for the effective investigation of the offence.

iii) Section 19 PACE 1984

1) Section 19 seizure: The power of seizure is available to a constable if he is lawfully on the premises.

2) Section 19(2): A constable can seize anything on the premises if he has reasonable grounds for believing:

   a) it has been obtained in consequence of the commission of an offence, and that it is necessary to seize it to prevent its being concealed, lost, altered or destroyed.

3) Section 19(3): A police constable can seize anything on the premises if he has reasonable grounds for believing:

   a) that it is evidence in relation to an offence he is investigating or any other offence, and

   b) that it is necessary to seize it in order to prevent its being concealed, lost, altered or destroyed.

4) Section 19(6): The power of seizure is not available in respect of items subject to legal privilege.

5) Section 22: Evidence seized can be retained 'so long as is necessary in all the circumstances'.

25.5 Unlawfully seized evidence

Section 78 PACE 1984 provides a court with a discretion to exclude such evidence if, in all circumstances, to admit the evidence would have such an adverse effect on the fairness of the proceedings that it should not be admitted.

26 FREEDOM OF ASSOCIATION AND ASSEMBLY

26.1 Introduction

In contrast to most foreign systems, the United Kingdom does not grant the rights to associate and assemble in a written Bill of Rights. Instead, English law places restrictions on activities, eg to prevent breach of the peace and any 'rights' are residuary, ie you can lawfully do what is not restricted by the law. To explain terminology:

a) *Association*: ie forming groups (eg political groups);

b) *Assembly*: ie gathering together (eg holding processions and meetings).

26.2 Association: restrictions

a) *Conspiracy*

To associate together and agree:

i) to do an unlawful act or to do a lawful act by unlawful means, constitutes the tort of conspiracy;

ii) to commit a crime, constitutes the crime of conspiracy.

b) *Section 2 Public Order Act 1936*

This is the section under which *quasi-military organisations* are prohibited. It is a *crime* to associate together to organise, train or equip; to usurp (assume) the functions of the police or the armed forces, or to use or display physical force to promote a political organisation. (This provision was used successfully against 'Spearhead', a fascist organisation in 1963 when its two leaders were sentenced to nine and six months imprisonment.)

c) *Prevention of Terrorism (Temporary Provisions) Act 1984*

i) *Part I* gives the Secretary of State power to proscribe in Great Britain organisations which appear to him to be connected with terrorism occurring in the United Kingdom and connected with Northern Ireland's affairs. The IRA and INLA are proscribed under the Act.

ii) *Part II* gives the Secretary of State power to make orders excluding from Great Britain, Northern Ireland, or the United Kingdom, persons involved in terrorism connected with Northern Ireland's affairs.

iii) *Part III* makes it an offence to make or receive a contribution towards acts of terrorism relating to Northern Ireland's affairs.

iv) *Part IV* applies to international as well as Northern Ireland terrorism and permits the arrest and detention of persons suspected of terrorist involvement.

NOTE: Apart from these specific restrictions, people are free to form groups and organisations, although there are many offences which lawfully associated groups can commit.

26.3 Assembly: restrictions

a) *Gathering on the highway: torts*

i) *Trespass*: The purpose of the highway is to allow passage and repassage and other incidental activities. Contravention of this principle constitutes the tort of trespass against the owner of the underlying soil (either local authorities or adjoining landowners). Prima facie, a stationary gathering on the highway constitutes this tort, but a procession does not. This tort has little practical application in this context.

ii) *Nuisance*: An 'unreasonable user' of the highway constitutes the tort of public nuisance. If this also interferes with the rights of an adjoining occupier or causes him special damage, it constitutes the tort of private nuisance. It was held in *Lowdens* v *Keaveney* (1903) that merely obstructing the highway was not an 'unreasonable user' of it, there had to be something more; eg a use of the highway which, having regard to its duration and when and why it took place, showed a 'reckless disregard for the rights of others'. This covers not only statutory gatherings, but could extend to cover processions too. Injunctions, including interlocutory ones, can be obtained from the courts to restrain the continuance of a nuisance, *Hubbard* v *Pitt* (1976).

b) *Gathering on the highway: crimes*

i) *Public nuisance*: is also a crime, but mere obstruction of the highway is *not* enough to constitute 'unreasonable user': *R* v *Clark* (1964).

ii) *Obstruction of the highway*: Under s137 Highways Act 1980, it is an offence wilfully to obstruct the free passage of the highway without lawful authority or excuse. Under s137(2) a police constable can arrest, without a warrant, a person suspected of this offence. It is lawful to use the highway for passage and repassage and for things incidental to such passage, eg, standing at bus stops, looking in shop windows, etc. Indeed, any reasonable use of the highway is lawful and cannot constitute s 137 obstruction, *Nagy* v *Weston* (1965), in which it was held that to determine reasonableness all the circumstances had to be looked at, including the length of time that the obstruction continued for and its place and purpose.

In *Arrowsmith* v *Jenkins* (1963) it was held that a partial obstruction of the highway was an offence, the fact that people could get round the obstruction, eg by crossing the road, was not a defence;

the fact that meetings had previously been held at the same place and the police had not done anything about them on those occasions, did not constitute a defence;

a person did not have to intend to obstruct the highway, to commit the offence, it was sufficient if he intentionally did something which constituted an obstruction.

Under s137, it would seem that any stationary gathering on the highway potentially constitutes an obstruction, whereas any procession does not, as to process is to use the highway for passage. Therefore, processions are prima facie lawful, stationary gatherings prima facie are not.

iii) *Open spaces*: Most parks are governed by by-laws which either prohibit the use of the park for meetings or require prior permission from the authority concerned, for a meeting to be held. There is no common law right to use an open space for meetings, even if it is dedicated to the public's use, *De Morgan* v *Metropolitan Board of Works* (1880). The use of Hyde Park Corner and Trafalgar Square for meetings is not authorised by common law, but by regulations.

c) *Football grounds*

The Football Offences Act 1991 creates a whole series of new offences which may be committed at designated matters.

They include: throwing anything at or in the grounds; racialist or obscene chants; going on to the pitch without lawful excuse.

26.4 Public order

a) *Introduction*

English law goes out of its way to protect the right of the State and its citizens to public peace and order. There are various crimes which can be committed where a breach of the peace occurs or is reasonably apprehended. The police and ordinary members of the public, are given extensive powers to prevent breaches of the peace from occurring and to control those that are occurring.

b) *The preventive powers of the police*

At common law, the police are under a duty to preserve the peace and to take whatever steps are necessary to stop breaches of the peace that are occurring and to prevent breaches of the peace that are reasonably apprehended (foreseen). When a police constable takes steps necessary to preserve the peace, he acts in the execution of his duty and can take steps that would otherwise be unlawful.

To illustrate

In *Humphries* v *Connor* (1864) C, a police constable, saw H walking through a predominantly Catholic area of an Irish town wearing an orange lily, the emblem of a Protestant party. People were provoked by this and to preserve the peace, C removed the lily from H. H sued C for assault. (If C had no lawful authority or duty to remove the lily, his action would have constituted an assault.)

It was held that:

> 'A constable is by law charged with the solemn duty of seeing that the peace is preserved. The law ... has announced to him ... that he is bound to see that the peace be preserved and that he is to do *everything that is necessary* for that purpose, neither more nor less.'
>
> per Hayes J.

Therefore, the police constable had acted lawfully, in committing what otherwise would have been an assault, to preserve the peace.

In *O'Kelly* v *Harvey* (1883) Court of Appeal, trouble was expected at a political meeting, not from those holding it, but from their opponents whom, it was believed, were to give those at the meeting 'a warm reception'. In order to prevent disorder caused by the opponents, H, a magistrate (having the same duties and powers as a police constable) decided to disperse those holding the meeting and in the course of doing this, laid his hand on O'K. O'K sued H for assault and battery. Did H have the lawful authority for his actions and, therefore, a defence to the claim?

It was held that H's:

> 'paramount duty was to preserve the peace unbroken ... by whatever means were available for the purpose ... if (H) believed and had just grounds for believing that the peace could only be preserved by withdrawing (O'K) and his friends from the attack with which they were threatened, it was ... the duty of (H) to take that course.'
>
> per Law LC.

Therefore, H had acted lawfully.

In *Thomas* v *Sawkins* (1935) High Court, a public political meeting was held. Police officers, who had heard that seditious speeches were to be made, were refused permission to enter the hall, but some did enter, sat in the front row and were told to leave. When T went to eject one of the police officers,

Sergeant S pushed T away. T prosecuted S for assault and battery, claiming that the police officers were trespassing and that, therefore, he had the lawful authority to use reasonable force to eject them.

It was held that the pos had the lawful authority to enter and remain on the premises, to preserve the peace.

> 'If a constable in the execution of his duty to preserve the peace is entitled to commit an assault ... he is equally entitled to commit a trespass.'
>
> per Lawrence J.

NOTE: This power is retained by s17(6) of the Police and Criminal Evidence Act 1984.

c) *Summary of principles so far*

The police are under a duty to preserve the peace and can do whatever is necessary to do so, including:

i) committing an assault (*Humphries* v *Connor*);

ii) dispersing a meeting (*O'Kelly* v *Harvey*);

iii) entering and remaining on premises (*Thomas* v *Sawkins*).

In *Albert* v *Lavin* (1981) House of Lords, A caused annoyance at a bus stop when he pushed past people to board a bus out of turn. L, an off-duty police constable, restrained A, but did not arrest him, to prevent further trouble. A struggle ensued. A was charged with assaulting a police constable in the execution of his duty, convicted and appealed.

A argued that L had no lawful authority to detain A without arresting him.

It was held that to the well established principle that a person could not be detained without being arrested:

> '... there is an equally well-established exception, not confined to constables, that is applicable to the instant case. It is that every citizen in whose presence a breach of the peace is being, or reasonably appears to be about to be, committed has the right to take reasonable steps to make the person who is breaking or threatening to break, the peace refrain from doing so, and those reasonable steps in appropriate cases will include detaining him against his will. At common law, this is not only the right of every citizen, it is also his duty, although except in the case of a citizen who is a constable, it is a duty of imperfect obligation.'
>
> per Lord Diplock.

The most important case of all in this sequence is:

In *Duncan* v *Jones* (1936) High Court, Mrs D was about to get onto a box in the street, outside an unemployment training centre, to address a meeting when a police officer told her that she could not hold her meeting there, but could hold it 175 yards away (at previous similar meetings there had been disorder). D refused to move and was arrested by a police officer. D was charged and convicted of obstructing a police officer in the execution of his duty. She appealed.

It was held that D had been rightly convicted. The police officer had a duty to preserve the peace and a duty to prevent anything which in his view would cause a breach of the peace. While taking steps to carry out that duty, he was wilfully obstructed (ie by D refusing his order to her to move) there could be 'no clearer case' of obstruction.

The importance of *Duncan* v *Jones* is that it decides that to make it more difficult for the police to carry out their duty to preserve the peace, eg by refusing to obey an order given where such an order is necessary to preserve the peace, constitutes an obstruction of the police constable in the execution of his duty. It is clear from *Wershof* v *Metropolitan Police Commissioner*, see para 24.4, that in such cases a police constable can arrest without a warrant for the obstruction. The decision in *Duncan* can be compared with the principle in *Beatty* v *Gillbanks* (1882) that a lawful Act does not become unlawful simply because others act unlawfully.

d) *Powers to arrest for a breach of the peace*

R v *Howell* (1982) Court of Appeal: the important points decided in this case are as follows:

i) There is a common law power vested in police constables and ordinary citizens to arrest for breach of the peace (without a warrant) where:

a breach of the peace is committed in the presence of the person making the arrest; or

the arrestor reasonably believes that such a breach will be committed in the immediate future by the person arrested, although he has not yet committed any breach, or

where a breach has been committed and it is reasonably believed that a renewal of it is threatened.

ii) For there to be a breach of the peace there must be an act done or threatened to be done which either actually harms a person, or in his presence his property or is likely to cause such harm, or which puts someone in fear of such harm being done. (A 'disturbance' alone is not a breach of the peace, there must be an element of violence.)

e) *Other preventive powers*

i) *Binding over*: Magistrates can bind a person over to keep the peace. This can be done when it is reasonably apprehended that a person will breach the peace at some future time. The person will be required to enter into recognisances which will be forfeited if he breaches the peace (ie he will forfeit sums of money).

ii) *Sections 11–14 Public Order Act 1986*

1) *Processions*

Section 11 – requires *6* days advance notice in writing of a public procession. An offence is committed if this requirement is not satisfied, unless it was not reasonably practicable to give such notice.

Section 12 – gives the 'senior police officer' the power to impose any conditions as appear necessary, including prescribing a route for, or prohibiting a procession from entering certain public places, where he reasonably believes that the procession may result in 'serious public disorder', serious damage to property or serious disruption to the life of the community, or that the purpose of those organising it is to intimidate others to act in a way in which they would otherwise not act.

Section 13 – allows the police to apply to a local council for an order banning all (or a class of) public processions for a maximum of *3* months (with the Home Secretary's consent) when section 12 powers are inadequate. Section 13(4) gives the same power to the police in London. BUT in London the Metropolitan Police Commissioner and the Home Secretary take the decision, local councils are *not* involved.

2) *Assemblies*

Section 14 – conditions may be impose upon public assemblies for the same reasons as in section 12 above – for example, conditions relating to the place of assembly, its duration and numbers present. 'Public assembly' means 20 or more persons assembled in a public place wholly or partly open to the air.

NOTE: In the case of assemblies there is *no* power to ban.

26.5 Public disorder – charges

The Public Order Act 1986 has substantially amended the law relating to public disorder. The Act repeals old offences under s5 Public Order Act 1936 and s70 Race Relations Act 1976. The 1986 Act abolishes the common law offences of riot, rout, unlawful assembly and affray.

Section 1 – Riot:

where 12 persons or more, present together, use or threaten unlawful violence for a common purpose and their conduct (taken together) is such as would cause a person of reasonable firmness present at the scene to fear for his personal safety. Maximum sentence: ten years.

Section 2 – Violent Disorder:

where three or more persons, present together, use or threaten unlawful violence and their conduct (taken together) is such as would cause a person of reasonable firmness present at the scene to fear for his personal safety. Maximum sentence: six months summary; five years indictment.

NOTE: Only three needed for offence and no requirement of common purpose.

R v *McGuigan* (1991) demonstrated some of the problems inherent in the requirement that three or more persons must together behave in such a way as to cause a reasonable person to fear for his personal safety. Three defendants were charged with violent disorder under s2(1). One was acquitted, two convicted. The Court of Appeal held that the other two convictions must be quashed because with one defendant acquitted the statutory criteria could not be satisfied.

Section 3 – Affray:

where a person uses or threatens unlawful violence towards another and his conduct is such as would cause a person of reasonable firmness present at the scene to fear for his personal safety. A constable may arrest without warrant anyone he reasonably suspects is committing affray. Maximum sentence: six months summary; three years indictment.

Section 4 – Fear or provocation of violence

where a person –

a) uses towards another person threatening, abusive or insulting words or behaviour, or

b) distributes or displays to another person any writing, sign or other visible representation which is threatening abusive or insulting,

with intent to cause that person to believe that immediate unlawful violence will be used against him or another by any person, or to provoke the immediate use of unlawful violence by that person or another, or whereby that person is likely to believe that such violence will be used or it is likely that such violence will be provoked. A constable may arrest without warrant where he reasonably suspects this offence is being committed. Maximum sentences: six months summary (and/or fine).

Section 5 – Harassment, alarm or distress

An offence occurs where a person

a) uses threatening, abusive or insulting words or behaviour, or disorderly behaviour, or

b) displays any writing, sign or other visible representation which is threatening, abusive or insulting.

within the hearing or sight of a person likely to be caused harassment, alarm or distress.

Defence: s5(3) – accused had no reason to believe there was anyone within hearing or sight likely to be caused harassment, etc, or that he was inside a dwelling and had no reason to believe anyone outside would hear or see the words, behaviour or writing, etc, or that his conduct was reasonable.

A constable may arrest without warrant anyone who engages in such offensive conduct after being warned to stop. Maximum sentence: summary fine.

NOTE: Offences under ss1–3 can be committed in public and private places.

Offences under ss4 and 5 can be committed in public and private places, although no offence will be committed by a person inside a dwelling provided the other person is inside that or another dwelling.

Intent (or awareness) is required for all offences. The criteria likely to be applied under s5(3) is best demonstrated by the recent case of *DPP* v *Clarke* (1991) in which four people demonstrating outside an abortion clinic carried placards showing a picture of an aborted foetus. They were charged under s5(1)(b) with displaying abusive and insulting signs within sight or hearing of persons likely to be caused harassment, alarm or distress. On appeal it was held that they had been correctly acquitted, because they had not intended or realised that their conduct was threatening, abusive or insulting, and on a subjective basis as under s5(3) were not aware of the effect their conduct was having on people.

27 FREEDOM OF SPEECH

27.1 Introduction

There is no right of free speech. To determine what a person can say or publish, various restrictive provisions of the law must be considered; whatever is *not restrained* is lawful. Some criminal and civil restraints on free speech are considered in this chapter, to illustrate the width of the restraints and their different purposes.

27.2 Public Order Act 1986, ss4 and 5

See chapter 26 above. (For interest, see cases of *Jordan* v *Burgoyne* (1963) and *Brutus* v *Cozens* (1973) under repealed s5 Public Order Act 1936.)

27.3 Public Order Act 1986, ss17–23

Section 17: Racial hatred means hatred against a group of persons in Great Britain by reference to colour, race, nationality or ethnic or national origins.

Section 18. An offence is committed by a person who uses threatening, abusive or insulting words or behaviour, or displays any written material which is threatening, abusive or insulting, if

a) he intends to stir up racial hatred, or

b) having regard to all the circumstances racial hatred is likely to be stirred up.

Similar offences, applying the same conditions as in s18, are found in:

Section 19: in respect of publishing or distributing written material which is threatening, abusive or insulting.

Section 20: with regard to the presenter or director of a public performance of a play.

Section 21: with regard to a person who distributes, or shows or plays, a recording of visual images or sounds.

Section 22: in respect of a broadcast or a programme in a cable programme service.

Section 23: a person in possession of written material or a recording with a view to, eg its display etc, or distribution etc, is guilty of an offence under the same conditions as in s18.

27.4 Contempt of court

See chapter 17.

27.5 Obscene Publications Act 1959

a) *Under s1*:

> 'For the purpose of this Act an article shall be deemed to be obscene if its effect ... is, if taken as a whole, such as to tend to deprave and corrupt persons who are likely, having regard to all relevant circumstances, to read, see or hear the matter contained or embodied in it.'

The definition of 'obscene' is wide enough to cover not only depictions of sexual acts, but also articles that encourage drug taking or which show violence. The key words are 'tend to deprave and corrupt'. The Act provides that it is an offence either to publish an obscene article or to have such an article for gain.

In *DPP* v *Whyte* (1972) House of Lords, it was held that:

i) an article could not be considered obscene in itself; it could only be so in relation to its likely readers;

ii) to define who 'likely readers' were of pornographic magazines sold in a shop, account had to be taken of 'all such persons as normally resort to such shops';

iii) the Act's purpose was to prevent the depraving and corrupting of mens' minds and this extended to cover 'the addict ... feeding or increasing his addiction';

iv) there was no necessity for an article to have an effect on a person's actions or behaviour.

NOTE too:

v) no expert evidence is admissible on the question of whether or not an article is obscene;

vi) an article is not obscene if it is so crude that it revolts people;

vii) no intention to deprave and corrupt is necessary.

b) *Section 4*

If an article is considered obscene under s1, then the Act provides a defence in s4, basically that the article should be published in the public interest, regardless of its obscenity:

i) '.. a person shall not be convicted of an offence ... if it is proved that publication of the article in question is justified as being "for the public good on the ground that it is in the interests of science, literature, art or learning, or of other subjects of general concern".'

ii) Expert evidence is admissible under s4.

iii) The s4 defence is not established by proof that the obscene article might have therapeutic effects on its likely readers.

One difficulty is that the Obscene Publications Act 1959 is not the only law on obscenity. There are various other statutes which allow customs officers, amongst others, to seize obscene material. In these statutes there may be no defence equivalent to s4 1959 Act. These inconsistencies bring the law into disrepute and reforms to the whole area have been recommended.

27.6 Official Secrets Act 1911 replaced by Official Secrets Act 1989

Under s2 of the 1911 Act an offence is committed:

a) If a person having in his possession any information which he has obtained owing to his position as a Crown servant ('official information') communicates the information to a person to whom he is not authorised to communicate it.

b) It is also an offence for a recipient of 'official information' to communicate it to another person without authority. It is also an offence to receive 'official information' knowing or reasonably believing that it has been communicated in breach of the above provisions.

These catch-all provisions cover:

i) any official information, ie any information learnt by a Crown servant in his capacity as such. Information does not need to be secret for s2 to apply. The relative importance or unimportance of the information is irrelevant;

ii) all Crown servants, including Ministers, all civil servants, the police, the armed forces and anyone who works in any government department. The relative importance or unimportance of the particular person's employment is irrelevant;

iii) the Act does not set out what constitutes authorisation. It seems that in practice the more senior a civil servant is the more implied authorisation he has to communicate information. Junior civil servants have little, if any, implied authorisation;

iv) it was held in the 'ABC' case in 1979 that it was irrelevant whether a person who communicated official information thought that such communication was in the interests of the State.

In practice, there have been few prosecutions under s2, but it has a pervasive influence and deterrent effect on civil servants especially. No prosecution can be brought without the Attorney-General's consent.

c) *Examples of s2 prosecutions*: See chapter 15 for *Tisdall* and *Ponting* cases.

In *R* v *Aubrey, Berry and Campbell* (1979) A, a *Time Out* reporter, and C, a freelance journalist, interviewed B, a former soldier, about his work in the interception and analysis of radio communications. A, B and C were charged under s2 and were convicted. B was sentenced to six months imprisonment; A and C were conditionally discharged.

d) The 1972 Franks Committee recommended the repeal of s2 and its replacement by provisions which would make unauthorised communication of the following an offence:

i) information classified as secret; or

ii) Cabinet documents; or

iii) information which would aid criminal activity; or

iv) which violated the confidentiality of information supplied to the Government

The main aim of these proposals was to narrow down the law. These criticisms and the cases of *Ponting* and *Tisdall* as well as *Spycatcher* prompted the reform of the law by the enactment of the Official Secrets Act 1989. The Act is not yet in force but it is to be brought into effect by a statutory instrument. The Home Office predict that this should occur before the end of 1989. The 1989 Act repeals s2 of the 1911 Act and replaces it with provisions designed to protect more limited classes of official information. It also clarifies the position of members of the security and intelligence services.

When the Act comes into force it will be an offence if a member or retired member of the security and intelligence services without lawful authority discloses any information relating to security received by virtue of that office or if a Crown servant or government contractor makes a damaging disclosure of any information relating to security or intelligence he receives. There is a defence if the defendant had no reasonable cause to know that the information related to security and intelligence (s1).

Similarly a Crown servant or government contractor is guilty of an offence if without lawful authority he makes a damaging disclosure in relation to defence or international relations or if he discloses information relating to criminal investigations. What is a 'damaging disclosure' is defined in clear terms in the sections relating to security and intelligence (s1), defence (s2), and international relations (s3). In each case there is a defence where the defendant was reasonable in a belief that the information did not relate to the relevant subject.

A person who receives unauthorised disclosures of information will himself commit an offence if he discloses the matters without lawful authority where he had reasonable grounds for belief that the information was protected by the Act. There is a defence if the disclosure is not damaging or if the discloser did not have reasonable cause to believe it would be damaging.

The Act has been criticised in that there is no public interest defence and insufficient protection for the press.

27.7 Sedition

Prosecutions for this common law restriction on free speech are rare. Its scope was set out by Cave J in *R* v *Burns* (1886):

> 'A seditious intention is an intention to bring into hatred or contempt, or to excite disaffection against the person of Her Majesty, her heirs, or successors, or the government and constitution of the United Kingdom, as by law established, or either House of Parliament, or the administration of justice, or to excite her Majesty's subjects to attempt otherwise than by lawful means the alteration of any matter in Church or State by law established, or to raise discontent or disaffection amongst Her Majesty's subjects, or to promote feelings of ill-will and hostility between different classes of such subjects.'

(but)

> 'An intention to show that Her Majesty has been misled or mistaken in her measures, or to point out errors or defects in the government or constitution as by law established, with a view to their reformation, or to excite Her Majesty's subjects to attempt by lawful means the alteration of any matter in Church or State by law established, or to point out, in order to their removal, matters which are producing, or have a tendency to produce, feelings of hatred or ill-will between classes of Her Majesty's subjects, is not a seditious intention.'

27.8 Defamation

A defamatory statement is a false statement which exposes a person to hatred, ridicule or contempt or which tends to lower him in the estimation of right-thinking members of society generally: *Sim* v *Stretch* (1936).

a) *Defamatory statements* are either:

   i) *Slander*: ie in a transitory form (spoken words). Special financial damage needs to be proved; or

   ii) *Libel*: ie in a permanent form (written words).

   Either party in a defamation action can require trial by jury, in which case the jury decides whether the plaintiff has been defamed and the amount of damages, if hc has.

b) *Defences*

   Some publications/statements are privileged:

   i) If absolute privilege applies, then the statement (etc) cannot found a defamation action. This privilege applies, among others, to:

   statements made by judges, counsel, witnesses, etc, during judicial proceedings;

   fair and accurate contemporaneous newspaper reports of judicial proceedings;

   statements made during parliamentary proceedings and in official reports papers etc published by order of Parliament;

reports by and statements to the Ombudsman;

State communications.

ii) If qualified privilege applies, then an action for defamation will fail unless it can be shown that the defendant acted with malice (spite, fraud, etc). This applies, among others, to:

fair and accurate reports of judicial proceedings (if contemporaneous see (i) point two above);

fair and accurate, unauthorised, reports of parliamentary debates;

fair and accurate, newspaper reports of the proceedings of

any public meeting and of local authority meetings.

iii) If a defendant proves that his statement was substantially true, then he has a defence ('justification');

iv) If a defendant proves that his statement, based on correctly stated facts, made without malice, was a comment on a matter of public interest, then he has a defence ('fair comment').

v) Under s4 Defamation Act 1952, if a defendant publishes defamatory statements 'innocently', eg if he did not know of circumstances that might lead people to think that the statement referred to the person allegedly defamed, and makes a formal offer to the plaintiff to, eg publish an apology, and correction ('amends') which the plaintiff does not accept, then he has a defence.

c) *Freedom of expression*

In *Application 14631* v *UK* (1990) a newspaper company complained to the European Commission on Human Rights that the unpredictability of the damages system in United Kingdom law – awards made by juries without judicial or other guidance or control – constituted a violation of the European Convention on Human Rights Article 10 (freedom of expression).

The Commission dismissed the application; the newspaper had failed to show that it had been deterred from publishing anything, nor could it show any award of damages (arbitrarily assessed or otherwise) had been made against it.

Article 10 was not meant to guarantee freedom to defame.

28 MARTIAL LAW AND EMERGENCY POWERS

28.1 Use of armed forces

At common law when there is serious public disorder, eg riots, which the 'civil authorities' (the police) cannot themselves control, the armed forces can be called upon to assist the civil authorities. The decision to 'send in the troops' would today be taken by the Home Secretary acting in consultation with the Ministry of Defence, the Chief Constable concerned and most likely the cabinet too. The armed forces could use whatever force was reasonable to control the disorder and restore order.

In *Attorney-General for Northern Ireland's Reference (No 1 of 1975)* (1977) Lord Diplock pointed out that:

> '... it may not be inaccurate to describe the legal rights and duties of a soldier as being no more than those of an ordinary citizen in uniform ... In theory, it may be the duty of every citizen when an arrestable offence is about to be committed in his presence to take whatever reasonable measures are available to him to prevent the commission of the crime.'

28.2 Martial law

If *grave* public disorder in the form of civil war, insurrection or rebellion occurred, which the civil authorities could not control, then the military, not subject to the control of the civil authorities, could impose regulations on citizens and decide what steps to take to end the disorder/emergency: this type of military government would constitute 'martial law' (rule by the military in times of grave emergency). The military authorities could, therefore, under 'martial law' apply rules that they had formulated and establish military courts to try those who break the rules. Certainly, in times of war:

> 'The civil courts have no jurisdiction to call into question the propriety of the actions of the military authorities.'

per Earl of Halsbury LC in the case of *Marais* (1902) Privy Council which involved action taken under 'Martial Law Regulations' published in a colony when it was being invaded.

This rule applies even though the civil courts are still functioning, although on the return of peace the ordinary courts could review the actions of the military authorities (*Marais*).

28.3 Emergency Powers Acts 1920, 1964

In times of peace emergencies may occur through, eg strikes in key industries or national disasters. The Emergency Powers Acts give wide power to Her Majesty in Council to make regulations during such periods. The provisions are:

a) *A Royal Proclamation* may be issued (which in practice would only occur on the advice of the Ministerial members of the Privy Council) to declare a state of emergency;

> 'If at any time it appears to Her Majesty that there have occurred, or are about to occur, events of such a nature as to be calculated by interfering with the supply and distribution of food, water, fuel, or light, or with the means of locomotion, to deprive the community, or any substantial portion of the community, of the essentials of life ...'

b) After such a Proclamation has been issued, Her Majesty in Council can make regulations by Orders:

'for securing the essentials of life to the community.'

And these regulations can give to Ministers, etc:

'such powers and duties as Her Majesty may deem necessary'

to secure the essentials of life to the community.

This is subject to three limitations: No regulation:

i) may be made imposing any form of compulsory military service or industrial conscription;

ii) is to make it an offence to take part in a strike or peacefully persuade others to do so;

iii) is to alter any existing procedure in criminal cases or confer any right to punish by fine or imprisonment without trail.

c) The issuing of the Royal Proclamation must be communicated to Parliament 'forthwith' and has a duration of one month, after which it can be renewed.

d) Any regulations made must be laid before Parliament 'as soon as may be' and expire if they are not approved by both Houses within seven days of laying.

The use of the Emergency Powers Acts:

1921 Coal Miners' strike

1924 Tramwaymen and Busmen's strike

1926 Coal Miners' and General Strike

1948 Dockers' strike

1949 Dockers' strike

1955 Railwaymen's strike

1966 Merchant Seamen's strike

1970 Dockers' strike

1970 Electricity Workers' work to rule, etc

1972 Coal Miners' strike

1972 Dockers' strike

1973 Electricity Engineers', Coal Miners', Railwaymen's overtime bans, etc.

NOTE: Under the 1964 Act the armed forces can be used in industrial disputes without the need for a proclamation of a state of emergency and without the need for parliamentary approval, if a Defence Council Instruction is issued. The powers, under Defence Council Instructions are more limited than the powers available under emergency regulations. Under Defence Council Instructions the army can be used on 'urgent work of national importance' eg the army and their 'Green Goddess' fire engines were used, under a Defence Council Instruction, to provide fire services during the 1977–8 Firemen's strike.

29 A BILL OF RIGHTS?

29.1 Introduction

Nearly every country guarantees certain rights and freedoms for its citizens in a written Bill of Rights which is part of the country's constitution. The United Kingdom does not. This chapter will consider whether a United Kingdom Bill of Rights is necessary, whether its provisions could be protected from repeal and what form it could take.

29.2 Does the United Kingdom need a Bill of Rights?

Due to the United Kingdom's unwritten constitution, there is no Codification of Civil Liberties and the restrictions on them. Also, the United Kingdom lacks statutes which codify 'groups' of rights in particular areas of the law, eg there is no statute which codifies the rights of citizens in relation to the police. However, some rights are well protected by common and statute law, eg the right to a fair trial (see Contempt of Court) the right to peace (see Public Order); but many of the great liberties are merely residual concepts (ie citizens can only do something which is not prohibited by law, eg freedom of speech) not positive rights. With no codification or fundamental guarantees of civil liberties, the supreme law-making power of Parliament becomes a matter of concern. It can make and unmake any law and the judges must obey. It could repress liberties and the judges could not declare the Acts concerned invalid.

> 'So long as English law is unable in any circumstances to challenge a statute, it is, in dangerous and difficult times, at the mercy of the oppressive and discriminatory statute.'
>
> Lord Scarman – 1974 Hamlyn Lecture.

29.3 How could liberties be better protected?

Parliament could pass individual statutes in certain important areas of the law, eg as it has done in the Race Relations Act 1976 to prevent racial discrimination. But, such a system of protecting rights is piecemeal, haphazard and lacks central purpose. It is also very slow. Pressure for reform from Royal Commission and similar reports is often either 'shelved' or acted upon with modifications a long time after the publication of the report.

The simplest and clearest method of protecting civil liberties is for Parliament to enact a Bill of Rights, setting out and codifying rights and the restrictions on them. But an important preliminary problem is what status a Bill of Rights should be given if enacted. Should it have the same status as any ordinary statute and be subject to express and implied repeal by Parliament, or should it have some form of specially entrenched status? In reality there are two points involved: (a) what method would best protect rights?; (b) could that method be adopted under United Kingdom constitutional law?

29.4 Entrenchment

a) *Against express repeal*

If some of the provisions of a Bill of Rights could be entrenched (protected) against repeal by a later Parliament, ie made unrepeatable and/or other provisions could be made subject to express repeal only by Parliament acting with a special majority, eg two-thirds of the Commons; then such entrenchment would very effectively guarantee the provisions. But under the United Kingdom's present constitutional system, neither of these types of entrenchment are possible. Both would lead the courts to having to consider the validity of statutes and would necessarily involve the reversal of the traditional constitutional doctrine that one Parliament cannot fetter future ones. Unless judges radically changed their traditional attitude to Parliament, a Bill of Rights could not be entrenched against express repeal.

b) *Against implied repeal*

If the provisions of a Bill of Rights could be entrenched against being repealed by later inconsistent statutes (which did not expressly repeal them) then this would guarantee the provisions to a certain extent. (Anything is better than nothing). While such entrenchment runs contrary to traditional theories of parliamentary supremacy, it seems that such entrenchment will be accepted and applied by the courts, as a political reality, in very important cases (eg s2(4) European Communities Act 1972 *Macarthys* v *Smith*).

29.5 Alternatives to entrenchment

To avoid constitutional difficulties the simplest method would be to have an entirely unentrenched Bill of Rights. This, though, would diminish one of the main aims of such a Bill, to act as a protection against the State. How effective an unentrenched Bill would be in practice would turn on the vigilance of the press and the public in watching for and seeking to prevent, statutory repeals of its provisions.

A position in between entrenchment and non-entrenchment was adopted in the Canadian Bill of Rights 1960 in which, after certain rights were declared, s2 provided that every law was to be construed and applied so as not to abrogate or infringe the rights, unless an Act expressly declared that its provisions were to take effect notwithstanding the Bill's provisions. On reflection, such a device would be the most suited to the United Kingdom Constitution, because it would merely introduce a rule of statutory interpretation. Parliament would still be free expressly to repeal or modify the Bill's provisions. The 1960 enactment is now the *Charter of Rights and Freedoms*, which is contained in the Canada Act 1982. Section 33 of that Act continues to provide that the provisions in the Charter can be overridden expressly by Federal and provincial legislation.

29.6 What form could a Bill of Rights take?

The most obvious model for a United Kingdom Bill of Rights is the European Convention on Human Rights (EC) to which the United Kingdom is a signatory. The EC clearly adopts a different position on many rights to that adopted in English law, eg the *Sunday Times* contempt of court case. The EC is a *treaty* which has not been incorporated into English law by statute and, therefore, at present it can only act as an aid to statutory interpretation and not as a positive source of rights and liberties. But, the EC could be easily enacted to form a United Kingdom Bill of Rights.

The disadvantages of using the EC as a United Kingdom Bill of Rights are:

a) The scope of the exceptions set out in its articles are potentially very wide and it is drafted in a European style, ie with bold provisions and no attention to detail. How would English judges, more used to strict and tight English statutory drafting, cope with the task of interpreting the EC?

b) The EC appears dated in places, it was formulated in 1950, and as it was drafted to find a common whole for the various European countries, it might not reflect very well the rights and liberties which the United Kingdom should seek to protect. (Or are rights universal?)

c) A further problem would be whether to incorporate the case law built up by the decisions of the European Court on Human Rights in interpreting and applying the EC.

Faced with these disadvantages, the main advantage of EC is that it exists! It is a ready-made model. How long would it take to formulate a Bill of Rights tailored especially for the United Kingdom?

29.7 Can we trust the judges?

If a United Kingdom Bill of Rights was enacted which sought to entrench its provisions, it would give the judges a great deal of power. The judges would be required either to question the validity of statutes inconsistent with the Bill, or at least not apply them. Could we trust the judges to carry out this task?

> 'The judges of England have always in the past – and always will – be vigilant in guarding our freedoms. Someone must be trusted. Let it be the judges.'
>
> Lord Denning – 1980 Dimbleby Lecture.

NOTE: At present though, there seems to be little popular interest in the question of whether the United Kingdom should enact a Bill of Rights and very little prospect of one being enacted in the foreseeable future. The House of Lords appears the most motivated, although attempts by the House to incorporate the European Convention into domestic law did not enjoy all-party support. A further attempt by a private member in the Commons in 1987 to introduce a Human Rights bill also failed for lack of support.

30 SCOTLAND, WALES, AND NORTHERN IRELAND

The United Kingdom consists of Great Britain and Northern Ireland. Great Britain consists of England, Scotland and Wales.

30.1 Scotland

a) *Union*

In 1603, the Crowns of England and Scotland were united when James VI of Scotland became James I of England, but the two kingdoms were not formally united and the Parliaments of England and Scotland were not united until over a century later. After negotiations between representatives of the two Parliaments, the Treaty of Union 1707 was drafted. This was approved by both Parliaments and the Act of Union 1707 was passed. Under the terms of the Act, the two kingdoms were united into Great Britain; and Scottish peers and commons became members of the Westminster Parliament. The Act also contains guarantees of certain conditions seen (by the Scots) as fundamental to the Union. The guarantees are:

i) that the Scottish private law will not be altered 'except for the evident utility of the subjects within Scotland';

ii) that the Scottish Courts of Session and of Justiciary and the Presbyterian Church were to continue for 'all time coming'.

It is arguable that, in legal theory, these guarantees place some kind of limitation on the supremacy of Parliament, because the Act itself created a new Parliament (the united one of England and Scotland) and if the Act states certain things that Parliament cannot alter, then the new Parliament was born unfree and limited.

This issue arose indirectly for consideration in the Scottish case of:

MacCormick v *Lord Advocate* (1953) Court of Session, in which the Lord President reserved his decision (ie came to no conclusion either way) as to whether an Act of Parliament which repealed or altered the 'fundamental' provisions of the Union could raise a justifiable issue. He made the following observations:

> 'The principle of the unlimited sovereignty of Parliament is a distinctively English principle which has no counterpart in Scottish constitutional law ... Considering that the Union legislation extinguished the Parliaments of Scotland and England and replaced them by a new Parliament, I have difficulty in seeing why it should have been supposed that the new Parliament of Great Britain must inherit all the peculiar characteristics of the English Parliament, but none of the Scottish Parliament.
>
> ... I have not found in the Union legislation any provision that the Parliament of Great Britain should be "absolutely sovereign" in the sense that that Parliament should be free to alter the Treaty at will.'

NOTE: it is difficult to conceive that a court would declare an Act invalid for breach of the fundamental provisions. As the Lord President observed:

> '... it is of little avail to ask whether Parliament "can" do this thing or that, without going on to inquire who can stop them if they do.'

b) *At present*

Scotland has its own and different legal, court, education and local government systems. There is a separate central government department to deal with Scottish matters, the Scottish Office, which is based in Edinburgh, exercises a degree of devolved administrative power and is headed by a Cabinet Minister, the Secretary of State for Scotland. In Parliament, bills that concern Scotland are considered by the Scottish Grand Committee and there is a Scottish Affairs Select Committee. Parliament frequently passes different laws for Scotland and the rest of the United Kingdom. On any issue in Parliament, Scottish Members of Parliament can, of course, be voted down by their English colleagues. These arrangements were not considered by many to give Scotland enough of its own governmental powers and pressure grew for larger scale devolution.

c) *Devolution*

In 1973 the Kilbrandon report of the Royal Commission on the Constitution was published. It recommended a devolution of legislative powers to an elected Scottish Assembly, with the Westminster Parliament retaining ultimate supremacy (along the lines of the Northern Ireland Stormont system). To partially give effect to the recommendations, a Bill was introduced in 1976, but was abandoned. In its place, the Labour government put forward the Scotland Bill 1978. Under this Bill: a single Chamber, Scottish Assembly, was to be elected, on a first past the post system and was to have legislative powers. The Scottish Assembly was, within defined areas, to have the power to pass Acts which altered or repealed Acts of Parliament. The 26 defined issues of competence for the Scottish Assembly included, eg health, social welfare, education, housing, transport, etc. There were limits, eg the Scottish Assembly could not impose or abolish any tax, or legislate for areas outside Scotland. To have effect as law a Scottish Assembly Act had to be approved by Order in Council, but the Secretary of State for Scotland could not put a Scottish Assembly Act before the Council for approval if:

i) the Judicial Committee of the Privy Council declared the Act to be ultra vires the powers of the Scottish Assembly; or

ii) the Secretary of State for Scotland was of the opinion that the Act conflicted with international or EEC obligations.

Also, the Secretary of State for Scotland could lay a bill passed by the Scottish Assembly before the Westminster Parliament to be subject to annulment under the negative resolution procedure if he considered that the Scottish Bill adversely affected an area which the Westminster Parliament had reserved powers over, ie if it affected a non-devolved legislative area.

In summary, the Scottish Assembly was to have devolved legislative powers, but subject to the supremacy of the Westminster Parliament and, in particular, the Secretary of State for Scotland's veto powers.

Under the 1978 Bill, the Secretary of State for Scotland was to appoint a First Secretary for Scotland and, on the First Secretary's recommendations, Scottish Secretaries, all of whom were to have ministerial powers in relation to the devolved areas of responsibility. The Secretary of State for Scotland was to have a power to veto decisions of the Scottish Executive, subject to receiving the backing of an affirmative resolution in Parliament. The Scottish Assembly was to receive a block grant of finance granted annually by Parliament and the Scottish Assembly was to decide its spending priorities. (It is interesting to note that the Scottish Assembly Acts were to be subject to judicial review for ultra vires, ie to ensure that the Scottish Assembly did not go beyond its devolved powers.)

The Bill became the Scotland Act 1978 but under its provisions it could not be brought into force unless approved by a referendum held in Scotland and if less than 40 per cent voted in favour the Act had to be repealed. A referendum was held in March 1979, at which only 32.5 per cent voted in favour and, therefore, Orders in Council were laid before Parliament which repealed the Act. Legislative devolution has not been a major issue since, although recent evidence shows a further upsurge in support for devolution. There has also recently been support for the idea of an independent Scotland within the EEC and nationalist support is in the ascendancy after the 1989 by-election victory of the Scottish National Party in Glasgow Govan, formerly a safe Labour seat. A conference on the constitutional position of Scotland has been in session.

30.2 Wales

a) *Union*

Wales suffered military conquest by the English in the thirteenth century and was annexed by the English Crown. It was not until the Act of Union 1536 (the 'Laws in Wales Act') that England and Wales were formally united. Under the Act, Wales was given an English style administration system, was granted representation in the English Parliament and the Welsh were required to speak English.

b) *At present*

English and Welsh laws are generally the same and England and Wales share a common legal and court structure. There is a separate central government department to deal with Welsh matters, the Welsh Office, which is based in Cardiff and headed by a Cabinet Minister, the Secretary of State for Wales. The Welsh Office exercises devolved administrative powers. There is a Welsh Affairs Select Committee in Parliament.

c) *Devolution*

Kilbrandon recommended legislative devolution to a Welsh Assembly, but the Wales Bill (1978) provided for the election of a single Chamber, Welsh Assembly which was not to have legislative, but only executive powers. The Welsh Assembly funded by direct grant from Westminster, was to have the power to make policy and executive decisions in relation to certain devolved areas, eg education, health, social services, etc. This power was to be exercised through sub-committees and was to cover powers in the devolved areas which various Ministers had previously exercised. The Secretary of State for Wales was to have veto powers over those Welsh executive decisions.

The Bill became the Wales Act 1978 but was subject to the same 40 per cent referendum provision as the Scotland Act. In the 1979 referendum in Wales, only 11.8 per cent voted in favour and, therefore, the Act was repealed by Parliament.

30.3 Northern Ireland

a) *Union and discord*

Northern Ireland has had, and is now suffering from, a tragic history. Its problems stem from its split community identity, some parts of its people wanting union with England, others wanting union with Southern Ireland. This divided community has provided United Kingdom governments with a constitutional problem which it apparently cannot solve.

The Union with Ireland Act 1800 united Great Britain and Ireland (North and South) and the Irish were granted representation in the Westminster Parliament. This Union was, for the vast majority of Irish people, an unwanted one and there was considerable hostility to it in Ireland. Various attempts were made in Parliament, in 1886, 1893, 1914, to give some degree of 'home rule' to the Irish to damp down the growing signs of trouble. In 1916 there was a violent uprising in Dublin and civil war ensued. Parliament, in the Government of Ireland Act 1920, set up separate and subordinate Parliaments for Northern and Southern Ireland, but the civil war continued. A treaty was signed in 1922 under which Southern Ireland was recognised as a self-governing Dominion, the Irish Free State. Southern Ireland declared itself a sovereign independent state in 1937 and in 1949 became the Republic of Ireland.

Northern Ireland though, ie the six northern counties, remained – and still remain – part of the United Kingdom. Under the 1920 Act, Northern Ireland had its own executive, ie a Governor, Prime Minister, Cabinet, Government Departments and its own two Chamber Legislative Assembly which sat at Stormont. The Stormont Assembly was subject to the ultimate supremacy of the Westminster Parliament and the United Kingdom government, which reserved to itself exclusive powers over certain areas, eg foreign relations, the armed forces and taxation. But, apart from those areas, Stormont had legislative powers. The Assembly was completely dominated throughout its 50-year life by the Protestant Unionist Party, which effectively cut the minority Catholics out of government. This eventually led to large-scale outbreaks of violence in the late 1960s and in 1972 Stormont was suspended and direct rule from Westminster, primarily by the Secretary of State for Northern Ireland, was put in its place: Northern Ireland (Temporary Provisions) Act 1972. An experiment was attempted by the Northern Ireland Assembly and Northern Ireland Constitution Acts 1973 under which a new Assembly and Executive system was selected and set up based on 'power sharing' between the two Northern Ireland communities. This only lasted a few months and the Northern Ireland Assembly Act 1974 dissolved the Assembly. Direct rule by the Secretary of State for Northern Ireland was resumed. Under the Northern Ireland Constitution Act 1973 Parliament declared that Northern Ireland would not cease to be part of the United Kingdom unless a majority of people in Northern Ireland consented to this in a special poll.

b) *Northern Ireland Assembly Act 1982*

In April 1982 the then Secretary of State for Northern Ireland, Mr Prior, put forward some new proposals for a form of 'rolling devolution' (gradual, flexible) to a Northern Ireland Assembly. These proposals were enacted in the 1982 Northern Ireland Act. However, these proposals have been continually frustrated, first by Catholic Members of Parliament boycotting the Assembly, and then by 'Unionist' Members of Parliament after the British government had signed the Anglo-Irish Accord in December 1985, an agreement giving the Irish Republic a say in the affairs of Northern Ireland. Because the functions of the Assembly had effectively broken down, the British government took steps in June 1986 to dissolve it.

31 LOCAL GOVERNMENT

31.1 Structure and functions

a) *In the past – Local Government Act 1972*

The Local Government Act 1972 established the following structure of local authorities in England and Wales (Scotland has its own separate system). Boundaries between the authorities are kept under review by the Local Government Boundary Commissions.

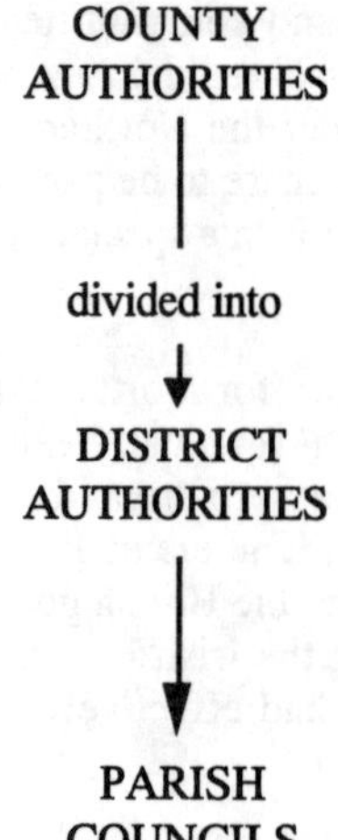

At each level, County, District, parish, each authority has its own council which has various functions:

Counties	*Districts*	*Parishes*
Education	Housing	Footpaths
Social Services	Public Health	Cemeteries
Libraries	Markets	Swimming baths
Transport (most aspects)	Refuse collection	Parks
Police, fire	Granting planning permission	Car Parks
Structure plan (for town planning)		
Refuse disposal		
Consumer protection		
Etc	Etc	Etc

London: had its own system established by London Government Act 1963.

Greater London Council (GLC)

|

32 Londons boroughs and City of London Corporation

b) *Recent Reforms – Local Government Act 1985*

The Conservative government in the Local Government Act 1985 provided for further reformation of local government by providing for the abolition of the Greater London Council (GLC) and the six Metropolitan County Councils on 1 April 1986.

This would be done, said the government, because these bodies did not provide a useful function (most functions were already carried out by district and borough councils) and were wasteful of resources (though there is a wealth of conflicting evidence as to whether abolition means greater economy of resources).

The existing functions of the GLC and Metro County Councils will ultimately be taken over mainly by the borough and district councils respectively. Opponents of the changes have suggested that abolition is merely a reflection of political manoeuvring on the government's part, in that the GLC and Metro Councils were all Labour controlled. There is certainly no clear evidence that abolition has been more economic, nor that it will lead to more adequate provision of local services.

Local Government Act 1988

This Act allows for (inter alia) local authority services such as refuse, cleaning, catering and maintenance to be put out to competitive tender. It also contains a much sought after provision preventing the 'promotion' of homosexuality.

Further reforms in the areas of education (the imposition of a 'national' curriculum, allowing schools to 'get out' of local authority control) and housing (with the emphasis upon the private sector) are forthcoming. They will further diminish the authority possessed by local government.

Local Government Act 1989

Of particular interest in this context is an updated 'Code of Local Government Conduct' issued as an appendix to Government Circular No 8/90 under s31 of the 1989 Act.

It deals with, inter alia, the following:

i) compliance by councillors with the law, and with standing orders;

ii) a failure to comply with the code itself may constitute maladministration;

iii) disclosure of pecuniary interests;

iv) conflicts between private interests and public duties;

v) gifts, hospitality and expenses;

vi) dealings with councillors and use of council facilities.

31.2 Councils

a) *Every authority has its own council* which exercises some of the authority's power itself, but which will also delegate the exercise of other powers to committees, sub-committees and officers.

i) A *County* council will have between 60 and 100 members.

ii) A *Metropolitan district* council will have between 50 and 80 members.

iii) A *Non-metropolitan district* council will have between 30 and 60 members.

b) *Councillors are elected* in elections governed by rules very similar to those for parliamentary elections, as follows:

i) *County councillors* – are elected every four years, and all retire together (en bloc) at the end of their four-year term of office.

ii) *Metropolitan district councillors* – one-third retire each year, elections are held to fill the vacancies.

iii) *Non-metropolitan district councillors* – use one of the above systems, at the district's choice.

iv) *In London* – elections are held every three years and all councillors retire together.

c) *Council meetings* presided over by a chairman elected annually, largely consider the reports and recommendations of the council's committees and its employees (officers). Under s101 of the Local Government Act 1972, a council has the power to delegate to committees, sub-committees and officers any of its decision making powers excluding decisions involving the raising of money. This wide power of delegation is frequently used. In turn committees can delegate to sub-committees and officers and sub-committees can delegate to officers. By statute, councils (where relevant) have to establish education, police and social services committees. Apart from these, councils in practice appoint many other committees to deal with the services the authority is responsible for and for special purposes too (ad hoc committees). A committee etc may be vested with the delegated power either to take decisions and merely report them to the council, or to consider something and make recommendations to the council for it to take the decision. Local authorities also employ many officials (officers) to carry out administrative and executive functions. There are some officers which every authority (where relevant) must appoint, eg a chief education officer. In practice, many powers are delegated to officers.

d) *Public Bodies (Admission to Meetings) Act 1960*

Under the Public Bodies (Admission to Meetings) Act 1960, the public and press are entitled to be present at council and committee meetings unless the authority concerned passes a resolution to exclude them in the public interest, eg where confidential business is to be considered at the meeting.

31.3 Finance

a) *The source of local authorities' income* are:

i) *Community charge ('poll tax')*: This source of finance replaced rates in Scotland in 1989 and in England and Wales in 1990. Unlike the rates it is a tax levied not on property but on each adult member of the population. Every adult over age 18 must register in their local area and pay an annual charge set by the local authority. There are certain exemptions for those in hospital, etc, and reductions for those on low incomes, but the charge has been severely criticised because it is not dependent on ability to pay. Whether a person occupies a council house or a luxury penthouse the charge levied per head is the same. The community charge is extremely unpopular and the levels of charge are much higher than foreseen by the Government, which has promised to review the working of the new system. The main reason for adopting the new system was to try to make councils more responsive and responsible to those in their area and to increase local government electors' involvement in local government. The community charge will continue only for one more financial year – 1992–93. The Government announced in 1991 a wholesale reform of the structure and finance of local government. In 1993 'council tax' will replace the poll tax. This will be based primarily on occupancy and property values. The Government will continue to have powers to 'cap' local authority expenditure.

ii) *Grants* from central government; which take the form either of grants for particular purposes, or block grants (the main form) which the authority itself decides how to allocate between its services. The amount allocated via block grants is determined each year by the Secretary of State for Environment, subject to affirmative resolution in the Commons;

iii) *Loans*: local authorities can borrow money for purposes approved by the Secretary of State for Environment;

iv) *Charges* for services and facilities.

b) *Local authority expenditure* is subject to the principles of the ultra vires doctrine (see chapter 14: Administrative Law – Principles); local authorities can only expend money for purposes which are either expressly or impliedly authorised by statute and furthermore they owe a fiduciary duty to their ratepayers to be thrifty. See *Bromley LBC* v *Greater London Council* (1983).

c) *Local authority accounts are audited* annually by a district auditor, a civil servant appointed by the Secretary of State for Environment (or sometimes by a private auditor, approved by the Secretary of State). If the district auditor discovers that expenditure has been incurred unlawfully (ultra vires) he can apply to the High Court for a declaration that the expenditure was unlawful. The High Court can also surcharge the councillors, ie order them to pay the sums unlawfully spent. In some cases, the court can disqualify councillors from office too. The Government has taken similar powers to limit the community charge which a council can levy ('charge capping') and the Secretary of State's action in charge capping some 23 authorities has been upheld by the courts. The government are indicating a preparedness to take on increased charge-capping powers.

31.4 Controls over local authorities

a) *Extra-judicial*

Local commissioners consider complaints of local authority maladministration and perform a similar task for local government as the Ombudsman does for central government.

b) *Judicial*

Local authorities must act in good faith: see *Jones* v *Swansea City Council* (1990).

The courts can review the actions of local authorities by applying the ultra vires doctrine.

Local authorities can sue and be sued, they are not Crown servants and do not enjoy any of the privileges or immunities of the Crown.

i) *Contract*

There is a general principle that public authorities, which includes local authorities, cannot enter into contractual undertakings that are incompatible with the exercise of their more important powers. This principle does not prevent l/as from entering into commercial contracts, but local authorities do not have the power to, eg limit their by-law making powers by contract (*Cory Ltd* v *City of London Corporation* (1951)).

The distinction appears to be between:

an authority giving away, or restricting, by contract its 'statutory birthright', ie its statutory powers which it cannot do; and

an authority entering into an ordinary commercial contract as part of the exercise of its statutory powers to enter into contracts – which it can do.

ii) *Tort*

Local authorities are vicariously liable for the torts of their employees and can be sued for them, as a private employer can. However, a local authority cannot be sued for its actions, which would otherwise found an action in tort, if the local authority is under a duty, or is given a power to do something which necessarily leads the local authority, in exercising its power or duty, to commit a tort: *Hammersmith Railway Co* v *Brand* (1869).

An ultra vires action by a local authority cannot by itself found an action in tort, for there to be such an action the local authority must have acted, eg ultra vires and negligently, *Anns* v *Merton LBC* (1978).

NOTE: some statutes which give local authorities decision-making powers, specially provide a remedy, eg on appeal, for persons aggrieved by the way in which the local authority has exercised its powers.

Recent examples of judicial review are:

i) *Hazell* v *Hammersmith and Fulham LBC* (1991) in which it was decided that local authorities had no statutory powers to engage in 'speculative trading' to increase their financial resources;

ii) *R* v *Greenwich LBC, ex parte Lovelace* (1991) in which it was held that a councillor might be suspended from council meetings or a council committee as a way of discipline by the party to which the councillor belonged. Provided the party acted in good faith, such disciplinary measures were not unreasonable.

c) *Central government*

In practice, central and local government generally co-operate with each other in exercising their powers. But, the central government has a wide range of powers which it can use to, directly and indirectly, control local authorities' actions. These powers are:

i) to make, withhold, and determine the levels of grants to local authorities. This is a most important power because it can be used to limit the money available to local authorities, thereby limiting their range of options and the services they can provide. This has been particularly effective with the passing of the 1980 Local Government Planning and Land Act. The Rates Act 1984 empowers the Secretary of State for the Environment to 'rate cap', ie to prescribe a maximum rate for local authorities in an effort to curb traditionally high-spending authorities. This capping power has now been extended to cover the community charge. Those who overspend may be subjected to financial penalties by the Secretary of State. These provisions severely restrict the power of local authorities to raise the amount of money which they feel is necessary in order to provide adequate public services;

ii) to control local authority borrowing;

iii) to lay down rules in the form of Statutory Instruments and also by less formal methods to govern the provision of services by local authorities;

iv) to inspect the way local authorities provide services; eg education and police;

v) to confirm/reject by-laws;

vi) to entertain appeals, eg in town planning where there can be an appeal against a local authority's refusal to grant planning permission, to the Secretary of State for Environment;

vii) to exercise default powers; such powers can be exercised when a local authority is failing to exercise properly its powers, to enable a central government Minister to take over the power himself to remedy the difficulty.

Example

R v *Secretary of State for the Environment, ex parte Norwich City Council* (1982) Court of Appeal. In this case the Housing Act 1980 gave council tenants the right to buy their houses at discounts. The Secretary of State received complaints alleging that Norwich City Council were delaying the implementation of this right by, for example, taking too long to make valuations, by 'counselling' all prospective purchasers, by making over-high valuations and by failing to employ the district valuer.

In the first seven-and-a-half months of the scheme, out of 803 cases, no sales had been completed. The Secretary of State and his department held various meetings with the councillors, but no real improvement was made. Eventually, the Secretary of State made an order under s23 of the 1980 Act by which the Council's powers to sell council homes were taken over by the Secretary of State, to be exercised by his Department. Under s23, the Secretary of State 'where it appears to the Secretary of State that tenants may have difficulty in exercising the right to buy effectively and expeditiously' could do 'all such things as appear to him necessary or expedient'. The Council applied for judicial review of the order.

The Court of Appeal held:

1. That a provision should be read into the s23 powers that they should be exercised in accordance with the rules of fairness.

   The Secretary of State had complied with this restriction, there had been meetings at which the councillors could explain their position and were advised and warned by the Secretary of State.

2. The decision of the Secretary of State was open to judicial review if he had acted ultra vires by misdirecting himself in fact or law (the Court of Appeal reiterated the established principles of judicial review) and the main question was whether:

   the Secretary of State could reasonably conclude that the terms of s23 were satisfied; per Kerr and May LJJ;

   the Council had acted unreasonably, as the Secretary of State could only exercise his s23 power if this condition was present; per Lord Denning.

Applying these tests, the Court of Appeal held that the Secretary of State had acted intra vires.

The importance of all these powers is that in combination with each other they give the central government extensive powers to limit and control local authorities.

32 NATIONALITY, CITIZENSHIP, IMMIGRATION, DEPORTATION AND EXTRADITION

32.1 British Nationality Act 1981

a) *Introduction*

The British Nationality Act 1981 enacted new provisions about citizenship and nationality. It is proposed to consider the British Nationality Act 1981 first and then the British Nationality Act 1948.

The most important aspects of the British Nationality Act 1981 are that it:

i) defines 'British Citizenship'; and

ii) provides that only British citizens have the right of abode in the United Kingdom. The 'right of abode' is fully considered under the Immigration Act 1971 below, but to explain briefly for now:

Under the British Nationality Act 1948 the status of 'citizen of the United Kingdom and Colonies' was established; citizens of the United Kingdom and Colonies though did not necessarily have the right to freely live in and to come and go from the United Kingdom (the right of abode) under the Immigration Act 1971. Therefore, the concept of citizenship under the British Nationality Act 1948 did not tie in with the concept of 'patriality' (persons having the right of abode) under the Immigration Act 1971. To remedy this, to tie citizenship and immigration provisions together, the British Nationality Act 1981 established the status of British citizens and that only British citizens have the right of abode in the United Kingdom. On commencement of the British Nationality Act 1981, the provisions of the British Nationality Act 1948 ceased to have effect.

b) *'British Citizenship' under the British Nationality Act 1981*

Acquisition is by:

i) Birth in the United Kingdom to a parent who is a British citizen or who is settled in the United Kingdom.

NOTES: this provision brings to an end the ancient principle that birth in the United Kingdom alone automatically entitles the person to be British;

it is sufficient if either parent satisfies the conditions;

to be 'settled' the parent has to be 'ordinarily resident' in the United Kingdom under the British Nationality Act 1981; a person is not ordinarily resident if he is in the United Kingdom in breach of immigration laws (see *R* v *Home Secretary, ex parte Zamir* below).

ii) *Birth* in the United Kingdom to a parent who becomes a British citizen or becomes settled in the United Kingdom. On the condition being satisfied, the person must be registered by the Home Secretary before he can become a British citizen.

iii) *Adoption*

iv) *Descent*: ie birth outside the United Kingdom to a parent who is a British citizen by birth, adoption, registration or naturalisation (NB: not by descent).

NOTE: this provision prevents chains of British citizenship by descent, because under its terms a British Citizen living outside the United Kingdom can pass on his citizenship to his children, but they cannot pass on their British citizenship to their children.

v) *Descent*: birth outside the United Kingdom to a parent who is a British citizen (by whatever method, including descent) *and* who is serving overseas in Crown service.

vi) *Registration*: The Home Secretary has the discretion to register persons as British citizens. The following (among others) are entitled to registration as British citizens:

a minor, within 12 months of his birth, born stateless to a parent who is a British citizen by descent *and* a grandparent who was a British citizen, by any method but not by descent, at the time of the birth of the parent;

a minor, born to a parent who is a British citizen by descent and the minor and both parents have been resident in the United Kingdom for the three years immediately preceding the application for registration;

'British Dependent Territories Citizens' or 'British Overseas Citizens' or 'British protected persons' (for definitions see below) who have been resident in the United Kingdom for the five years immediately preceding the application for registration. An applicant must not have been in breach of the immigration laws during the five-year period;

Gibraltarians;

a wife of a citizen of the United Kingdom and Colonies (the British Nationality Act 1948) who applied within five years of the commencement of the British Nationality Act 1981.

vii) *Naturalisation*: an adult may apply for naturalisation. He must be of good character; have a sufficient knowledge of English; have been resident in the United Kingdom for the five years immediately preceding his application (and not in breach of the immigration laws at any time during that period); and intend the United Kingdom to be his home.

viii) *Acquisition at commencement of the British Nationality Act 1981*: a person who was a citizen of the United Kingdom and Colonies under the British Nationality Act 1948 *and* who had the right of abode in the United Kingdom under the Immigration Act 1971 immediately before the commencement of the British Nationality Act 1981 (1 January 1983) automatically became a British Citizen under the British Nationality Act 1981 on its commencement.

c) *Other types of citizenship under the British Nationality Act 1981*

The British Nationality Act 1981 created various forms of citizenship; the 'first class' citizenship is a British citizen because *only* a British citizen has the right of abode in the United Kingdom. The other forms are:

i) *British Dependent Territories Citizenship*: British Dependent Territories are listed in the British Nationality Act 1981 and include: Gibraltar, Hong Kong and the Falklands.

ii) *British Overseas Citizenship*: a citizen of the United Kingdom and Colonies under the British Nationality Act 1948 who does not, on commencement the British Nationality Act 1981, become either a British citizen or British Dependent Territories citizen.

iii) *British Protected Persons*: Mostly persons in Brunei.

NOTE: Basically (i),(ii) and (iii) are entitled to passports, (ii) and (iii) are entitled to consular protection and aid. None have the right of abode in the United Kingdom.

iv) All types of citizens under the British Nationality Act 1981, apart from British Protected Persons, are also designated as 'Commonwealth citizens'.

d) *Aliens* (under the British Nationality Act 1981) are persons who are neither 'Commonwealth citizens' nor British Protected Persons nor citizens of the Republic of Ireland.

e) *Losing British citizenship (British Nationality Act 1981)*

A British citizen by registration or naturalisation (only) can be deprived of his citizenship by the Home Secretary if he is satisfied of disloyalty, disaffection, or where the person has served a 12-month period of imprisonment within five years of his registration or naturalisation and the Home Secretary is satisfied that it is not conducive to the public good for the person to remain a British citizen.

NOTE: A British citizen can renounce his citizenship.

32.2 British Nationality Act 1948

The provisions of the British Nationality Act 1948 ceased to have effect on the commencement of the British Nationality Act 1981, but it is still important to understand the provisions of the British Nationality Act 1948, mainly because of the British Nationality Act 1981 provisions for acquisition of British citizenship at commencement of the British Nationality Act 1981 (see above).

a) The British Nationality Act 1948 defined those entitled to citizenship of the United Kingdom and Colonies. A person who was either a citizen of the United Kingdom and Colonies or a citizen of a Commonwealth country listed in the British Nationality Act 1948, was also a 'British subject' who could also be described as a 'Commonwealth citizen'.

b) *Citizenship of the United Kingdom and Colonies was acquired by*:

i) *Birth* in the United Kingdom (note, no additional conditions);

ii) *Adoption*;

iii) *Descent*, ie birth, where the father was a citizen of the United Kingdom and Colonies at the time of the birth, but if the birth took place in a foreign country *and* the father was a citizen of the United Kingdom and Colonies by descent, the birth had to be registered at a United Kingdom consulate.

NOTE: chains of citizenship by descent could be established under the British Nationality Act 1948; a citizen of the United Kingdom and Colonies by descent could pass his citizenship onto his children and so on, provided each birth was registered as described above.

iv) *Registration*, eg a wife of a citizen of the United Kingdom and Colonies was entitled to be registered by the Home Secretary as a citizen of the United Kingdom and Colonies; and

v) *Naturalisation*.

NOTE: Citizens of the United Kingdom and Colonies could renounce their status. Citizens of the United Kingdom and Colonies by registration or naturalisation could be deprived of their status.

32.3 Immigration Act 1971

a) *Introduction*

The provisions of the British Nationality Act 1948 were very widely drafted. In order to control immigration, the Immigration Act 1971 was passed. Immigration Act 1971 separates the concepts of right of abode (those entitled to live in the United Kingdom) from the status of citizen of the United Kingdom and Colonies, ie being a citizen of the United Kingdom and Colonies does not give that person the right of abode in the United Kingdom.

It is important to realise:

i) That until the commencement of the British Nationality Act 1981 (1 January 1983) persons having the right of abode in the United Kingdom were 'patrials' in the Immigration Act 1971.

ii) That on commencement of the British Nationality Act 1981, the concept of patriality was repealed and instead a British citizen under the British Nationality Act 1981 had the right of abode in the United Kingdom.

but

iii) NOTE: Under the British Nationality Act 1981, all those persons who immediately before the commencement of the British Nationality Act 1981 were both citizens of the United Kingdom and Colonies under the British Nationality Act 1948 and patrials under the Immigration Act 1971, were British Citizens under the British Nationality Act 1981 and, therefore, had the right of abode in the United Kingdom.

b) *General principles*

i) All those having the right of abode in the United Kingdom are free to live in and to come and go into and from the United Kingdom without let or hindrance, ie without being subject to the restrictions of immigration control.

ii) Those not having the right of abode, are subject to immigration control. They must obtain leave to enter the United Kingdom, which may be for a limited or indefinite period, with or without conditions attached. Immigration officers have the power to grant or refuse leave of entry to such persons, with or without conditions, under the Immigration Rules laid down by the Home Secretary. The Rules are laid before Parliament but are not Statutory Instruments. They are rules of practice not law. The Immigration Act 1971 and Immigration Rules provide a complete code of immigration control and rights under international law to settle (if any) are *not* preserved; *R* v *Home Secretary, ex parte Thakrar* (1974).

c) *Patrials*

Patriality is acquired by:

i) A person who is a citizen of the United Kingdom and Colonies by birth, adoption, naturalisation or registration.

ii) A person who is a citizen of the United Kingdom and Colonies by descent, ie by virtue of being born to a parent who was a citizen of the United Kingdom and Colonies, where the parent was himself a citizen of the United Kingdom and Colonies either by birth, adoption, naturalisation or registration (NOTE: not by descent) or by descent from a parent who was a citizen of the United Kingdom and Colonies by birth, adoption, naturalisation or registration (NOTE: not by descent).

NOTE: This apparently complicated provision simply means that patriality can be 'passed' by a person who is a citizen of the United Kingdom and Colonies by any method other than descent, to that person's child and grandchild, but no further. Patriality by descent is limited.

iii) A person who is a citizen of the United Kingdom and Colonies settled in the United Kingdom and ordinarily resident there for at least the five preceding years.

iv) A 'Commonwealth citizen' under the British Nationality Act 1948, born to or adopted by a parent who was a citizen of the United Kingdom and Colonies by birth.

v) A woman who is a 'Commonwealth citizen' under the British Nationality Act 1948 and who is married to any citizen under (i)–(iv) above.

32.4 EEC nationals

Under the Treaty of Rome, EEC nationals have the right to accept offers of employment within the EEC and to move freely, ie not subject to the restrictions of national immigration controls, within the EEC for this purpose and to remain in the member state for this purpose and to remain there after the employment finishes. This right of free movement and entry also extends to such a person's spouse, dependant children, dependant parents and grandparents. The Immigration Rules reflect these EEC provisions. EEC nationals are in a very special category. These EEC principles are directly applicable and the validity of any deportation order against an EEC national can be adjudged by the provisions of the relevant directly applicable EEC Directive (*Van Duyn* v *Home Office* (1975)).

32.5 Illegal immigrants

The Immigration Act 1971

An illegal immigrant is a person who enters, or remains in, the United Kingdom in breach of immigration control, eg without leave as required, or in contravention of conditions attached to a leave.

Also note these important cases:

R v *Home Secretary, ex parte Zamir* (1980) House of Lords, in which Z, who was born in Pakistan, applied for an entry certificate. Z was entitled to it, under Immigration Rules, because he was unmarried and a dependant of parents settled in the United Kingdom. Z was granted the certificate, but before Z used it to enter the United Kingdom, he got married. When Z entered the United Kingdom he was asked no questions and he volunteered no information. Later, Z was detained as an illegal immigrant. He applied for habeas corpus.

It was held that an alien seeking entry to the United Kingdom owes a positive duty candidly to disclose all material facts which denote a change of circumstances since issue of the entry clearance.

Therefore, Z was an illegal immigrant.

When does this positive duty of disclosure exist?

In *R* v *Home Secretary, ex parte Jayakody* (1982) Court of Appeal, Jayakody was a married man who, to gain entry to the United Kingdom, stated that he was single. He later applied for an extension of his leave and admitted that he had previously lied about his marital status. An Immigration Adjudicator held that Jayakody was an illegal entrant because he had entered the United Kingdom by deception. An application for judicial review of the decision was made.

The Court of Appeal held that while every immigrant is under a positive duty candidly to disclose material facts (*R* v *Home Secretary, ex parte Zamir* (1980)), there was no duty to disclose non-material facts. To be 'material' a fact had to be decisive, it had to be of such a nature that, if disclosed, the immigration authorities would have been bound to, or would in all probability, refuse leave to enter.

Applying that test to the facts of the case; the fact that had not been disclosed, that Jayakody was married, was not decisive and if the facts had been disclosed the immigration authorities might have granted leave to enter.

NOTE: It was held in *R* v *Home Secretary, ex parte Khawaja* (1984) Court of Appeal that the principles above (in *Zamir* and *Jayakody*) applied to cases of obtaining indefinite and limited leave, by non-disclosure.

32.6 Deportation

Under the Immigration Act 1971, a person who does not have the right of abode in the United Kingdom can be deported under an order made by the Home Secretary:

a) if he does not observe a condition attached to his leave to enter; or

b) if he remains beyond the time limited by the leave; or

c) if the Home Secretary deems his deportation to be conducive to the public good; or

d) if another person to whose family he belongs is, or has been, ordered to be deported. NOTE: This covers wives, but not husbands and children under 18 of the 'another person'; or

e) if he is convicted of an offence for which he is punishable with imprisonment and, on his conviction, he is recommended for deportation by a court; or

f) if he is an illegal immigrant.

32.7 Appeals

NOTE: All immigration decisions are subject to judicial review on normal principles (*ex parte Zamir*).

The Immigration Act 1971 establishes appeal procedures:

a) A person is entitled to appeal to an Immigration Adjudicator:

   i) Against a refusal of leave to enter, but not while the person is in the United Kingdom. There is no appeal against such refusal, if made by the Home Secretary on the grounds of public good.

   ii) Against a variation of the conditions attached to a limited leave to enter. There is no appeal if the Home Secretary certifies that the person's departure would be conducive to the public good in the interests of national security or international relations or other political reasons.

   iii) Against a deportation order. There is no appeal if the order was made on the grounds that it is conducive to the public good in the interests of national security, or international relations, or other political reasons. (In such cases, the deportee may be given a 'hearing' in front of the three Civil Service Advisers – the 'Three Wise Men' – but such proceedings are not subject to the rules of natural justice or the duty to act fairly; *R* v *Home Secretary, ex parte Hosenball* (1977).)

   iv) Against a deportation order made on the grounds of illegal immigration, but not while the deportee is in the United Kingdom.

   v) Against the terms of a deportation order, on the grounds that the deportee ought to be deported to a different country to that specified in the order.

b) An Immigration Adjudicator will allow an appeal if he considers:

   i) that the decision was not in accordance with the law or the Immigration Rules; or

   ii) that a discretion should have been exercised differently.

Appeals from Immigration Acts lie to an Appeal Tribunal.

32.8 Extradition

Extradition has been defined as:

> 'the *formal surrender* by one State to another *of a person* who, being found in the former State, is *accused or* has been convicted of an offence committed within the jurisdiction of the latter.'
>
> Wade and Phillips.

a) *Extradition to foreign states*, ie non-Commonwealth countries, is governed primarily by the Extradition Act 1870.

i) *Conditions*:

For an extradition between the United Kingdom and a foreign state there must be:

an extradition treaty between the states; and

'double criminality', ie the criminal act in the foreign state must also amount to a criminal act if it had been committed within English jurisdiction. (*R* v *Governors of Pentonville and Holloway Prisons, ex parte Budlong and Kember* (1980)); and

the offence must be listed, as an extraditable offence between the states, in an Order in Council.

ii) *Procedure*

Requests for extradition are in practice made to the Home Secretary by foreign diplomats. The Home Secretary can then order a magistrate to issue a warrant for the arrest of the 'fugitive criminal'. The magistrate must be satisfied of the condition of double criminality before he can issue a warrant. On arrest the fugitive criminal is then taken before a magistrate who will decide whether the necessary conditions for extradition are present. If the magistrate decides that they are, the Home Secretary can (he is not bound to) order the fugitive criminal to be surrendered to the foreign state (extradited) after the expiration of 15 days, during which time habeas corpus can be applied for to test the legality of the extradition.

iii) *'Political offences'*

Under s3 Extradition Act 1870, a fugitive criminal cannot be extradited if the offence has a political character.

It has been held that:

shooting and killing a member of the (Swiss) Government during a political rising was a political offence: *Re Castioni* (1891);

Polish sailors who, dissatisfied with conditions in Poland, mutinied and locked up their officers, causing some injuries, committed political offences; *R* v *Governor of Brixton Prison, ex parte Kolczynski* (1955).

It appears that if the offender has an ulterior motive of a political kind when he commits the offence, then it has a political character.

NOTE: But under the Suppression of Terrorism Act 1978 certain *listed* offences are *not* to be regarded as 'political offences' between signatories of the European Convention on the Suppression of Terrorism, which includes the United Kingdom and the other EEC members.

The listed offences include murder, manslaughter, rape, kidnapping, false imprisonment, assault, various explosives and firearms offences, criminal damage, hijacking.

b) *Extradition to Commonwealth countries*

This is governed by the Fugitive Offenders Act 1967 which lays down better safeguards against unfair surrender than the 1870 Act.

i) *Conditions*

For an extradition between the United Kingdom and a Commonwealth country:

the offence must be one of those listed in the 1967 Act; and

there must be 'double criminality'; and

the offence must be punishable with at least 12 months imprisonment in the Commonwealth country.

ii) *Procedure*: similar to the 1870 Extradition Act procedure.

iii) *'Political offences'*

There is a similar bar on extradition for political offences as in the 1870 Extradition Act, although if a Commonwealth country signs the European Convention on the Suppression of Terrorism, then the 1978 Suppression of Terrorism Act will apply to it.

iv) *Discharge by the High Court*

The High Court has the power to order the discharge of a fugitive criminal if it considers that it would be unjust or oppressive to extradite him because:

the offence is trivial; or

of the time that has elapsed since the offence; or

the accusation was not made in good faith in the interests of justice.

NOTE (1): The High Court has no similar power under the 1870 EA.

NOTE (2): Special and separate provisions apply for extraditions to Ireland under the Backing of Warrants (Republic of Ireland) Act 1965.

33 THE COMMONWEALTH

33.1 Introduction

'The Commonwealth of Nations is *a voluntary association of independent sovereign states*, each responsible for its own policies, consulting and co-operating in the common interests of their peoples and in the promotion of international understanding and world peace.'

Commonwealth Declaration, Singapore (1971).

The one common factor shared by the members of the Commonwealth is that they had some connection with the British Empire. It is proposed to outline first the important steps in the transformation of Empire to Commonwealth.

33.2 Empire to Commonwealth

a) *The Colonial Laws Validity Act 1865*

British Colonies generally had their own legislative assemblies, but these were subject to the overriding authority of the Westminster Imperial Parliament. The Colonial Laws Validity Act 1865 established the exact relationship between the Westminster Parliament and the colonial legislatures. Under the Act:

i) Section 1: an Act of the Imperial Parliament only applied to a colony when it was 'by express words or necessary intendment' (implication) made applicable to it.

ii) Section 2: the laws of a colony were to be read subject to the Acts of the Imperial Parliament which applied to the colony and if a colonial law was incompatible with such an Imperial Act, then the former was void to the extent of the inconsistency.

iii) Section 3: a colonial law was not void merely because it was incompatible with English common law.

iv) Section 5: a colonial legislature had full power to make laws changing the constitution, powers and procedure of the legislature, provided that such laws were passed in accordance with any existing requirements laid down by an applicable Act of the Imperial Parliament, or Colonial Law. (For the effect of s5, see *Attorney-General for New South Wales* v *Trethowan* in chapter 3.)

b) *The Statute of Westminster 1931*

Gradually some of the Colonies developed, through convention, a status of near independence from the Empire, 'Dominion' status. The 1926 Imperial Conference (in the Balfour Report) declared that the United Kingdom and the Dominions were 'autonomous Communities within the British Empire, equal in status, in no way subordinate one to another in any aspect of their domestic or external affairs, though united by a common allegiance to the Crown ...'

By convention, the legal authority of the Westminster Parliament to enact laws for the dominions (which were in law still colonies) was only exercised at the request of and with the consent of, a dominion. Then, the Dominion status of Canada, Australia and New Zealand was recognised by the Statute of Westminster 1931 which enacted that:

i) Section 2:

> '(1) the Colonial Laws Validity Act 1865 shall not apply to any law made by the Parliament of a Dominion.
>
> (2) No law and no provision of any law made by a Dominion shall be void or inoperative on the ground that it is repugnant to the law of England, or to the provisions of any existing or future Act of Parliament of the United Kingdom ... and the powers of the Dominion shall include the power to repeal or amend any such Act in so far as the same is part of the law of the Dominion.'

ii) Section 4:

> 'No Act of Parliament of the United Kingdom passed after the commencement of this Act shall extend to a Dominion as part of the law of that Dominion unless it is expressly declared in that Act that that Dominion has requested and consented to the enactment thereof.'

Under these provisions, the Dominions were effectively given legislative independence from the Imperial Parliament. Whether Parliament could enact a law for a Dominion in breach of s4 raises conflicting points of legal theory and political reality, see *Blackburn* v *Attorney-General* below.

NOTE: Section 4 was used in the Canada Act 1982, for judicial comment on its provisions, see *Manuel* v *Attorney-General* (1982) in chapter 3.

c) *Independence Statutes*

Since World War II, nearly every country that was part of the British Empire has been granted full independence from Great Britain and the legislative authority of the Westminster Parliament. Grants of full independence have been made in various Independence Acts, as each occasion arose, and such Acts go beyond the provisions applied by the Statute of Westminster 1931 to Dominions because: in an Independence Act the Westminster Parliament declares that it has *no* authority to enact laws for the independent state. (Often, as a symbol of total independence, an independent state will enact its own Constitution in place of the one given to it by Westminster in its Independence Act.)

Whether Parliament could enact a law for an independent state in breach of these principles raises conflicting points of legal theory and political reality:

> 'We have all been brought up to believe that, in legal theory, one Parliament cannot bind another and that no Act is irreversible. *But legal theory does not always march alongside political reality*. Take the Statute of Westminster 1931 ... Can anyone imagine that Parliament could or would reverse that Statute? Take the Acts which have granted independence ... Can anyone imagine that Parliament could or would reverse those laws and take away independence? Most clearly not. *Freedom once given cannot be taken away. Legal theory must give way to practical politics.*'
>
> per Lord Denning MR in *Blackburn* v *Attorney-General* (1971).

NOTE: On independence most states become and remain thereafter, full members of the Commonwealth.

33.3 The Commonwealth

The Commonwealth 'is a voluntary association of independent sovereign states', which evolved from the British Empire. Its full members (47 states) are:

United Kingdom	Fiji	Maldives	Sri Lanka
Canada	Gambia	Malta	Swaziland
Australia	Ghana	Mauritius	Tanzania
New Zealand	Grenada	Nigeria	Tonga
Antigua	Guyana	Papua New Guinea	Trinidad and Tobago
Bahamas	India	St Kitts-Nevis	Tuvalu
Bangladesh	Jamaica	St Lucia	Uganda
Barbados	Kenya	St Vincent	Vanuatu
Belize	Kiribati	Seychelles	Western Samoa
Botswana	Lesotho	Sierra Leone	Zambia
Cyprus	Malawi	Singapore	Zimbabwe
Dominica	Malaysia	Solomon Islands	

(Nauru is a 'special member', ie some rights as others, but no separate representation at meetings of the Commonwealth Heads of Government.)

NOTE: In 1989 Fiji is presently outside the Commonwealth after a coup d'etat. It is hoped it will shortly be reinstated. Pakistan is now seeking to re-enter the Commonwealth.

Also there are various territories which are part of the Commonwealth by virtue of being Colonies of the United Kingdom (or dependencies of the United Kingdom or Australia or New Zealand) eg: the Colonies of Hong Kong, Gilbraltar. These are not members in their own right.

NOTE:

a) Most members of the Commonwealth are parliamentary democracies.

b) Some of the members recognise the Queen as their Head of State, eg Australia, New Zealand and in such countries the Queen is represented by a Governor General. Governor Generals are appointed by the Queen in accordance with the recommendation of the Government of the particular state. Governor Generals have the same position and powers in relation to the State to which they are attached as the Queen does in the United Kingdom. This arises from the 1926 Imperial Conference. Governor Generals can, therefore, enter into political controversy, as in 1975 when the Governor General of Australia dismissed the Australian Prime Minister after his Government had failed to obtain support from Parliament.

c) Many of the members are Republics with Presidents as Heads of State. India set an important precedent when it became a Republic but remained a full member of the Commonwealth; the London Declaration 1949, India became a Republic in 1950.

d) Other members have their own monarchs as Heads of State, eg Tonga. Malaysia has an elected Monarch.

e) All members accept the Queen as the symbol of the free association of the member nations of the Commonwealth and as such, the Head of the Commonwealth.

33.4 Features of the Commonwealth

a) The Commonwealth evolved gradually, as the Empire disintegrated, to provide an association of states that were once closely connected to Great Britain.

b) Because the Commonwealth was not formally created, it does not have written constitutional rules; inter-member relations are governed by conventions.

c) The Commonwealth does not have an international status, as eg the EEC does. It is not an independent international power.

d) The Commonwealth has no legislative, executive or judicial organs. There is no authority over and above the governments of member states.

e) The Queen has no constitutional functions as Head of the Commonwealth; she is merely a symbol.

f) To become a member, a state has to: be independent, be accepted by the existing members and recognise the Queen as Head of the Commonwealth.

g) Some nations have left the Commonwealth, eg Eire (1949), South Africa (1961), Pakistan (1972).

h) Members conduct their own defence and foreign policies and enter into treaties, ie there is no Commonwealth defence or foreign policy. (A notable example of a member entering into a Treaty solely for its own benefit occurred when the United Kingdom signed the Treaty of Rome to become a member of the EEC, thus re-aligning its trading patterns which had formerly depended heavily on the Commonwealth.)

i) Periodic meetings of the Heads of Governments of the members are held, at which the heads of government discuss, eg major issues of international affairs. They do not formulate binding policies, but sometimes formulate general statements of principle.

   For example, the issue of sanctions upon South Africa discussed at the Nassau Conference 1985 (though no definitive agreement was reached). Note also the role of the Eminent Persons Group (EPG) who visited South Africa in 1986 and strongly criticised the continuance of apartheid in that country.

j) There are various other Commonwealth meetings, eg between finance ministers and between officials responsible for trade, education, etc. There are also various official and unofficial consultative and advisory organisations; interchanges of technical knowledge; and other types of mutual co-operation.

k) In 1965 a Commonwealth Secretariat, headed by a Secretary General, was established, with a headquarters in London. The Secretary General has no executive powers but the Secretariat distributes information and facilitates the holding of Commonwealth meetings and inter-member co-operation.

l) Most members have abolished the right of final appeal from their own courts to the Judicial Committee of the Privy Council (which was an incident of membership of the Empire).

m) The Commonwealth is in fact 'a minor consultative and co-operative international body whose members have certain special relationships with one another' (de Smith).

ON FROM 'A' LEVEL

One of the great misconceptions surrounding 'A' Level studies is that all subjects must be chosen with a specific career in mind. This fallacy probably arises because most people now know that certain science subjects are stipulated for such careers as Medicine, Dentistry and Pharmacy. But, as with most rules, there are always some exceptions, for some universities are now offering a preliminary year to enable students to receive a foundation course in science or engineering subjects before starting on a scientific or technological degree course, even though they may have taken non-scientific subjects at 'A' Level.

Advanced Level subjects therefore should be seen as a universal currency. The student who takes science 'A' Levels can still apply for Business Studies or Accountancy courses, whilst those who have not taken Law at 'A' Level can still apply for law courses. An 'A' Level course in Constitutional Law, however, when combined with other 'A' Level subjects, is an acceptable subject for a wide range of non-scientific careers and courses. Even so many students take it simply because they are interested in following law as a career.

A degree course in Law is certainly an advantage for anyone who is ultimately aiming for a career as a solicitor or barrister. By way of a Law course, students will receive lectures from practising lawyers and will have the opportunity to meet and discuss many aspects of law from people involved in day-to-day legal matters. Conversely, however, a degree in Law is not in itself a licence to practice. Many students take the course because they want to study a challenging subject, one which above all will train you to think in a precise and methodical way.

It is for this reason and because a study of Law is regarded as an excellent all-round 'education' that employers hold Law graduates in high esteem. Statistics show, however, that Law graduates go into many other and various careers including accountancy, banking, information technology, marketing, business management and the media.

There are many degree courses in Law offered by the universities and colleges in the UK. These include the Scottish Law courses offered by the Scottish institutions and specialised courses such as Business Law and joint courses with law and languages, sociology, politics and economics.

Most Law courses follow a similar pattern with many specialised options being available in the second and third years, such as international law, land law, medico-law and many others.

An important proportion of the legal profession is now educated at the country's new universities (old polytechnics). Approximately 1,500 Law graduates qualify each year from these institutions offering the LLB course. Part-time Law degree courses will further swell this total.

Two of the new universities in England and Wales (De Montfort and Nottingham (Trent)) even provide an LLB on a 'sandwich' basis. At Trent, for instance, students spend six months of their first year and nine months of their third year undertaking practical training in a solicitors' office.

The most new university courses generally tend to concentrate on the practicalities of life and have responded to the needs of industry, commerce, and the professions and Law is no exception. Not only do all LLB Honours courses exempt graduates from Law Society and Bar Council Examinations, but in many cases they also meet the very special requirements of Europe. Indeed, they are ready for the day when Brussels puts its rubber stamp to the mutual recognition of degrees and diplomas, and when a British lawyer will be able to stand up in a French or German court as readily as his or her counterpart will be able to plead a case at the Old Bailey or in the High Court.

There are those courses, for example, which include an important element of EC Law (such as at the new universities of Central England, Central Lancashire, De Montfort, John Moores, North London, Staffordshire and Wolverhampton), while others include International Law and Comparative Law (John Moores has an option in International Law of Human Rights, at Westminster it is possible to study Public International Law in the second year, and Guildhall has a course in Law of International Trade and

Law of Transnational Business Transactions in the third year. East London University offers four subjects in Year 3 that reflect a student's interest in international affairs and Sheffield Hallam offers International Business Law, whilst Glamorgan and Wolverhampton each offer International Trade Law).

Manchester Metropolitan has an LLB Honours course in Law with a French option which will allow a student to spend a year abroad between Years Two and Three. Bristol (UWE) has a four-year honours course in European Law and Languages which provides a year's work or study abroad where two Community languages are used. Coventry's European Business Law has undergraduates studying a language in the first two years and concentrating on law in another European country in Year Three. There are also good modern language options at several other universities including De Montfort, Nottingham (Trent), Sheffield Hallam and Glamorgan.

Within the University of Central Lancashire's LLB course, there are sections on International Terrorism and International Civil Liberties. Civil Liberties are also included at Middlesex and Staffordshire while North London has sections on International Relations and International Protection of Human Rights. Nottingham (Trent) has a section on Immigration and Race Relations Law. De Montfort provides a programme in Law and Medicine, and Oxford, Brookes, which pioneered the modular degree, provides a full-time modular LLB which allows a wide range of legal subjects to be offered.

But getting into law courses is not easy. Because of the popularity of the subject there are many applications each year. Twenty, thirty or forty applicants for each place is not uncommon. Such popularity means that high grades are set for admission. Several universities such as Bristol, Edinburgh, Exeter, Kent, Hull, Leeds and Warwick are now asking for 'A' Level grades at ABB and almost all other universities are asking for BBB. Some applicants, however, feel that a joint course such as Law and French, German or Italian would be an ideal preparation for work in Europe, and of course they are right. They should, however, realise that on any one such course there may only be eight or nine places available, compared to fifty or sixty on single honours law courses. Thus competition for places will be even greater and academic excellence will be the admissions tutor's main priority. (For details of all offers and selection procedures see *The Complete Degree Course Offers – How to Choose your Course*, £13.95, Trotmans, 12 Hill Rise, Richmond, Surrey.)

While 'A' Level grades, therefore, are of considerable importance, the grades you have already achieved at GCSE are also going to be scrutinised and students with a range of subjects at grade A or B will obviously receive priority when offers are made.

'A' Level grades, of course, carry an equivalent score in points (A = 10pts, B = 8pts, C = 6pts, D = 4pts, E = 2pts) and, while most popular university offers will be made by way of grades to be achieved, all is not lost if you do not achieve the exact grades, for some institutions will consider equivalent points scores, where offers are generally made in the 20pts to 24pts range.

Again, however, there is an exception to the general rule, with the minimum entry requirement made for some courses at Holborn College. The College offers LLB Hons Degree in conjunction with Wolverhampton University, and also the London University LLB (Hons) external degree. Holborn College offers a unique and highly structured teaching system which has resulted in a high success rate among students. Additionally it is also possible to take degree courses in Law by way of distance learning in which students can take their degrees externally which allows students to transfer to some other universities at the end of the first year.

But in preparing your application for law degree courses there is another factor which must be considered, that being the section on the UCAS form which requires applicants to provide 'further information'.

This section is the only section of the form on which the applicant can try to impress the admissions tutor! Probably the best way to impress the admissions tutor is by indicating how your interest in a study of law has developed and ideally this should be done by way of work experience or work shadowing in a lawyers' office. Alternatively, attendance in courts of law – in the public gallery – where you can watch the 'law in action' is useful. When attending court cases do not forget to make notes on various aspects of the cases you follow since you may be asked questions about them at interview.

Interviews are usually very important and invariably questions will be asked concerning recent major law cases and on aspects of current international legal issues. Hence the importance of keeping up to date on legal topics in the national press.

Ultimately, however, admissions tutors are looking for thoughtful, intelligent people capable of undertaking a challenging course and giving a great deal of attention to detail. If you are one such person, then a course and a career in law could be ideal!

Good luck!

Brian Heap

INDEX